Contemporary
Political
Philosophers

Contemporary Political Philosophers

Edited by

Anthony de Crespigny
UNIVERSITY OF CAPE TOWN

and

Kenneth Minogue
UNIVERSITY OF LONDON

Dodd, Mead & Company
NEW YORK   1975

Library of Congress Catalog Card Number: 74-26158

ISBN: 0-396-07095-7

Printed in the United States of America

Designed by JEFFREY M. BARRIE

Contents

Introduction

Political philosophy is the natural product of a society in which men relate to each other not as kinsmen, fellow-subjects, or comrades, but as citizens. This observation is needed to remind us that most men at most times have known nothing of citizenship. Sometimes they have lived in huge empires, ruled by remote emperors whom they were powerless to influence except by the desperate expedients of rebellion and riot. At other times they have lived in tribes, and imagined themselves to be members of a large family. But what would happen if there were no well-supported emperor to frighten them into submission and if tribal cohesion broke down? Such a situation has occurred on several memorable occasions in the history of Europe. One such occasion was during the confusion following the entry of the Dorians into Greece, and led in time to the development of the Greek polis. Another such occasion followed on the barbarian invasions of the Roman empire, and led to the creation of mediaeval realms. The result in both cases was the creation of communities whose cohesion depended upon the recognition of officers (such as king, pope, prime minister, *strategos*, consul) possessing defined authority. The community, moreover, was sustained by a continuous activity of accommodation which we call (following the Greeks, and particularly Aristotle) "politics." The word is elastic, and is often extended to cover everything from disputes between trade unions to family quarrels. But politics is primarily the activity by which some persons conduct the public business of a community whose members are recognised to be diverse in such characteristics as age, sex, belief, and social background. Sometimes, of course, this activity fails in its object. Civil war and revolution result.

Men have torn their communities apart quarrelling over who should be eligible for the highest offices, over the question of whether two or more religious beliefs may legitimately be held within the community, and for many other such reasons.

The condition of tranquility in civil societies depends upon that readiness to tolerate others which is often called "civility." This character was supremely exhibited by the Romans, both in the way patricians and plebeians worked out their differences and in the way they accommodated the gods of the nations they conquered. Such civil tolerance in the matter of religion was threatened by the appearance of a religion which put much stress upon the jealousy of its God and the unique efficacy of its message. The ancients wore their cults lightly, but from the time of the Emperor Theodosius onwards, the Christian religion introduced into public affairs a zealous concern for true doctrine; and ever since that time, Europeans and those who have inherited their culture have only with difficulty been able to sustain communities containing a variety of fundamental beliefs. From late mediaeval times, spiritual and secular authority came increasingly into the same hands, and orthodox belief became one of the requirements of citizenship. The results included civil wars, persecutions for heresy, inquisitions, purges, and many other more casual examples of human intolerance. Modern secular ideologies have inherited this fanatical spirit in full measure. Indeed, since the thrust of orthodoxy has passed from theologians to theoreticians, the intensity of persecution has increased rather than diminished, for the theologian merely demanded faith, whereas the theoretician believed himself possessed of demonstrable truth. This pretension has made life difficult for political philosophers, since they are always in danger of arriving at conclusions incompatible with the currently received orthodoxy. One of the philosophers treated in this book, the late Leo Strauss, has argued that this situation is so much a constant of the experience of political philosophers that their discipline is inherently an esoteric one whose truths must be carefully hidden from the carelessly profane and from potential persecutors. From Socrates to Trotsky, the advancing of political doctrines has been attended with danger of death or persecution. But we should not conclude that political philosophers are themselves a harmonious body of men. They disagree on many questions profoundly, and at times vitriolically. The problem is that one man's philosophy is another man's pretentious mysticism, or, alternatively, logic-chopping pedantry. The philosophers in this book are, on the whole, a tolerant set of thinkers, but there is no doubt that some of them will deplore the company in which they find themselves.

Political philosophy is a speculative inquiry into the assumptions of the practical activity of politics. It can be conducted in a confusing variety of ways, and at an equally confusing variety of levels. The fact that, as a discipline, it has not provided a growing body of agreed truths has often led people to the mistaken belief that philosophical disagreements merely reflect the profound divisions of politics itself. For what could be more obvious than that politics is largely about conflicts that arise within and between states, or that these conflicts produce many incompatible statements of viewpoint? Blue and Green, Guelph and Ghibelline, Whig and Tory, Bolshevik and Menshevik, Republican and Monarchist, are but a few of the names of competing parties, each of which has produced a doctrine in its own support. One of the worst confusions of nomenclature which bedevils political inquiry today is the common practice of referring to a bundle of arguments advanced in favour of such presumed desirabilities as democracy, monarchy, or the single-transferable vote, as a "philosophy." This vulgar use is but one more example of that grandiose elevation by which the undertaker becomes the "mortician" and the greengrocer a "fruitologist"; but whereas a rose by any other name would smell as sweet, a political doctrine believed to be a "philosophy" can easily unhinge the understanding. So far as this volume is concerned, the term "philosophy" describes a theoretical inquiry into the logical relations holding between the most general ideas used in the understanding of some area of reality. The important point is that, whilst the political doctrines produced by parties are attempts to *persuade,* philosophy is an attempt to *understand.* There is always, of course, the risk that we shall smuggle our preferences into our understandings, but it is not at all inevitable that we should do so. Academic criticism inspects arguments for their weaknesses, and any contraband of preference will sooner or later be contested. And it is certainly true that men of the most varying political attitudes will agree perfectly on what is a conclusive argument and on what evidence would be decisive in case of a disagreement.

The real quarrel between political philosophers arises entirely from within philosophy itself, for, being pre-eminently a self-conscious form of understanding, it never fails to be preoccupied with its own character. This character is purely argumentative. Whereas other forms of understanding, such as science or history, are, to put the matter crudely, anchored to an "outside" world of fact and evidence, philosophy is free to move speculatively according to its own internal motion. It has long been disputed whether this makes philosophy the highest form of understanding to whose conclusions all other inquiries must conform (as Plato thought); or whether it is (as John Locke thought) a conceptual underlabourer only useful in keeping in sharp logical repair the concepts employed in other business. Philosophers become, on this unassuming view, the caretakers of the conceptual toolshed, but they are never allowed actually to use the tools on a proper job of understanding. When refined, this question becomes vastly complicated, and leads to a situation in which some philosophers (particularly, though by no means exclusively, in Germany and France) have been regarded as the creators of incomprehensible and pretentious speculations, whilst others (particularly in Britain and America) have been regarded as trivial and pedantic explorers of the meanings of words.

Such disputes between philosophers partly explain a parochial comedy played out in the 1950s in Britain and America in which political philosophy was announced to be dead, with the result that political theorising took on the character of obituary. The device of dramatising an issue or an institution by announcing its death seems to have been invented by the publicist Nietzsche in relation to God—unless we wish to trace its ancestry back to Burke's announcement that the age of chivalry was dead. It has proved a felicitous device for gaining attention, and has led intellectuals to inquire whether the novel, or the proscenium arch, or the nation-state (to name but a few on the danger list) ought to be declared dead. In 1956, political philosophy was authoritatively pronounced extinct by a Cambridge don, Peter Laslett, in the course of introducing a collection of essays on *Philosophy, Politics and Society*. Nothing could better illustrate the instability of worldly things, however, than the confession, within six years, that the same authority had detected a slow pulse rate and a few heartbeats. The corpse was declared to be living once more: indeed his very life was modestly attributed to the very volume in which his death had been announced. No doubt in the Midsummer Night's dream of philosophy there must always be room for Bottom the Weaver; and the writers of introductions to collections of essays should always (being a species of salesman) be regarded with suspicion. But the oddity of this premature death-certificate is that virtually all the philosophers with whom this book is concerned were then in full philosophical flow. No doubt this particular episode ought to be attributed to the comedy of cultural diagnostics by which intellectuals try to cheat the historian of his work, but it could only have taken the form it did because of the currency of an erroneous view to the effect that political philosophy is essentially prescriptive or "normative."

This is an error with which we may deal summarily by insisting that there are at least three kinds of assertion likely to be made by students of politics. One of these consists in trying to explain what actually goes on in politics: it may be done in the historical manner of a Bagehot or a Tocqueville; or with the apparatus of quantitative data often assembled by modern political scientists. In either case, the material is, broadly speaking, descriptive. Alternatively, we may be interested in advancing some political policy (such as more money for social services or the restoration of capital punishment) or some general attitude towards policies (favouring change in general, for example, or judging policies in terms of their supposed bearing on liberty or the national interest). In this case, we shall clearly be prescribing what ought or ought not to be done, or thought. Many of the landmarks of political thought, such as Milton's *Areopagitica*, Paine's *Rights of Man*, and Marx's *Communist Manifesto*, are clearly of this character. But there is a third, and quite distinct, kind of interest we may take in political affairs. When Hobbes discusses in *Leviathan* the logic of terms like "representation," "authority," and "law of nature," he is exploring our understanding of the state in terms of a materialist doctrine about reality, and an individualist doctrine about society. He is certainly not in any sense describing what goes on, nor is he prescribing what anyone should do. To treat him as doing so is to regard him as a pamphleteer; it is plausible, but it misses an important distinction. The *Leviathan* is a complicated argument from which nothing at all follows directly and logically about what, in terms of the quarrels of seventeenth-century England, should be supported. Confirmation of this assertion may be found in the fact that *both* sides in the English Civil War were capable of appropriating fragments of the Hobbesian argument, and at the same time both sides regarded this very argument as dangerous and unsatisfactory. Similarly, whatever ambitions Plato may have had about being a philosopher king, the *Republic* is an attempt to exhibit the rationality of political associations in terms of the different capacities of human beings. Aristotle relevantly criticised Plato's argument, not by disagreeing with any supposed "prescriptions" it contained, but by arguing that it made communal diversity a contingent excrescence of political life rather than (as seemed a better understanding) the cause and centre of the activity itself. These issues are philosophical, and are both vulgarised and misunderstood if they are reduced to the level of a contest of "prescriptions" or "norms."

It is true, of course, that someone who advocates a highly abstract attitude and argues his case in terms of liberty, justice, or some similar idea, and who selects materials for his pleading from the repertoire of philosophical argument, may make pronouncements difficult to distinguish from political philosophy in the strict sense. John Locke's *Second Treatise* is a good example of just this problem of identification, and is now more easily understood in what seems to be its true light only because of the passage of time. Readers had long been puzzled by the presence of unexplained characters, such as the servant who cuts the turfs in the state of nature.* They had wondered at the appearance of an intuitionist doctrine contrary to what Locke had argued in the *Essay on Human Understanding*. Such problems made it clear that this was a work of political advocacy, couched in a philosophical mode, which could not be understood on its own terms the way a proper work of philosophy should.

These few simple considerations are advanced in an at-

* V, 28.

tempt to weaken the intellectually disastrous belief that argument can only be concerned with one or other of two loosely specified things called "facts" and "values"; or, in other words, that our intellectual life consists of two general kinds of activity called "describing" and "prescribing." And the objection is not that the distinction cannot be made, for it can, and it is often useful; but rather that there are other kinds of intellectual activity (such as philosophy) which are badly maimed if forced through the crude sieve of such a distinction. Besides, it generally happens that one side or other of the distinction has the greater prestige. Hence, in the idealist atmosphere generated in political discussion by the work of T. H. Green, Bernard Bosanquet, and later L. T. Hobhouse, a concern with values and ends was taken as a sign of elevation, and political thought tended to degenerate into uplift in which the conspicuous merit of the heart was thought to compensate for the muddles of the head. If anything died in Anglo-Saxon political thought around the middle of the century, it was tolerance for this inspirational combination of idealism and utilitarianism.

At other times, however, prestige has gone to the facts. Positivism has demoted values to the level of mere preferences and exiled them to the very periphery of the intellectual world. For if values are simply matters of taste, then *de gustibus non disputandum;* and understanding abdicates. To point the finger at someone's assertion and remark that it is a value-judgement has been (particularly among simple people) regarded as a lethal move in the game of argument. Fortunately, recent decades have produced some extremely rigorous investigation into the structure of preferences, of which the work of John Rawls is a notable example. But it remains necessary to insist upon two things: first, that political philosophy is a special kind of attempt to *understand* politics, and is logically unrelated to prescription; and secondly, that values are not mere preferences, but things having an investigable rational structure of their own.

The problems of mapping this confused intellectual region have been intensified in recent times by the appearance of an intellectual construction which purports *both* to explain the world, *and* also to elucidate for us the nature of our political duties. This type of construction is called an "ideology," and its main concern is to destroy political activity as it has previously been known in Western Europe. Thus some versions of nationalist doctrine have sought to expel all foreign influences from the community and have promised that once this has been achieved, the need for abstract laws, coercive institutions, and remote officeholders—indeed conflict itself—will disappear. Men will live with each other as brothers rather than as citizens. This is an attempt to replace the artificial bonds of politics by the natural bonds of an imagined kinship; the state will revert to the tribal status from which it seems to have emerged. Similar promises have been made about the benefits of racial homogeneity. But undoubtedly the most popular of these doctrines promises that the extinction of politics will be the result of the ending of class divisions—putting an end to the necessity for difficult choices. The conditions of brotherhood, as they appear in Marxism, are that all men should live the same kind of life in a classless society. That these doctrines look forward to an end of politics would in itself be enough to distinguish them from such properly political doctrines as liberalism, republicanism, conservatism, and legitimism. But they are, in addition, intellectually quite different. They present themselves not as the expression of a political preference (which is all that political doctrines can be) but rather as keys to the fundamental structure of reality. Like religions, ideologies assume themselves the possessors of the one true belief. And they invariably take the form of explaining the history of mankind in terms of the adventures of whatever abstract entity has been chosen to unlock the secrets of life: race, nation, or class. The intellectual level of this type of political thought is usually low; but that of its Marxist versions is both abundant and, on occasions, formidably intelligent. For the most part, the policy of the editors has been to exclude ideological writing, but Marxism clearly presents a hard case. Part of our solution has been to treat Marcuse (who is certainly a distinguished Hegel scholar) at considerable length as a representative figure.

Philosophy appears to be a form of understanding akin to art in that individuality is an important part of it. For the whole business of philosophers may best be described as the finding of problems in what most people take for granted. Most politicians are too busy pursuing power to worry much about the ac-

tual concept of power; and the first man who wondered about
the real existence of the material world no doubt looked to his
fellows like someone in danger of going off his head. A significant philosopher is generally a man who discovers a problem
where none was found before, and usually he goes on to
suggest a certain type of solution. These types of solution are ir-
reducibly individual. They may be imitated, or plagiarised, but
they cannot be absorbed without remainder into the "findings"
of an intellectual tradition. Hence it is that whilst physicists
have left Newton to the historians of science, philosophers still
read Aristotle. This is also why a book on "problems of contemporary political philosophy" has a somewhat abstract look. Each
philosopher works out a nexus of problems and solutions which
constitute a style of thought, and particular arguments can only
be abstracted at the risk of distortion.

Can we extract from these essays some central theme
which has been at the centre of the philosophical interest of our
century? Philosophers, by contrast with scientists and historians, are men who survey the world from the mountain top; but
the world is surrounded by many peaks of vantage, and the
view is significantly different from each one. Many of the moun-
taineers discussed in this volume have, for example, seen our
times as those in which human freedom was threatened by the
strains of modern civilization. Thus Popper presents us with the
contrast between the open and the closed society as the fundamental option facing mankind, and Hayek (signposting the
road to serfdom), Jouvenel, and Rawls write on a not dissimilar
intellectual wavelength. But another group of thinkers—Marcuse, Macpherson, Sartre—have at the forefront of their minds
the knots that something they recognise as "capitalism" has tied
us in. Each of them responds to a version of the human predicament conceived after the manner of Marx. Still others—Arendt,
Strauss, Voegelin; possibly in some respects Oakeshott and
Aron—have seen the modern world attempting to abandon political activity in favour of some panacea: technological prob-
lem-solving, rationalism, positivism, society by contrast with
the state, or (in Popper's version) utopian social engineering. In
the classical world, and whilst Christian assumptions were
taken for granted in the European understanding of the situation of mankind, politics was recognised as both essentially

human and (partly by consequence) limited in terms of what it could achieve. Heaven was elsewhere, or nowhere. The modern world has seen a surge of optimism about human possibilities, and now it is impossible to philosophise about politics without taking up a position on the question of whether this optimism is justified or not. Here, if anywhere, is the preoccupation which links together all the subjects discussed in this book. But within its interstices, modern political philosophers can still be found discussing in terms of new conditions a number of familiar questions found in the classical writers: What is the logic of political discourse? What is the character of the modern state? What is the relation between politics and what we may rather pompously call "time and eternity"?

There is, of course, a considerable risk of misunderstanding when the philosophical work of a lifetime is discussed in essays of a few thousand words. Clearly it would be a gross error to imagine that the essays that follow are digests of the philosophers' work. But such bodies of thought are complex and difficult countries which confuse the visitor. What he may hope for in this book is a general account of the terrain, and a number of useful compass points for future exploration, supplied by experienced travellers who are in many cases engaged in setting up realms of their own.

Here then is a collection of essays which attempt to indicate the philosophical individualities of a dozen writers who have all, by general consent, contributed much to the understanding of the twentieth century. They philosophise in a variety of styles, and they are certainly not presented in terms of any single coherent philosophical position. Some deal with what are immediately recognisable as philosophical questions; others have at the forefront of their preoccupation questions of economics, political policy, or intellectual history. All, however, have some kind of philosophical position. Each of them is, furthermore, firmly rooted in the experience of the twentieth century; indeed, all but two were born within ten years of the turn of the century, and most found their mature voices in the period between the wars. Most have produced their major work since 1945. Such a collection as this can lay no claim to canonical status, and some notable thinkers have certainly been omitted. But each of the philosophers dealt with here has responded to some or many of the excitements of this most melodramatic of centuries, and each has said something likely to capture the attention of later generations.

The subjects of the essays are arranged chronologically, by order of date of birth. Spelling and usage in the essays follow English, Canadian, or American style, according to the preference of the individual authors.

ANTHONY DE CRESPIGNY
KENNETH MINOGUE

Contemporary
Political
Philosophers

Herbert Marcuse:
Alienation and Negativity

by DAVID KETTLER

Since Montesquieu and Hume, political thought has been faced with a problem of "civilization." Two considerations enter into the problem. The first is a judgment that modern men live within a comprehensible network of circumstances significantly different from those of earlier times. While there is much controversy about the ways in which these circumstances interconnect and about their sources, there is a good deal of agreement about the indicators which signal the civilized condition. Earlier writers on the subject stressed the emergence of a market economy and then the eruption of industrial production; drastic refinement in the division of labor; dramatically higher levels of national wealth and rates of increase; new forms of poverty; the spread of the work-ethic and habits of utilitarian calculation; the establishment of scientific inquiry, dissemination of its findings, and the application of findings in technology; new standards of education and the rise of public opinion; innovations in forms of organization and the displacement of traditionalist elites; and, generally, the decline of violence and "enthusiasm" and the rise of orderly new matter-of-factness and civil conventionality. Recent writers devise operational measures of social and economic "development" and may well concede the term "civilization" to a certain high range of readings on their indices. In any case, it is widely acknowledged that a distinctive constellation of social and economic factors somehow sets the scene for modern political life.

The second consideration defining the problem of civilization is uncertainty whether these new circumstances represent progress or corruption in morals and politics (or whether, as some would insist, they simply define a new context for implementing unchanging principles). Early treatments of the problem tempt us to simple classifications, although even there closer scrutiny reveals complexity. We contrast the celebration of "Enlightenment" in the *Encyclopedia* with Rousseau's gloomy assessment of progress in the arts and sciences, or we compare James Mill's zestful appreciation for the new reign of commerce, calculation, and invention with Adam Ferguson's dismay about the eclipse of civic virtue in a polished and commercial society. But certainly in the next generation—as shown, for example, by John Stuart Mill's noted essay on "Civilization"—the problem appears to many to require a response more subtle than approving or decrying the new constellation. Civilization opens vast new opportunities for human achievement and satisfaction, Mill argues, but it also brings overwhelming new distractions from the cultivation of excellence as well as new forms of power prone to tyrannical abuse and impervious to existing controls.

For Mill and many of his contemporaries, the problem of civilization presents itself as a dilemma. More recent political writers sharing these concerns may well be classified by their response to the dilemma. Some conclude that moral and political life must find ways of *managing* the irremovable tensions and conflicts attending the dilemma. Others see the possibility or necessity of *transcendence:* the dilemma can and perhaps must be overcome through radical transformation of the factors and of their impact. Herbert Marcuse exemplifies the latter response in our time.

Some commentators, in attempting to explain Marcuse's influence, have charged that he appeals to an immature incapacity for sustaining the demands of contemporary civilization, that he offers an emotional retreat from moral and political responsibility. We are not concerned here with the psychology of intellectual influence; we shall respect and consider Marcuse's claim to offer something very different. He undertakes to show that proposals for moral and political survival through piecemeal, continuous management of difficulties generated by civilization are untenable, that such proposals misjudge or misstate the forces at work. And he presents reasoned arguments on behalf of radical alternatives. But interpreting and assessing his work are complicated by a circumstance which has attended discussions of civilization throughout.

However civilization has been conceived it has usually involved the idea of a new and perfected philosophical method congruent with the findings and procedures of the new natural sciences. Critics of civilization have consequently commonly considered themselves obliged to vindicate alternate approaches to argument and evidence, or, more generally, to define alternate roads to truth. Since Marcuse's presentations are strongly influenced by such considerations, systematic evaluation would seem to require primary attention to his discussions of philosophical method and epistemology. Yet such a course is not only very difficult—requiring as it does fairly elaborate treatment of idealist philosophical traditions—but also quite possibly unrewarding, since there is some reason to believe that Marcuse's *operating* method is not identical with his systematic reflections on method. For present purposes, then, we will not take Marcuse's work as the expression of a philosophical system. Instead, we shall look at his criticisms of the social and political thought which project continuous management of civilizational dilemmas, and then at his projection of transcendent alternatives. We shall limit ourselves to his writings since 1955. The whole treatment must, in all fairness to Marcuse, be considered provisional, since it does not take the work on the terms he has set, but rather takes it on the terms implicit in conventional discourse among English-speaking students of political thought. We are interested in the bearing of this thought upon an idiom of political thought strongly marked by the liberal-democratic approach to the problem of civilization.

A paper by John Chapman well summarizes this approach and indicates its response to our central theme.[1] Chapman contends that liberal thought builds upon an "ideal of human perfectibility, understood as that form of development of our potentialities, the outcome of which is a harmonious meshing of moral freedom and psychological need, in terms of both character and institutions." In relation to this ideal, the social changes

[1] John Chapman, "The Moral Foundations of Political Obligation," in J. Roland Pennock and John W. Chapman, eds., *Political and Legal Obligation* (New York, 1970), pp. 148 f.

commonly referred to by the expression "civilization" manifest themselves as "individuation and rationalization." Far from assaulting the liberal idea, these tendencies are the "psychological, or characterological aspects of perfectibility." Civilization, in other words, generates the kind of man required by liberalism. This is so because the "harmony" envisioned involves an "ambivalence" held in "equipoise." Chapman finds "at the heart of liberalism a vision of the rational individual, capable of both competition and cooperation, a polarized and yet integrated personality, a man who was both economic and moral."

On this view, liberalism welcomes the very breakdown of emotional unity within and among individuals that is commonly decried by critics of civilization, who contrast the impact of this breakdown with the integral mobilization and unification presumed to have been involved in virtuous classical republics. The case is similar with regard to the erosion of institutional loyalties and their displacement by rational calculations of instrumental worth. Contrary to the fear of critics is "the liberal persuasion that individuality and rationality are processes that make for social and political integration." With all this said, it might appear that such a liberalism represents an unqualified affirmation of civilization. But there are darker echoes. The conditions described by liberal moral psychology as necessary to autonomy impose profound strains upon individuals and institutions, and the maintenance of the equipoise requires the most astute management. On balance, however, it may be said that Chapman sees in civilization at least as much opportunity as dilemma.

Marcuse accepts the liberal emphasis on "individuation" and "rationalization," but he denies that these processes—at least in the forms they have assumed in what he qualifies as "bourgeois" or "technological" civilization—contribute to the formation of moral personality, as the liberal writers epitomized by Chapman contend. Taking Max Weber as the prime theorist of rationalization and Sigmund Freud as the theorist of individuation, Marcuse attempts to show that these theories, when properly and thoroughly understood, reveal the contemporary system of civilization as a system of total domination. As civilization advances, Chapman maintains, men constitute themselves as individuals having interests, duties, and rights; and they see the conditions which shape their destinies more and more as constellations of forces which can be understood so as to be mastered (or at least counted on). Marcuse responds that individuation culminates in a complete loss of self; and rationalization, in universally self-destructive irrationality. Civilization cannot be managed; it must be transcended. Thus, Marcuse believes that he has undermined the moral psychology of liberalism, that the moral personality whose autonomous operations are said to provide ethical legitimation for "free" institutions cannot exist without the most radical overturn of the world made by civilization and preserved by such institutions. Contrary to the claims of Chapman and others who agree with him, Marcuse concludes that modern social and political institutions do not embody a complex strategy required by modern civilization for managing tensions between freedom and authority, virtue and commerce, duties and interests, autonomy and dependence; they are, rather, repressive agencies staving off liberating revolution which will transcend existing civilization.

After reviewing the arguments attempting to show the "necessity" for such transcendence, we will consider Marcuse's accounts of the transcendent order. Chapman alleges, in the essay cited earlier, that Marx and his followers (including Marcuse) enter upon a "project of displacing institutions based on political and economic rationality by ones based on emotional and moral solidarity," in keeping with a "new vision of human 'perfectibility,' in which psychological unity replaces ambivalence as the defining category of human nature." If it should prove that Marcuse has in fact put forward such an alternative, the outcome would clearly contradict his own intentions. Marcuse's projections always intend a complex social entity characterized by distance among participants as well as by harmonious interplay. In a recent work, Marcuse assaults those who claim more than symptomatic significance for the emotional antiart of the counterculture: "order, proportion, harmony," he writes, "the idea, ideation of a redeemed, liberated world—freed from the forces of repression. . . . This is the static of fulfillment, of rest: the end of violence; the ever-renewed hope which closes

the tragedies of Shakespeare—the hope that the world may now
be different." [2] But Marcuse is not content to show the necessity or to explicate the hope for such an alternative.

He means to guide the political practice of his reader, to
identify the forces and activities that can achieve what is necessary, that can fulfill the hope. It would appear a hopeless undertaking. If the forces pervading the existing order are not merely
antithetical to ideals of perfectibility, but systematically destroy
the capability for perceiving these ideals, let alone acting upon
them—as Marcuse claims—what conduct can be meaningful,
what can be done? Marcuse finds in Marxism a model for breaking through the vicious circle: a quantum of social and political
energy is cast aside by the normal operations of the system, but
not destroyed; its spontaneous reaction to this destiny sets in
motion a chain of changes, first within itself, so that new potentialities are uncovered and vast new effective powers brought
into play; these powers come to attack and then to transform the
system. Putting the case so abstractly and in terms of physical
metaphor removes it a considerable distance from Marx's quite
historical expectations about the proletariat, the communist
movement, and the revolution. But it is necessary to put it so if
we are to identify the common elements in Marcuse's shifting
strategies. At different times Marcuse sees the revolutionary
force in the Marxist proletariat, in the rationalist tradition of
philosophy, in social outsiders, in deeply repressed erotic instincts, in intellectuals, in the modes of high culture—in various
combinations, never to his own satisfaction. What remains constant and seems firm is his determination to orient political
practice to whatever appears to be the "revolutionary movement" at a given time. Inquiries into the sources and precise
characteristics of the movement's revolutionary nature and debates about ways of fulfilling its mission are then to be carried
on within the orbit of the movement itself. Marcuse's political
views, in the narrow sense of that term, are consequently the
least settled and the most difficult to expound systematically in
relation to the major traditions of political philosophy. But they
form an important part of Marcuse's thought and will be considered.

[2] *Counter-Revolution and Revolt* (Boston, 1972), p. 94.

The problem of civilization in political thought is thus to be seen in three compartments: questions of *necessities*, questions of *ideals*, and questions of *instrumentalities*. In the first, we want to know whether civilization imposes or reveals new tasks which social and political actors must perform if they are to survive. In the second, we ask whether and how our understanding of civilization affects our vision of a perfect order. In the third, we inquire into the norms constituting morally justified political conduct, asking whether these must be accommodated in some important way to our perception of the civilized condition. Marcuse shares with the liberal tradition here illustrated by reference to John Chapman the conviction that civilization makes a profound difference. He differs markedly in his reading of that difference. We shall consider his contentions and arguments as best we can within the limits we have set ourselves. The objective is not to judge Marcuse, but to advance inquiry into questions that contemporary political thought must answer.

Marcuse maintains that the political and social institutions established in the most civilized countries during the nineteenth and twentieth centuries cannot manage the social strains generated by civilization, despite appearances to the contrary.[3] At first, and perhaps for a prolonged period, the failure is disguised. Social order prevails; social production booms; social satisfaction abounds. Yet, for Marcuse, the fact of failure needs but to be uncovered: the seemingly liberal and democratic management proves to harbor a subtle despotism maintaining itself in important part by destroying the very civilization it purports to secure. Surface manifestations of civilization flourish, but the energizing principles are systematically corrupted. And, according to Marcuse, the new barbarism of refinement bred up in place of the principles cannot in the long run sustain *any* order, not even a blatantly despotic rule resorting to tyrannical techniques. Periodic political crises—rebellions and repressions— betoken and foreshadow the ultimate manifest failure. In the

---

[3] A popular statement of the opposing view can be found in Reinhold Niebuhr and Paul E. Sigmund, *The Democratic Experience: Past and Prospects* (New York, 1969), especially pp. 3–87, by Niebuhr.

end, the "system" stands revealed as the ever more violent war of all against all; the center cannot hold.[4]

Writing in the 1930s, Marcuse had been satisfied that his critique of Hegel revealed the untenability of the liberal adjustment to civilization. The liberal tradition, which Marcuse saw as culminating in German idealism, does not identify the "constitution of liberty"; it misinterprets a phase in an ongoing historical process. And the contradictions become blatant in fascism. Under these conditions, to proclaim the old principles is to animate practices which will subvert and transcend the old order. "Happiness" has the central place among these proclamations. Once the working class inquires into the "use values" of the objects it is constrained to produce, once it demands the satisfactions of which it is so manifestly deprived, the movement toward liberation gets under way. "Reason" comes to imply comprehensive social and economic planning: even the most ordinary public discourse recognizes the irrationality of securing the economic realm from purposive human regulation. In the face of frank fascist oppression, even the call for political freedom in a principled liberal form, Marcuse maintained, points in a progressive direction: the struggle against the totalitarian state merges with the struggle against the social order whose fatal weaknesses such a state epitomizes. The crisis of revolutionary transformation was upon civilized society, Marcuse thought. Its own historic principles mobilize the forces arrayed against it, and the defenders of "civilization" against communism and subversion are revealed as bloody tyrants.[5]

When Marcuse returned to theoretical work, almost ten

---

[4] Marcuse concludes a characterization of contemporary society thus: "As long as this is the history of mankind, the 'state of nature,' no matter how refined, prevails: a civilized *bellum omnium contra omnes*, where the happiness of the ones must coexist with the suffering of the others." *An Essay on Liberation* (Boston, 1969), p. 14. In this preview of Marcuse's argument, we are deliberately invoking the memory of such eighteenth-century political thinkers as Montesquieu. Marcuse does not use "despotism," "barbarism," and "corruption" as they did. But the pattern of his argument, we suggest, corresponds quite closely to their earlier one. This observation says nothing about the merits of his case, it simply makes the case more familiar.

[5] In retrospect, Marcuse maintains that these conceptions were conditioned by the impressions of the Spanish Civil War and the united front against fascism. See "Foreword (1965)" to *Negations* (Boston, 1968).

years after World War II, he could no longer speak of "crisis" in this sense, and he could no longer call up such a dynamic toward transcendence by invoking the old principles. The pursuit of reason, freedom, and happiness has been rendered coherent within the limits of the old system; that pursuit has been transformed so as to reflect and support the civilizational order.[6] And yet Marcuse remains convinced that this order is to be judged not simply as undesirable because failing to meet criteria laid down by Marcuse as reflecting man's highest aspirations, or something of the sort, but is indeed to be judged as "impossible"—so antithetical to the needs of man in society that it must be transcended if humanity is not to be destroyed. But what can it mean to say that the "impossible" is existent and stable and seemingly invincible? Marcuse's distinctive argument during the past fifteen years has been above all a psychological one.[7] The adjustment now demanded on behalf of civilization generates ever-mounting measures of aggression in all social actors; however, this manifests itself, quite possibly for a long time, in attitudes and actions supportive of the existing order or, at most, in outbursts which harm individuals while leaving the system intact. But at some fatal point, Marcuse expects, there will be cataclysmic destruction.

Such a reading of modern dynamics breaks sharply with the view that civilization vindicates itself by creating the space within which morally autonomous man can exist and function. On that view, illustrated above in John Chapman's argument, rationalization and individuation as social processes make it possible for a man to manage, with the help of liberal attitudes and institutions, the strains and challenges of civilization. The confrontation between the two positions can be seen as a contest in the area of "moral psychology": on the one side, a view of modern man ever more subservient to external forces and storing up ever greater potentialities and needs for viciousness;

[6] See the "Epilogue (1954)" to the second edition of *Reason and Revolution* (New York, 1959) for a convenient summary of Marcuse's revised assessment.

[7] Marcuse's social commentary is extensive and often polemical, and he often draws on earlier themes as well as on the contentions of other social critics. We cannot recreate the atmosphere of his writings, but must isolate what seems to be the central line of argument.

on the other, a view of modern man gaining in moral autonomy and responsibility so long as he does not lose his nerve. At its most interesting, this contrast does not appear to be an argument between "collectivism" and "individualism," or between "irrationalism" and "rationalism." Instead of depicting such universes in collision, we shall examine Marcuse's rendering of Max Weber and Sigmund Freud as theorists of the decisive social processes, and then consider his application of what he claims to be *their* most important insights for the diagnosis of our time.

While Marcuse's earlier work consistently treats fascism as an irrational reaction against the failure of liberal civilization to fulfill the promises of reason, he now commonly contends that he had been deceived by the irrationalist *doctrines* of fascism and that he now understands that fascism in *practice* is a consistent implementation, in rather special conditions, of the program implicit in the liberal conception of rationality. In his earlier view, liberal civilization appears to uncover the possibilities of rational mastery over circumstances but fails to pursue them, both because it equates reason with technology-directed science and because it remains committed to private property. Yet even these limitations define a productive one-sidedness, in Marcuse's earlier view: they create the conditions for their own transcendence, notwithstanding such crisis-manifestations as fascism. The logic of social reason, Marcuse thought, drives toward human liberation, and the obstacles in the way seem ever more evidently illogical and unreasonable, even to common sense. But in the work we are now considering, Marcuse credits the corrupt forms of rationality with extensive capacities for survival and self-perpetuation, without a recourse to political totalitarianism except for special circumstances such as those now seen to have produced nazism in Germany. Logic, reasonableness, and rational problem solving (and planning), as they are conceived and established in advanced technological societies, generate no revolutionary dynamic. It is the conception of revolution which now appears patently unreasonable and utopian, to disciplined thought as well as to general opinion, regardless of class. Dominant political agencies and social institutions can solve or at least manage the problems which become visible, and the needs perceived by most individuals are met.[8]

According to Marcuse, it was Max Weber who identified and labeled the social process which gives modern industrial society its distinctive character. "Rationalization," as the process is called, structures the experiences and actions of men so as to make them calculable in terms of costs and benefits, and it organizes social action so as to allow maximally efficient implementation of decisions based upon such calculations. To subject events to human reason so understood, Marcuse comments, is to subject them to a "technical" mode of encountering the world, a vision of a universe of ultimate facts—including the needs of individuals and the requirements of systems—and a search for the manipulations requisite for optimal satisfaction of these demands. For Weber, rationalization is inseparable from industrialization. Moreover, in contrast to Marcuse's view, rationalization is seen to create the condition under which the responsibility and choice of individuals have their greatest impact; although it is also said to test men's moral and political capacities to the utmost—and perhaps beyond their strength. Once reason is restricted to the calculation of means and consequences, individuals cannot evade personal responsibility for their choice of ends. Weber acknowledges that such a high charge of responsibility may exceed the moral capacities of individuals and may paralyze some or even drive them to irrationality. Similarly, on this view, the development of legal-rational structures of authority, with the attendant emergence of bureaucracy and legalism, vastly enhances the possibilities for purposive political control on behalf of public objectives. This development too has its dark side in that it renders less probable the emergence of political leadership able to wield the new instruments: the bureaucratic structure of means comes to equate its self-preservation with ends of policy, and there is a loss of direction and vitality only too likely to be countered by a resurgence of charismatic or otherwise irrational power. Weber

---

[8] "Thus irrationality becomes the form of social reason, becomes the rational universal." "Freedom and Freud's Theory of the Instincts," *Five Lectures* (Boston, 1970), p. 3. Marcuse shares with the Young Hegelian tradition the penchant for pointed paradoxical formulations.

himself had grave doubts about the outcome of these counter-
tendencies which, in his view, accompanied rationalization.
But, when he allowed himself speculation upon the moral implications of his findings, he saw the situation as the closest it
was possible to come toward realizing liberal hopes for man.
And many contemporary liberals find in Weber a sophisticated
model for a theory affirming civilization, a model which specifies the social and psychological conditions for autonomy and
analyzes the special dangers which accompany these conditions
and to which they frequently succumb.[9]

Marcuse presents his own contrasting assessment of rationalization as a deepening of Weber's insights, as a consistent
pursuit of the inquiry implicit in Weber's concepts, but illogi-
cally (and ideologically) aborted by Weber and his followers so
that they could produce conclusions compatible with liberalism. But before considering Marcuse's distinctive adaptation of
Weber's work, it should be noted that throughout his comments
on technical rationality there also runs the familiar Marxist
argument: that capitalist interests *distort* the inner logic of rationalization. According to this argument, Weber unreasonably
equated the operating requirements of an industry producing
for the sake of capitalist profits with the functional requirements
of industry and modernization as such. Marcuse contends, on
the other hand, that they are in fact increasingly in conflict.
"The repressed final cause behind the scientific enterprise," he
writes, is "pacified existence." [10] The "consummation of technical reason" could really make for liberation,[11] and systematic
public administration tends in its own nature toward the "administration of things," not the domination of man.[12] Even in its
technical form, thus, rationalization sometimes appears in Mar-

[9] Weber's argument on these points is conveniently available in his best-
known essays, "Science as Vocation" and "Politics as Vocation," in H. Gerth
and C. W. Mills, eds., *From Max Weber* (New York, 1958). In addition to John
Chapman, influential writers drawing on Weber's argument in this connection
include Raymond Aron, Daniel Bell, Reinhardt Bendix, Benjamin Nelson, and
Edward Shills.

[10] *One-Dimensional Man* (Boston, 1964), p. 235.

[11] "Industrialization and Capitalism in the Work of Max Weber," *Negations*, p. 233.

[12] *Ibid.*, p. 218, 223; see also *Soviet Marxism* (New York, 1961), especially
"Preface (1960)."

cuse's later writings as a progressive and revolutionary concept whose full recognition in theory yields a damning indictment of capitalism and whose full realization in practice would constitute a liberated society.

From this standpoint, Marcuse charges that Weber misunderstands the tensions within modernity. Weber had imagined a conflict between rationalization and irrational resistance. In fact, according to Marcuse, there is conflict between rationalization and the historical forces which have brought it into being. Rationalization can provide a systematic ordering of resources for the satisfaction of human needs, but capitalism produces coerced subordination to the requirements of infinite productivity as well as destructive domination over nature; rationalization promises a "technification of domination," which implies a noncoercive coordination of social effort, but capitalism rests upon domination in the interest of a narrow ruling class.

Marcuse's more distinctive recent position is found superimposed upon this line of discussion, often in the same texts. Here he attacks technical rationality as such, and its presumed psychological bases and social manifestations. Capitalism corrupts society, from this standpoint, because it *perfects* technical rationality, not because it perverts it. Especially striking is the suggestion that an ordering force antithetical to human perfection can itself appear perfectible. A society ordered by and for technical rationality, it seems, need not frustrate men's expectations although it stifles their capacities: it will not be shaken by ever more intense crises; it may not generate ever more threatening resistances to its order. "When technic becomes the universal form of material production," Marcuse writes, "it circumscribes an entire culture, it projects a historical totality—a world." Although terms like "capitalism" and "socialism" continue to play an important part in Marcuse's writings, the focus turns from such social units of analysis as private property or commodity production to units of the sort more commonly studied by psychologists. Marcuse insists that these psychological units also require social and historical interpretation, that even so seemingly timeless a matter as human instinct must be seen as an historical product in some basic way. But it remains striking that Marcuse now assesses social patterns in terms of their impacts upon and implications for human nature, and much less in relation to other social forces. His most elaborate treatment of technical rationality occurs under the headings of "one-dimensional society" and "one-dimensional thought," but these are found in a work significantly entitled *One-Dimensional Man.* The "world" defined by technical rationality is taken up within the man at home in it and willingly recreated by him in his actions. To understand this process and, as he conceives it, to show its ultimate irrationality and destructiveness, Marcuse professes to build upon Freud.

Marcuse understands Freud to have shown first, that mankind creates and recreates civilization as the "reality principle" gains superiority within the psychic economies of individuals, and, second, that the psychic effort to create and sustain such superiority exacts heavy costs. According to Marcuse, the "reality principle" has been in fact equivalent to the "performance principle"; and this requires above all the delay and restriction of pleasurable gratifications, so that psychic energies can be applied in a disciplined way to the tasks imposed upon men by a natural scarcity of the things men need and by the multiplicity of competing, gratification-seeking men. Man has to work, in short, and man must be governed; and the reality principle epitomizes the psychological organization which best adapts man to these requirements. In Marcuse's rendering at least, Freud's thesis resembles the utilitarianism of Hobbes and Hume, except that there is greater emphasis on the strains which attend such an order founded on renunciation. The performance principle, in any case, is presented as the psychological counterpart of technical rationality as a social fact.

Marcuse emphasizes Freud's conclusion that the psychological costs accompanying such organization of energies mount steeply as civilization progresses. Instinctual renunciation requires repression of instincts, and this can be achieved only by turning one expression of instinctual force upon others. Aggression, much of it turned by the individual upon himself, comes to be a major form of psychic energy. And civilized men are thus unhappy, often disturbed, and periodically wild. Freud saw these strains and disadvantages as ameliorable but ultimately inescapable costs of a process which he seems in general to value. When he concluded "Where id is, let ego be," he suggested that men escape complete dependence on dark natural forces and the terror of uncontained warfare only if they accept painful renunciations and controls, since the generation of ego is closely linked to the experience with superego and to the rise of the reality principle. Like Weber Freud offers sparse and precarious prospects to the autonomous civilized man of liberalism, but cannot envision a better alternative.

Marcuse considers Freud's conception of the individuation supposed to accompany and in some measure to outweigh the sufferings produced by progressive civilization as not so much wrong as obsolete. Marcuse maintains that the processes which now order and control men's instincts no longer bring about the possibility of the individual somehow discovering an autonomous self within the interplay of developmental pressures and resistances which Freud describes. Social institutions for production and control harness men's instincts to institutional requirements without depending on the complex familial drama depicted by Freud. Men are socialized to their role as instruments of the apparatus by a pervasive and seemingly automatic system of rewards, penalties, and alternatives foreclosed. Marcuse argues in effect that the descriptions which contemporary behavioral psychologists offer correspond more closely to the facts of contemporary society than does Freud's account of civilization, but that the facts must be subjected to an interpretation informed by Freud. Marcuse sees the contemporary pattern of psychological formation directly comparable to the regression of the ego which Freud discovered in mob psychology. Individuation is shortcircuited. Men submit to a depersonalized ego-ideal to enter a mass collectively enlisted in the service of technical reality. No one is in charge. The institutions reproduce themselves.

Corresponding to this, in Marcuse's account—and proof in his view that Freudian theory is vastly superior to that of the behaviorists, even though their descriptions are more up-to-date—is a constant increase in aggression and destructiveness. The smooth and comprehensive regulation of impulses generates aggressive energies, but denies them outlet in acts of self-defence and self-assertion, since there are no controllers in sight. Repression of instincts produces guilt and anxiety. Aggression and destructiveness pervade society in ways which cannot but lead to their further escalation. Marcuse stresses the aggressive component in modern uses of technological products; he returns constantly to automobiles which kill, in symbol and in fact, to aggressive intrusions upon remaining private spaces by noisy repetitions, militarization, mobilization against the enemies within and without, and escalating warfare. Freud had imagined that the costs of civilization could be borne. Marcuse argues that this judgment rests on an incomplete accounting. When the performance principle assumes full sway, Marcuse contends, civilization begins to undermine itself. At the apex of success and stability, civilized society becomes quite literally impossible.

The existing social order requires and induces a transformation in man, generating the "qualities which enable him to get along with others in his society." [13] Marcuse constantly speaks of this effect as being produced by "systematic manipulation and control" (p. 253), but—as will be seen in connection with the supervening theme of domination—deliberate shaping seems not to be the most basic process Marcuse has in view. Social structures interact in a transformative way with psychological makeup, according to Marcuse, through a myriad of pushes and pulls which can only be comprehended as "tendencies, forces which can be identified by an analysis of the existing society, and which assert themselves even if the policy makers are not aware of them." "These objective tendencies become manifest," he asserts, "in the trend of the economy, in technological change, in the domestic and foreign policy of a nation or a group of nations, and they generate common supraindividual needs in the different social classes, pressure groups and parties." (p. 252.) All social actors, it would appear, collaborate in this transformation work. Marcuse insists, against the neo-Freudian revisionists, that the adaptation reshapes the very

[13] "Aggressiveness in Advanced Industrial Society," *Negations*, p. 256. This useful synopsis of the argument Marcuse has been developing since *Eros and Civilization* (Boston, 1955) will serve as a reference for the ensuing discussion, with page numbers in parentheses. Marcuse's interpretation of Freud cannot be evaluated here. For contrasting assessments, compare Peter Sedgwick, "Natural Science and Human Theory," *The Socialist Register 1966* (London and New York, 1966) and Paul A. Robinson, *The Freudian Left* (New York, 1969), p. 147.

organization of human instincts, not simply personality or character. The changes which have taken place, though imperfectly effectuated as yet, involve a whole new structure, an integral breach with the past. Similarly, no mere reform or adjustment can inaugurate a transcendent alternative. That too will have to involve, according to Marcuse, an instinctual revolution. But that issue will concern us later.

The existing psychological order subordinates life to death, Eros to Thanatos. Marcuse explains:

> Now the (more or less sublimated) transformation of destructive into socially useful aggressive (and thereby constructive) energy, is, according to Freud . . . a normal and indispensable process. It is part of the same dynamic by which libido, erotic energy, is sublimated and made socially useful; the two opposite impulses are forced together and, united in this twofold transformation, they become the mental and organic vehicles of civilization. But no matter how close and effective their union, their respective quality remains unchanged and contrary: aggression activates destruction which "aims" at death, while libido seeks the preservation, protection and amelioration of life. Therefore, it is only as long as destruction works in the service of Eros that it serves civilization and the individual; if aggression becomes stronger than its erotic counterpart, the trend is reversed. *Negations* (p. 257).

And it is precisely such a reversal which marks the present age. Men's circumstances elicit mobilization of aggressive energy, especially against the individual himself, and this must take strength from the erotic. Marcuse cites, in this connection, what he calls "military mobilization" of societies, the radical divorce between productive work and satisfaction, the "conditions of crowding, noise, and overtness characteristic of mass society"; and he associates all this with the elimination of counteracting spheres, especially the devaluation of truth and aesthetics through an "administered language" and entertainment. The details of Marcuse's social and cultural criticism, although often pungently formulated, are not so very distinctive, after all. What makes his argument formidable as a whole is his conception of a "system" whose primary dynamics have been internalized within the structure of needs characteristic of its "victims" as well as its "beneficiaries," and whose momentum leads to universal death. Marcuse concludes:

If Freud's theory is correct, and the destructive impulse strives for the annihilation of the individual's own life no matter how long the "detour" via other lives and targets, then we may indeed speak of a suicidal tendency on a truly social scale, and the national and international play with total destruction may well have found a firm basis in the instinctual structure of individuals. (p. 268)

Triumphant technical rationality proves ultimately irrational not merely because it imposes deprivations far more stringent than could be justified by contemporary conditions of supply, and not merely because it generates within its administrators as well as its subjects a steadily mounting danger of lethal explosion, but also and above all because it converts into aggressive form the erotic libidinal energies required for the integration of any social order. Marcuse insists that sociality depends upon a good deal of instinctual energy in erotic form. If existing civilization converts this into aggressive and destructive drives, society reproduces itself in a manner ever more tenuous and susceptible to catastrophe. As noted earlier, the argument as a whole is strongly reminiscent of the way in which Montesquieu and his followers thought about tyranny and its presumed corrosive effects upon social union in progressive societies.[14]

In the older tradition tyranny was commonly defined as a political system constituted by power in its harshest form: the ruler's command secures obedience simply by virtue of his violent might and his subjects' fear. Marcuse says comparatively little about political power and might; his key concepts are, rather, domination and repression. The significance of this conceptual shift will become clear. Just now it is important to note that for Marcuse the ordinary, politically relevant conduct of

[14] "Freedom and Freud's Theory of Instincts," *Five Lectures*, especially pp. 22 f. The earlier writers distinguished between societies where despotism may well be appropriate, where it is sustained by a pervasive and stable slavishness generated by climatic, cultural, and other long-term factors; and societies where despotism arises as a result of abuses of power, but where it cannot sustain the links among men necessary for its own long-term existence. E. V. Walter has explored this tradition. See, for example, his *Terror and Resistance* (New York, 1969). This distinction is often conceived as a distinction between despotism and tyranny.

men in contemporary society must be understood as a product
of "domination" just as, for the older tradition, such conduct
was elicited, in tyrannies, by the ruler's exactions and imposi-
tions. "Domination is in effect," Marcuse writes, "whenever the
individual's goals and purposes and the means of striving for
and attaining them are prescribed to him and performed by him
as something prescribed." [15] But that definition appears broad
enough to include any sort of ordered conduct, and Marcuse
goes on to focus upon a more restrictive sense of the term. Like
the conception of tyrannical power in the tradition, Marcuse's
"domination" is to be contrasted with "rational authority":

> The latter, which is inherent in any societal division of labor, is
> derived from knowledge and confined to the administration of
> functions and arrangements necessary for the advancement of the
> whole. In contrast, domination is exercised by a particular group
> or individual in order to sustain and enhance itself in a privi-
> leged position.[16]

Under conditions of domination in the narrow sense, "social
needs have been determined by the interests of the ruling
groups at any given time, and this interest has defined the
needs of other groups and the means and limitations of their satisfactions." (p. 3.) At its extreme, "there is an irrational transfer
of conscience and the repression of consciousness." [17] But we
are left with an important uncertainty.

Is it indeed the case that "domination," as Marcuse understands it, requires a dominator as well as the dominated? When
he speaks of the "exercise" of domination by groups of individuals having certain purposes, or when he refers to "ruling
groups," it certainly seems so. Yet he also claims that "domination can be exercised by men, by nature, by things—it can also
be internal, exercised by the individual on himself and appear
in the form of autonomy." (pp. 1–2) Even if we remove from the
last passage some overpointedness produced by Marcuse's decision—apparent in this essay only—to label all forms of repres-

---

[15] "Freedom and Freud's Theory of the Instincts," *Five Lectures*, p. 1.
Numbers in parentheses will now refer to this essay.
[16] *Eros and Civilization*, p. 36. See also "The End of Utopia," *Five Lectures*, p. 81.
[17] "Obsolescence of the Freudian Concept of Man," *Five Lectures*, p. 50.

sion "domination" in some sense, there remains a question. Marcuse has never resolved it in full.

In his discussion of "mass democracy," the major political form within which contemporary domination operates, in his view, this matter becomes quite important. At first he seems to be echoing C. Wright Mills's thesis in *Power Elite:*

> Having control of the [giant production-and-distribution] apparatus [of modern industry], or even of its key positions, means having control of the masses in such a way, in fact, that this control seems to result automatically from the division of labor, to be its technical result, the rationale of the functioning apparatus that spans and maintains the whole society. Thus domination appears as a technical-administrative quality, and this quality fuses the different groups that hold the key positions in the apparatus— economic, political, military—into a technical-administrative collective that represents the whole. (p. 15)

Despite the puzzling ascription of a universal representative character to the dominant collective, Marcuse appears to describe a ruling group controlling the rest in furtherance of its own interests. But he goes on to build on the notion of representation instead:

> This technical-administrative collectivization appears as the expression of objective reason, that is, as the form in which the whole reproduces and extends itself. All freedoms are predetermined and preformed by it and subordinated not so much to political force as to the rational demands of the apparatus. . . . (p. 16)

To the extent that there are individuals in ruling positions, it now emerges, they function more like Hegel's universal administrative class than like Mills's power elite: what is crucial is that the "reason" they represent is the antireason of technical rationalization, not that they rule for the sake of their privileges. Marcuse confirms this impression: "There is no longer an autonomous subject across from the object, a subject that governs and in doing so pursues its own definable interests and goals." (p. 16)

That would seem to reduce the distinction between domination and rational authority altogether to a judgment about what is "necessary for the advancement of the whole," and leave altogether out of consideration the mode of control as such. While it is not meaningless to say that domination is any constraint upon action which steers it so as to uphold a system judged to be irrational or vicious, such a definition would not allow one to adduce the prevalence of domination as a major proof of irrationality or viciousness. Marcuse escapes the tautology only insofar as he shifts the locus of domination from the social or political, as ordinarily understood, to the psychological. Domination then proves to be a condition of individuals, not a condition of relations between individuals (although that does not mean that the individual's condition may not be a function of relations with others). There need not be a dominator, although there often is one.

To be dominated, it is only necessary to have one's instincts attuned to external demands emanating from the process which supplies and creates material needs, whether these demands come in the forms of commands or suggestions or even opportunities. Domination becomes complete, according to Marcuse, when individuals abandon the capacity of opposition or resistance. Without resistance, there is no way in which individuals can express their power. This is how Marcuse interprets the widely remarked decline of political conflict during the 1950s and early 1960s, and denies that it has anything to do with "consensus" in any sense of that term relevant to liberal conceptions of consent. Stating Marcuse's argument in the older language, we may say that for him domination has at its core the corruption of civic virtue.[18]

Enslavement in the ordinary sense, the enjoyments of individual liberty, consumer-sovereignty, man's ever-growing mastery over nature, totalitarian dictatorship, pluralist liberal democracy—all may be forms of domination if they build upon and reinforce an incapacity for saying "no," if they preempt the human power of resistance. But in the last analysis, on this

[18] As so often, Marcuse's argument strikes classical chords: " 'I am free,' you claim. But on what grounds—you who are enslaved to do so many things. . . . No literal bond of slavery compels you, no force from without moves your muscles; but if tyrants arise within your sick soul, how do you escape unpunished?" Persius, *Satura* 5, ll. 124, 127–31; cited in Robert D. Cumming, *Human Nature and History* (Chicago, 1969), I, 340, n.104. Cumming locates the passage in the context of "sermonizing in the Cynic-Stoic Tradition."

reading, each man reproduces his own domination, especially if he simply minds his own business. Though not only then. Political activity within the ordinary channels of such a society of dominated men—if it speaks the ordinary language and utilizes the ordinary instruments—cannot lift people out of their dependence upon the processes making for domination, and so simply reinforces the existing order, whatever the sincere professions of the individuals involved. Marcuse concludes that men are satisfied within a system approaching total domination. They are also, in his view, doomed to be destroyed by it—doomed to destroy themselves through it.

Marcuse himself calls his diagnosis "apocalyptic" and "eschatological," and he insists that his vision of a transcendent alternative must properly be designated "utopian." In the next section we shall describe that vision as best we can and, in the last, we shall try to follow what Marcuse has to say about the implications of his theory for political practice. Since the whole of the foregoing has been remorseless summary, it will hardly do to summarize once again. What is most noteworthy for the political theorist in the work reviewed so far, it has been suggested, is its insistence upon examining the social relationships and psychological attributes presupposed by the central principles and maxims of political theory, and its conclusion that liberal political language and practice fails to comprehend the problems posed by these factors under conditions of advanced civilization. The postwar period of Marcuse's productivity revealed the shattering fact that liberal arrangements can create contentment without liberation.[19] To express and explain this

---

[19] There is also the very important fact, little reflected in the bulk of Marcuse's most influential writings, that Marcuse served for fifteen years as political commentator on Central and Eastern Europe. *Soviet Marxism* presumably reflects these activities. In many ways this book is pivotal to any understanding of Marcuse's thought. Soviet political life, as Marcuse described it, is marked by political despotism in its most direct sense, by moral preachings which almost parody the repressive morality of Western civilization, but also by the elimination of capitalist private property. Marcuse seems to conclude that the underlying spirit of communism as liberating alternative is nevertheless somehow there, manifested above all in the failure of the people to internalize the repressive norms (as witnessed by the reliance on violent techniques of rule and blatant interminable propagandizing); that there remains the live possibility therefore that the people will rise against their ruling institutions, once these

conception Marcuse develops a theory of despotism or tyranny relying on criteria very different from those found in the political tradition. There is a common factor, here designated as "corruption," but it is treated very differently. We shall return to these themes in the last section.

Marcuse's qualifications as utopian visionary are somewhat unusual. His thought and his writing lack the ingenious specificity and sensuous concreteness which mark great utopias: he always seems to tell rather than show. Nevertheless he conveys, to some influential audiences at least, a conviction that there is something out there, an actual alternative whose vital principles can be grasped. Perhaps it is as some of his harsher critics suggest, that his abstract categories offer empty though imposing vessels to be filled by the reader with whatever stuff his dreams are made of. As we shall see, Marcuse might not find such an objection as telling as the objectors might think.[20] We reserve judgment. If we are at all right about the logic of Mar-

---

institutions have performed their historically necessary task of building production beyond the constraints of scarcity; and that, since the internal masters are not in command, such an attack on external governors would yield liberation. Marcuse suggests that the Soviet political and social order provides a temporary and radically imperfect framework within which the major advances of civilization can be accumulated without incorporating its fatal dangers. That accumulation then makes possible a wholly new order. Schematically, in brief, his understanding of the Soviet order is very similar to his understanding of Western civilization: it is somehow possible to discern the "spirit" or "idea" or ultimate rationale moving a society, and that force has its locus, in the last analysis, in the psychological structure within its inhabitants. Though produced and reproduced by the institutional matrices defining men's existences, these congruent "spirits" cannot be extrapolated from an account of social and political arrangements as such. Thus, "free" institutions may sustain despotism, and "despotic" institutions may foster liberation. Since Marcuse sees the need for a revolution against the Soviet state, his position can hardly be called pro-Soviet. His position does, however, imply a preference for the Soviets in any struggle with the Americans because their gains would be less likely to secure despotism in its most important sense. In any case, it may well be that Marcuse's sustained attention to the harshness and ineffectiveness of the East contributed as much as his recognition of the tolerance and success of the West toward his turn from history to human nature as an ultimate framework for theoretical discussion.

[20] See David Kettler, "The Vocation of Radical Intellectuals," *Politics and Society*, 1, no. 1 (1970).

cuse's ideas, his critique of liberal responses to civilization could stand without a projected alternative, as a doleful prophecy. But such an outcome would be altogether alien to Marcuse's own design. The notion of a transcendent alternative is not a consolation somehow added to a bleak prognosis, a "lullaby-song of Heaven" to soothe our dismay. There is an authentic ring of optimism in Marcuse's work.[21] He is serene in the depiction of evil because he is confident that there is another world.

Marcuse would offer us a joyful science. The good order is above all an order in which men are happy. Priding himself upon continuities with Epicureanism, Marcuse claims that he can show how "the ancient desideratum of hedonism" can now be fulfilled. Happiness and truth need no longer conflict; happiness need no longer be located in the interstices of a harsh order required by imperious necessities. The structure of necessity itself, Marcuse argues, now commands that men make themselves happy. Marcuse conditions happiness upon a revolutionary restructuring of instincts. His account of utopia does not address itself to the problems of political power, as these have been stated in the liberal tradition of political theory. Like Marxist writers, Marcuse claims that these "problems" pertain to the irrational circumstances of contemporary civilization and not to the ordering of social relationships as such. He goes beyond the Marxists in anticipating a state of affairs which will dispense with power as a source of problems, and thus in attempting to undermine the premises upon which rest so many questions of political theory. Political power is indeed oppressive in existing civilization; but this whole mode of relating men, according to Marcuse, arises from the structure of human instincts as they have adapted themselves to the requirements of production and progress. And this can change. The "will to gratification" must replace the "logic of domination." In the happy society, no one would enjoy power. Marcuse insists that there can be a radically different organizing principle and or-

[21] It would be worthwhile to compare Marcuse in this respect with Max Horkheimer and Theodor Adorno, with whom he shares so many ideas. They are also speaking of "hope," but the impenetrability of their writings on these themes may testify to their despair. Marcuse's utterances, in contrast, bear the marks of having glad tidings to tell.

dering force within the individual as within the society. As in his earlier work, liberation implies order. In depicting this alternate order, Marcuse refers primarily to two related classes of experience available to men at the present time and contends that these prefigure the essential qualities of all experience in utopia: love and aesthetic sensibility. We shall look first at these new human capabilities, as Marcuse sees them, and then at the patterns of relationships and actions corresponding to them, insofar as we can tell what Marcuse has in mind.

Marcuse argues that humankind created the instinctual structure depicted by Freud in a revolutionary adaptation to scarcity in nature and the promise of social productivity. The reality principle orders libidinal energies so that man can encounter necessities in a practical way. But the established form of the reality principle, says Marcuse, is the performance principle; repression and guilt purchase progress and civilization. Now, Marcuse holds, what was necessary and rational has become unnecessary and irrational. There can and must be a change in the political economy of the psyche: the "aesthetic principle as form of the reality principle" [22] will structure and direct the instincts. Marcuse tries in several different ways, drawing extensively on poetry and mythology, to convey the quality of the hoped-for new principle. We must be content to summarize his claims. Marcuse maintains that human fantasy, forms of eroticism which do not seek to master others, the capacity for play and artistic creation, and aesthetic sensibility all testify to the possibility that man can encounter the world in a meaningful way without the lust for domination and the repression, calculation, and anxiety which that lust implies.[23]

That these modes of experience now largely serve as mere consolations and recreations supporting the dominant system does not negate their ultimate subversive significance, Marcuse contends. Libidinal energies can be redirected from their present channels of aggression, technical rationality, and exploitative genital sexuality. The sum total of human relationships

[22] *Essay on Liberation*, p. 90. See also *Eros and Civilization*, pp. 150–51.

[23] See pt. II of *Eros and Civilization*, "Beyond the Reality Principle," p. 129. See also "Progress and Freud's Theory of the Instincts," *Five Lectures;* "A Biological Foundation for Socialism?" *Essay on Liberation;* "Nature and Revolution," *Counter-Revolution and Revolt*.

and activities can be charged with a diffuse but joyful erotic satisfaction. In the earlier writings of this sort, especially in *Eros and Civilization,* Marcuse distinguishes between the repression presumably necessary for the unavoidable self-discipline involved in socially necessary work and the "surplus repression" which attends the prevailing system of alienated labor and domination. Only the latter could be eliminated, while the former would simply be displaced from its central place in man's makeup. But that qualification is steadily eroding, as Marcuse comes to decide that work itself must be an integral part of the new happiness, providing direct gratification for new sorts of needs.[24]

Marcuse nowhere discusses the ontogenetic process which would reproduce in the individual the instinctual structure corresponding to such a pattern of impulses and actions. In some measure, however, his conception is implicit in his judgment that Freud's account has become obsolete and that the organization of the instincts has in any case become a product of social-political forces and not of the intrafamilial dialectic. Just as the last revolution presupposed that radical transformation in the family which Freud recounts in the primal slaying of the father and its aftermath, so the forthcoming liberation of men, although measured by the reconstitution of the soul, presupposes social and political overturn. As already noted, Marcuse gives no more than a very general account of the social and political arrangements corresponding to this new psychological structure and presumably capable of sustaining it once it has been somehow established.[25]

Obviously he envisions some kind of collective ownership of productive means and pretty certainly he intends an end to formal institutions of government.[26] Although "technology and

[24] *Essay on Liberation,* p. 91; see also pp. 20–22, where he expressly cites Nietzsche against Marx on this point.

[25] In *Essay on Liberation,* Marcuse appropriates the Soviet Marxist distinction between socialism and communism, speaking of a "First Phase, that is, the authoritarian bureaucratic development of the productive forces," p. 89. But he also insists that such a phase could only contribute to liberation if the new sensibility were already operative within it.

[26] There is considerable lack of clarity about this in the texts. In *Essay on Liberation* and "Repressive Tolerance," Marcuse talks about "direct democ-

technique" are now central to the logic of domination, they must be retained and converted to the rhythms of the new order, since the triumph over scarcity which is the material foundation upon which utopia rests depends on the new productive capabilities. As already noted, Marcuse imagines that the continued operation of these resources can be freed from "technical rationality" and the rage for productivity. Marcuse speaks of "creative experimentation with the productive forces" and "play with the potentialities of human and non-human nature." "The productive imagination," he continues, "would become the concretely structured productive force that freely sketches out the possibilities for a free human existence on the basis of a corresponding development of material productive forces." [27]

To fill in these very vague indications, Marcuse has turned in his most recent work toward some of the ecological writers, especially Murray Bookchin's notion of "liberatory technology." [28] Very importantly, the society would cease to be "pro-

---

racy" and rule by a genuinely "free and sovereign majority," whose members have somehow been educated for autonomy. In these passages, his position moves very close to that of a classical Rousseauist democrat, with added Kantian elements. But there is so little room in the ambitious discussions of the new psychological structure for the psychology of such citizenship that we cannot take these political arrangements as an integral part of the new society, but must refer them rather to the period of transition, seeing them as an alternative to the "educational dictatorship" which is also discussed in this context. In "The Left Under the Counter-Revolution," Marcuse expressly describes "a 'direct democracy' of the majority" as "the form of government or administration for the *construction of socialism." Counter-Revolution and Revolt*, p. 54. But the limits of this stage remain unclear. Marcuse's inconclusiveness on these vital political questions is part of a pattern to be further discussed. See also *Essay on Liberation*, pp. 68–69 and 69n.; "Repressive Tolerance," in Robert Paul Wolff, Barrington Moore, and Herbert Marcuse, *A Critique of Pure Tolerance* (Boston, 1965, 1968), p. 105, and "Postscript 1968," pp. 122–23; cp. "Freedom and Freud's Theory," *Five Lectures*, p. 23 f. for an attack on the "idealist" conceptions of freedom and autonomy.

[27] "The End of Utopia," *Five Lectures*, p. 66. "A productivity that is sensuousness, play, and song," *Eros and Civilization.*

[28] *Counter-Revolution*, p. 61. Marcuse's own imagination flags rather badly whenever he wants to illustrate this conception, and he turns up with banal talk about parks instead of parking lots and an occasional romanticizing of folk crafts. See "The End of Utopia," *op. cit.*, p. 65.

gressive," in the sense of the old political economy; genuine contentment is a "stationary state." In a striking passage, Marcuse remarks that "freedom would no longer be an eternally failing project." He goes on to say:

> Productivity would define itself in relation to receptivity, existence would be experienced, not as continually expanding and unfulfilled becoming but as existence or being with what is and can be. Time would not seem linear, as a perpetual line or rising curve, but cyclical as the return contained in Nietzsche's idea of the "perpetuity of pleasure." [29]

As all this suggests, the release of eroticism which Marcuse espouses had astoundingly little to do with the pleasures of genital sexuality, and the cooperation and solidarity he has in mind involve no fusion of identities into some libidinal mass. He does speak of a "libidinous civilization," but soon makes it clear that he means by this the "idea . . . of an aesthetic sensuous civilization," as it had been foreseen by Friedrich Schiller in the letters *On the Aesthetic Education of Man*.[30]

Writing in 1795, Schiller had sought a solution to two overlapping problems: how to recapture the classical capacity for civic virtue under conditions of commercial civilization—a question suggested to him by his study of Rousseau's *Discourses* and Adam Ferguson's *Essay on the History of Civil Society*—and how to bridge the gap between the requirements of morality laid down by Kant and the impulsions governing human conduct discerned by Hume, Helvetius, and other psychologists. When Schiller speaks of an "aesthetic state," it should be noted, it is as a dimension of existence intermediate between the "dynamic state" of powers in motion and the "ethical state" of unconditional duties. The playful involvement with beauty which constitutes this state affects the life of the whole community, but its actual denizens are few. Schiller

---

[29] "Progress and Freud's Theory," *Five Lectures*, pp. 40–41; see also *Eros and Civilization*, pp. 124–46.

[30] "Freedom and Freud's Theory," p. 23, pp. 41–42. The standard edition and translation of the work by Schiller is now Friedrich Schiller, *On the Aesthetic Education of Man*, edited and translated by Elizabeth M. Wilkinson and L. A. Willoughby (Oxford, 1967). Marcuse built especially on the series of letters between the Sixth and the Ninth, pp. 31–61, and then the Twenty-Seventh, pp. 205–19.

writes: "But does such a state of Aesthetic Semblance really exist? And if so, where is it to be found? As a need, it exists in every finely attuned soul; as a realized fact, we are likely to find it, like the pure Church and the pure Republic, only in some few chosen circles. . . ." [31] Marcuse acknowledges that the aesthetic ideal serves Schiller at least in important part as supplement and consolation for the requirements of life in a modern commercial civilization, but he contends that it is possible to abstract the design from its restrictive context and to pattern an entire countercivilization upon it.

This must not be misunderstood as a contention that all men can somehow become "artists." Following surrealist poets, Marcuse sees in art at its best an anticipation of the happiness which liberation can bring. But he insists that its embodiment in artistic work, in the narrow sense of "high culture," is itself a product of the repressive social order. If "the aesthetic function is conceived as a principle governing the entire human existence," [32] it may be that there is no place in utopia for artists, as there seems to be none for critical theorists. In any case, Marcuse is persuaded that Schiller offers the vital clue for the "solution of a 'political' problem: the liberation of man from inhuman existential conditions." "The play impulse," he contends, "is the vehicle of this liberation." In restating "the idea behind the *Aesthetic Education*," Marcuse emphasizes the moral intentions of the work, as well as its conception of order:

> It aims at basing morality on a sensuous ground; the laws of reason must be reconciled with the interest of the senses; the domineering form of impulse must be restrained . . . To be sure, if freedom is to become the governing principle of civilization, not only reason but also the "sensuous impulse" energy must conform with the universal *order* of freedom. However, whatever order would have to be imposed upon the sensuous impulse must itself be an "operation of freedom." The free individual himself must bring about the harmony between individual and

---

[31] *Ibid.*, p. 219. On the question of sexuality, Schiller writes: "taste throws a veil of decorum over those physical desires which in their naked form, affront the dignity of free beings; and, by a delightful illusion of freedom, conceals from us our degrading kinship with matter."

[32] *Eros and Civilization*, p. 188. See in the same work "The Aesthetic Dimension," pp. 172–96.

universal gratification. In a truly free civilization, all laws are self-given by the individuals: "to give freedom by freedom is the universal law" of the aesthetic state; in a truly free civilization, "the will of the whole" fulfills itself only "through the nature of the individual." Order is freedom only if it is founded on and sustained by the free gratification of the individual.[33]

Such a conception of order can be imagined to govern "human existence" in its entirety, rather than (as Schiller had thought) a narrow realm, only on the assumption of the psychological revolution that Marcuse has in view. He writes:

> The life instincts themselves strive for the unification and enhancement of life; in nonrepressive sublimation they would provide the libidinal energy for work on the development of a reality which no longer demands the exploitative repression of the Pleasure Principle. The "incentives" would then be built into the instinctual structure of man. Their sensibility would register as biological reactions, the difference between the ugly and the beautiful, between calm and noise, tenderness and brutality, intelligence and stupidity, joy and fun, and it would correlate this distinction with that between freedom and servitude.[34]

The "aesthetic state," it must be recalled, is not offered as the vehicle of that revolution, but rather as the condition congruent with its triumph.

Marcuse asks that we encounter this utopian projection through our imagination. We shall be content to observe it. In particular, Marcuse is concerned to deny that man must suffer deprivation and anxiety if he is to rise and remain above animal existence. Repressive civilization and domination had its justification so long as scarcity necessitated modes of labor discipline which in turn involved the generation of aggressive impulses necessitating coercive government. On the basis of plenty, men can attain to a new and higher humanity.[35] The projected Golden Age is not an age of prehuman passivity or angelic stupidity; it is a universal dance measure—complex, active, self-justifying. And, increasingly, Marcuse seems to

[33] *Eros and Civilization*, pp. 190–91.
[34] *Essay on Liberation*, p. 91.
[35] Cp. David Hume, *Treatise of Human Nature* (Oxford, 1888; 1958), p. 494.

suggest that there are harmonies in nature which can set the tempo, if humanity will be receptive.[36] As with the critique of modern civilization, we cannot but be struck by the affinities between Marcuse's thought and the classicism of the eighteenth century. Although there are formulations borrowed from Nietzsche and vitalist writers, and there is an insistence on resources of the unconscious, all these materials are assimilated to the intellectual habits of the Enlightenment. Such historical comparisons have very limited use, given the complexity of the phenomena and the diversity of interpretations, but they will serve to underline the distance between Marcuse and the "irrationalist" tendencies of the nineteenth and twentieth centuries. Marcuse offers an account of an educational order when he turns to a consideration of the "best state," as did Plato and Aristotle, each in their way, and as did the modern rationalist writers, through John Stuart Mill and John Dewey, when they set out to counter what they took to be the dehumanizing consequences of commercial civilization. It is a practical education, measured by the character it builds and not by the knowledge it accumulates. And, almost certainly, it is an education without educators, a self-cultivation through participation in cultivating forms.

Marcuse will not allow us simply to contemplate this joyful alternative. If we regard it thus, it would be simply another of the cultural products which, in his view, lead us to forgetfulness of our mission even while they remind us of the possibilities, because the reminder itself gives a soothing joy. Marcuse insists that the transcendence of power politics and technical rationality must be perceived as an ideal. He demands that we order our moral and political practice according to this

[36] On the image of dance, see "Introduction," to Schiller, op. cit., p. cxxxi f. The editors cite Goethe, Pope, Valéry, Nietzsche, T. S. Eliot, as well as Schiller himself. See also Herman Hesse, Steppenwolf, and Ingmar Bergman, The Seventh Seal. In a recent essay, Marcuse takes as the epitome of the vision he intends Bertold Brecht's poem, "The Lovers," depicting the dancelike flight of the two cranes. Counter-Revolution, p. 119 f. On the question of nature, Marcuse speaks increasingly of the "liberation" and "domination" of nature. "Liberation of nature is the recovery of life-enhancing forces in nature, the sensuous aesthetic qualities which are foreign to a life wasted in unending competitive performances." Counter-Revolution, p. 60. See also the work of Marcuse's student: William Leiss, The Domination of Nature (New York, 1972).

ideal and, in effect, denies it all value if it is not a present possibility. Marcuse's attempts to depict a revolutionary politics and
morals which will be a pursuit of happiness must concern us
next. But we can say even now that Marcuse considers the projection of the utopian alternative as itself an integral part of
such politics: it is necessary to reinforce the fleeting intimations
which all men have that things can be altogether different.
Breathing life into such a spark is a delicate matter; an excess of
fuel can smother it. This is why, as hinted earlier, Marcuse may
well be quite indifferent to charges that his utopian vision is
vague precisely with regard to many of the matters which generated the "realistic" compromises of his intellectual predecessors. Then too, it must be recalled, Marcuse's critique of liberal
civilization aims to show that those compromises are untenable.
Taken as a whole, Marcuse's argument depends on his conception of the revolutionary movement. If the conception stands,
the critique of civilization is a diagnosis of an infinitely promis-
ing crisis, and the utopian projection, the regulative ideal of an
efficacious practice; if the conception fails, the critique may be
Spenglerian prophecy, and the ideal, nostalgic invocation of
antiquated cultural glories.

Marcuse's work contains, as we have seen, a critique and a
utopia. His account of the universe within which meaningful
political activity must be comprehended falls between these
two. The principles of neither the old civilization nor the new
can apply to it. The revolution must be seen as an entity having
boundaries in political space and time like any other domain.
Paradoxical as it may seem, Marcuse means to oblige his
readers to citizenship within this polity. When he speaks of a
"right of revolution," he may be understood to use the term
"right" in the dual sense common in most Western European
languages other than English: there is a lawful structure defining duties as well as secure claims against other conflicting
demands. A revolution, in this sense, is not simply the forceful
negation of some existing legitimacy. It is a counterregime, having its beginnings long before the old regime fails and continuing in power until it can be somehow displaced by the new
order. Marcuse's writings on these subjects address themselves
to problems at two very different levels. First, he means to char-

acterize the revolution in general, depicting its basic principles, powers, and processes. Second, he offers political commentary on the present state of the revolution, its particular prospects and requirements. Marcuse's thought at the first level is confident and quite clear. At the second level, however, Marcuse encounters grave problems, including periodic doubts whether there is anything more than a vague idea of revolution in existence and consequently whether there is anything at all that it makes sense to do. We shall consider some of these difficulties, as well as their implications, in conclusion.

In contrast to his earlier Marxian confidence, Marcuse comes increasingly to view the revolution as project rather than as burgeoning actuality. This shift in attitude has to do with the consolidation of welfare-state capitalism after World War II and with disappointment in the Soviet Union and communist parties. The shift also involves a reexamination of the tasks assigned to revolution: it is no longer a matter of radicalizing and completing trends already present in the existing society and in the immediate reactions against it, but a matter of tapping energies and capabilities which lie more or less securely passive—repressed and absorbed by the major forces shaping men's experiences. The revolution stands outside the society, wholly reforming the human resources which are somehow made available to it, transforming them into men fit for combat and other action. If we have understood the spirit of the happy society correctly, moreover, there is almost as sharp a divide between it and the requirements of revolution. Revolution demands direction, effectiveness, repression, organization, super- and subordination, violence; the utopian aesthetic state will constitute its order altogether differently. But then the question arises whether it will require another revolution to move from the revolution to its presumed result, and we might find ourselves caught up in the paradox of infinite divisibility.

Raising such a possibility forces us back to a fundamental issue which we have expressly sought to set aside in this treatment: the matter of philosophic method. Marcuse, after all, is justly renowned as a writer who introduced many to the Hegelian dialectic and to its place in Marx's thought; and the dialectic presents itself precisely as a logic or intellectual strategy able to comprehend qualitative change, the analogue in philosophical and historical method to the mathematical techniques which dissolved Zeno's paradox. Has our account of Marcuse's thought brought us to incomprehensible changes and interminable transitions because we have left out his dialectical approach? Are we encountering problems which we have ourselves created? These are questions which a systematic treatment of Marcuse's thought would have to entertain in detail. We can simply assert a conclusion that it was Marcuse who was unable to make the dialectical conception work in attempting to deal with the relationships among corrupt society, utopia, and the revolution which is to intervene. Our recourse to the comparatively static models of Montesquieu as aids in expounding Marcuse's argument rests on the conviction that Marcuse actually organizes his materials into such structures, notwithstanding all the dialectical language. These remarks are not meant to suggest an assurance that dialectical methods *could* be made to work in political and social theory, in the way that Marcuse's philosophical program proclaims. It is possible that his departure from that program is a justifiable or even necessary accommodation to the substantive findings of his inquiry. Such questions cannot be addressed here. The main points are that Marcuse's later writings more nearly portray society as undergoing a sequence of distinct morphological incarnations than as caught up in a developmental dynamic, and that the epoch of transition itself takes on a surprising measure of integration, so that it is hard to say how it could begin or why it would end.

Let us turn to Marcuse's account of the structure of revolution in general. Marcuse's initial definition is quite ordinary: "the overturning of a legitimately established regime and constitution by a social class or movement having the objective of transforming the social as well as the political structure." [37] The expansion of the concept, so that it no longer refers simply to a certain class of events but also to a type of social entity, turns on the key word "movement." Marcuse constantly uses the term "movement" equivocally for revolutionary events and for the social actors—organizations and agencies as well as individuals—intending or acting in them. The problem of justifying

[37] "Ethik und Revolution" (Ethics and Revolution), *Kultur und Gesellschaft* 2 (Frankfurt, 1965), p. 131.

revolutions, for example, quickly becomes a problem of justifying revolutionary movements and revolutionary regimes. In the tradition, we can distinguish two general approaches to the right of revolution. The first stresses the corruption which attends tyranny and sanctions a resistance which will purify the polity and displace the tyrannical regime with one having contrasting qualities of reason and morality. The second sees resistance as defensive, the resumption of a natural right to the use of violence for the securing of vital properties. From this standpoint, the prime objective is to force public power back into its legitimate channels. The major actor in the former conception is a virtuous competitor for power; in the latter, it is an innocent victim of abuse. Marcuse's critique of liberalism brings him clearly within the former camp. The right of revolution is a right of revolutionaries; it depends far more on their righteousness than on their having been wronged.

The measure of right, then, is the capacity to promote human freedom and human happiness when these are being systematically repressed. If justified in this way, the revolutionary movement may use violence against existing powers and the revolutionary regime may subject the people to a "compulsory education" which will strip away the accumulated slavish patterns of thought and action, the domination within.[38] General moral arguments against the use of violence do not apply, according to Marcuse, because they are always only selectively applied to actions against established regimes. The infliction of hurt is a pervasive fact of human history; the ethically relevant distinction is that between reactionary and revolutionary violence. The same applies to indoctrination and "totalitarianism." According to Marcuse, all systems rest upon the psychological formation of men; and, as we have seen, none, in his view, is more total in its control than the system reproducing modern civilization. The fact that the present political system takes the form of democracy does not alter the basic situa-

[38] "Repressive Tolerance," p. 100 f. For some revealing parallels, see the discussion of Savonarola in J. G. A. Pocock, "Custom, and Form, Grace and Matter: An Approach to Machiavelli's Concept of Innovation," in Martin Fleischer, ed., *Machiavelli and the Nature of Political Thought* (New York, 1972), pp. 162–65.

tion, although, as will be seen, Marcuse frequently seeks democratic legitimation for the revolution. Existing democracy he variously describes as simply a sham behind which elites and interests rule or as a tyranny of a tyrannized majority. Controlled and/or corrupted wills cannot create obligation. In effect, Marcuse reverses the conventional presumptions. Once a revolutionary movement is constituted, meeting the criteria stated above, it is to be treated as the legitimate regime, presumably by its adherents as well as by all others within its claimed sphere; force attempted against this regime is then to be seen as illegitimate resistance. Marcuse repeatedly terms the violence perpetrated by revolutionaries "counter-violence," citing Robespierre as well as Marx in his support.

The revolution is an ethical entity, not only in its purpose but also in its means and in its inner constraints. Marcuse insists that "there are forms of violence and repression which a revolutionary situation cannot justify, because they negate the end to which revolution serves as means. Of this sort are arbitrary violence, terrorizing tactics, and indiscriminate terror." [39] But he appears confident that a revolutionary regime generates its own ethos, placing restraints on its own conduct as well as on that of others, to replace the internalized norms appropriate to the earlier condition. In no sense, then, can revolution be conceived as force out of control. There may be all sorts of violent risings against existing governments, revolutionary or repressive, but many of these, it appears, must be classed as "rebellions" or called by some other term expressly referring to the kinds of actions involved. Such events may be evaluated in relation to the revolution, being seen as preparatory or supportive or hostile, but unless they can be incorporated within the revolutionary movement itself, they lack ethical character, even if the standards of right they violate are no longer valid.

But actors involved in such actions all claim to be promoting human freedom and happiness. How can one know whether a particular claim is valid? Marcuse argues that the criteria are in principle objectively calculable. It should be possible to compare a projected alternative with the present, in regard to human freedom and happiness; and it should also be possible to

[39] "Ethics and Revolution," p. 139.

incorporate within the "brutal calculation" an estimate of the harm to be inflicted in the process of transformation for comparison with the harm attending nontransformation. He admits, however, that such a calculation can never be complete or certain. The real judgment can only come after the fact; we must now estimate probabilities, accept individual responsibility for involvement in an "historical experiment." Given a negative assessment of an existing system, there is a presumption in favor of forces moving against it—although that presumption can be overridden by recourse of those forces to impermissible means or some other substantial loss of ethical right. Marcuse places the individual actor in a curious and difficult position: on the one hand, he appears to be morally obliged to support the revolution, which is justified in punishing those who oppose it; on the other, he is given very little help in evaluating any particular claimant to the revolutionary role, especially if there should be competitors. Marcuse's position presumably is that this is an inescapable part of the human condition, not to be evaded by submission to presently dominant forces, whatever moral norms may be conventionally established.

Yet the discussion cannot remain at so general a level. Marcuse claims, after all, that social theory must provide an orientation to practice, that it must deal with the concrete historical present. We must then consider whether and how Marcuse sees the revolution in his own time. In an attempt to systematize ideas which are scattered in diverse political commentaries, we will relate his judgment to three aspects of revolutionary right. First, given the resources available to the society, can there be a social order which imposes substantially less repression on man, greatly enhancing his "freedom" and "happiness" as Marcuse understands those terms? Marcuse's critique and utopia say yes, without question. Existing legal and political institutions lack all moral right. This yields what we may designate an abstract right to revolution. The second aspect of the concept, as Marcuse applies it, refers to the actual availability of revolutionary forces—that is, some effective social energy which embodies the movement or gives quite specific promise of doing so. After Marcuse gives up the expectation that the industrial working class, operating through the organizations which have grown up since the time of Marx, represents such a force, he links this aspect directly to the third: the question of a revolutionary ethos. The concrete right to revolution, then, depends on the existence of a movement, at least potentially powerful enough to capture power and integrated by a purposive will to attain the revolutionary end. In dealing with past revolutions, Marcuse treats this third aspect as a completion of right which often can only be discerned in retrospect, after the revolutionary regime has consolidated itself, and the rationale for actions motivated by quite diverse concerns becomes clear. It is a historical judgment.

With regard to the present, however, it does not appear as though the revolutionary force can be mobilized without the awareness of domination—presumably because the domination is so insidiously pervasive within the subjects of the existing order. As repeatedly remarked, Marcuse has great difficulty deciding whether men are now subject to revolutionary right and if so what it might dictate. He has no doubts about insurgents in national liberation movements, in relation to their own situations; but he does not appear to believe that partisanship with those forces extends their right to individuals and groups operating in metropolitan centers. His writings constantly monitor the activities of oppositional groupings in the advanced countries, and his judgments there are not clearly stated. Speaking to radical students in 1967, Marcuse said:

> In monopolistic industrial society [the violence of suppression] is concentrated to an unprecedented extent in the domination that penetrates the totality of society. In relation to this totality the right of liberation is in its immediate appearance a particular right. Thus the conflict of violence appears as a clash between general and particular or public and private violence, and in this clash the private violence will be defeated until it can confront the existing public power as a new general interest. As long as the opposition does not have the social force of a new general interest, the problem of violence is primarily a problem of tactics.[40]

This statement would appear to sanction "violence" against the system, where tactically justified, even though the revolutionary movement is not sufficiently well-established to

[40] "Problem of Violence and the Radical Opposition," *Five Lectures*, p. 90.

appear as more than the arbitrary actions of individuals or narrowly defined special groups. But the explication of Marcuse's "tactics" links them to that "brutal calculation" which is part of the criterion of revolutionary right itself, so that acts of violence which are tactically unsound would also appear not to be right. In his most recent essay then we find:

> In the counterrevolutionary situation of today, violence is the weapon of the Establishment. . . . The revolutionary force which is destined to terminate this violence does not exist today. . . . Action directed toward vague, general, intangible targets is senseless; worse, it augments the number of adversaries.[41]

Despite some fluctuations, then, we can say that Marcuse finds the revolutionary right to be defective at the present time. The primary task he sets for "the left," or "the opposition," or even "the movement" to which he speaks, is the perfecting of this "right," the constitution of the revolutionary force. As a practical matter he denies the movement the full powers which pertain, in his view, to such a force. His diagnosis of the present situation consists of two parts: first, repeated surveys of recent social trends, in search of social energies antithetical to the prevailing system, energies which could presumably be converted to resources of revolution; and second, commentary on the political aspirations and activities of those who think of themselves as radical if not revolutionary opponents of the system, primarily students. The first sort of inquiry brings Marcuse repeatedly to the possibility that the working class is being pushed, despite everything, into conflict with the requirements of the system, especially with regard to work discipline. He also points in various ways to the presumed mounting frustration of technicians, the bitterness of outcast segments of society, the undermining of power by external foes of the system, the breakthrough of erotic and aesthetic forces in the form of various refusals. But he acknowledges most of the time that these have no necessary cumulative impact and that they need not propel events in a revolutionary direction. In the last analysis, everything depends on the activity of those who must found the revolutionary movement itself. At the conclusion of one

---

[41] "The Left Under the Counterrevolution," *Counter-Revolution*, p. 53.

essay, in fact, Marcuse writes: "The search for specific historical agents of revolutionary change in the advanced capitalist countries is indeed meaningless. Revolutionary forces emerge in the process of change itself; the translation of the potential into the actual is the work of political practice." [42] And that brings us to the political practitioners he has in view.

Theirs is primarily an educational task: they must generate the vision and the will able to provide the ethos for revolution. They must act so as to enhance their own critical understanding of the society and its alternative. They must foster in themselves that sensibility which can generate a "vital need for radical change" in themselves. They must build a new morality. And they must work against a total ethical closure within a society, helping to loosen social morale, where possible, so that other people may at some time become open to new and revolutionary possibilities. In Marcuse's terms, the present function of radical oppositionists is to develop the "consciousness" which may at some time integrate and animate a genuinely revolutionary movement. In the present situation revolutionary consciousness exists only in attenuated and uncertain form, and then only in social forces not "capable of subverting the established system in order to build a socialist society." [43] Even in dealing with forceful actions directed against major institutions of the society, Marcuse assigns primarily educational objectives and significance to the political activities he supports. Those activities are at most creating the barest outline of the political entity whose concerted effort will transform the society; they are incubating the spirit which will move the revolutionary force.

This view of contemporary radical political practice helps to account for an otherwise puzzling (or morally offensive) feature of Marcuse's writings on these matters. As we have seen, he assigns the most sweeping rights and powers to a revolutionary movement, especially with regard to violence; but his specific examples of the "violence" he approves are always instances of "disruption," usually quite innocuous cases of blocking traffic. [44] This is not disingenuous evasion of the conse-

---

[42] *Essay on Liberation*, p. 79.
[43] "The Left Under the Counterrevolution," p. 53.
[44] *Ibid.; Essay on Liberation*, p. 77.

quences of approving violence, it would appear, but application of a consistent though unclear principle—almost as though oppositionists were denizens of some Lockeian state of nature which anticipates the norms of a proper civil order but concedes very few of the powers which such an order involves. The Lockeian parallel becomes even more tempting when it is recalled how little membership in the oppositional movement requires of those who associate themselves with it. But we do not want to labor a suggestion intended to clarify only one aspect of a body of thought which is otherwise so antithetical to such models. Oppositionists can act in hopes of revolutionary vindication, but they may not presume too far upon such expectations.

Drawing on eighteenth-century parallels, Marcuse refers to the present as "the period of enlightenment," preparing the ground for the revolutionary movement and practice yet to come. Activities which many of the actors and their opponents see as direct steps in revolutionary politics, Marcuse interprets as steps in the self-definition of an intellectual and moral force which may in turn create the spiritual conditions within which revolutionary politics may flourish. Marcuse even places prime stress on such considerations in evaluating the significance of successful revolutionary movements outside the "advanced capitalist countries":

> The Cuban Revolution and the Viet Cong have demonstrated: it can be done; there is a morality, a will and a faith which can resist and deter the gigantic technical and economic force of capitalist expansion. More than the "socialist humanism" of the early Marx, this violent solidarity in defense, this elemental socialism in action, has given force and substance to the radicalism of the New Left.[45]

From another perspective, we can see Marcuse's appeal to his readers as moral exhortation to free themselves from the slough of corruption which presumably surrounds them, almost without regard to further consequences. "And even if we see no transformation," he said at the end of a lecture on "The Problem of Violence and the Radical Opposition," "we must fight on. We must resist if we still want to live as human beings, to

[45] *Essay on Liberation*, pp. 81–82.

work and be happy." [46] This almost-stoic undercurrent only rarely comes to the surface in Marcuse's work, not least because he doubtless does hope that it will be possible to create a world completely consonant with the needs of whole men, as he understands them. But there is an important interplay between Marcuse and his readers, in which he suggests to them that their ability to read and to understand what he says is already a sign that they are not wholly subject to the system of domination. Taking seriously what he is saying is already a "political" act, because it is opening themselves to possibilities within themselves which the corrupting system seeks to extirpate. If the "politics of transcendence" is revolutionary in character, it is preceded by a "politics" of "hope," which may be defeated in all of its encounters with the power system. When revolutionary politics in the narrower sense actually commence, very few of the activists from the intellectual movement may be involved. Such a politics may even presuppose the destruction of that movement. [47]

It is against this background that we must consider the question of Marcuse's "elitism," his notion of "educational dictatorship," and his relationship to political democracy overall. Many commentators allege that Marcuse simply sweepingly assigns political authority to the self-styled radical intelligentsia, licensing all actions that they, as possessors of truth, might take. There are doubtless passages which justify such a reading; but the final argument—especially as amplified in his recent work—appears to be somewhat more interesting. Marcuse clearly insists that present political activity must not defer to the will of a majority which, in his view, has been turned tyrannical by the forces which dominate it. Those who have "knowledge and sensibility" must proceed, even if their actions are met with incomprehension or hostility by the masses of men. [48] Moreover, Marcuse urges special attention to the "intellectual and moral qualities of the leaders," in assessing political groupings professing to be revolutionary; and he sometimes flirts with and sometimes simply advocates the idea of an "educational dictatorship" to replace the old regime and to force men to be free,

[46] *Loc. cit.*, p. 94.
[47] *Essay on Liberation*, p. 69.
[48] *Counterrevolution*, p. 32.

until they have been educated to the autonomy and sensibilities required by the new order.[49] But there is a distinction to be made. Elitism and intellectualism are the *necessary* attributes of the politics of hope—the prophetic and educational movement seeking to define and somehow to make available the "idea" of revolution. Revolutionary leadership, not to speak of "educational dictatorships," pertain to a phase in a political movement having a far more popular character and pushed by forces far more widely dispersed than the special excellences of the prophetic order.

In discussing the political structure of the revolution, in other words, Marcuse reverts to the complex ambiguities of the republican democratic tradition, as they are also found in the work of Marx and throughout the history of Marxism. He speaks of "direct democracy" in the revolutionary regime, which "would assure, on all levels, genuinely free selection and election of candidates, revocability at the discretion of the constituencies, and uncensored education and information." He adds, however, "such democracy presupposes equal and universal education for autonomy." [50] In an attempt to depict a possible convergence between working-class oppositionism founded on the experiences of the work-place and revolutionary consciousness, Marcuse invokes the memory of the workers' councils of 1919–20 as well as the Paris Commune, and he expressly denies the general suitability of the Leninist party with its avant-garde.[51] The constitution of the revolution is heir to the *Social Contract* of Rousseau, with all of its difficulties concerning the preconditions of the general will and the relationships between lawgivers and people. It is not simply elitist, a direct rule by those presumed to be wise. And the erection of such a constitution is, in any case, not on the agenda at this time. Pursuing the parallel, we can say that the "politics of hope," as we have called it, involves the formation of a prophetic order able to serve as lawgiver, not as tyrant or prince. Marcuse prefers the language of "education," or, far more modestly, "potential catalysts of rebellion."

[49] "Repressive Tolerance," especially "Postscript, 1968," p. 117 f.; and "Ethics and Revolution," p. 135.
[50] *Essay on Liberation*, p. 69n.
[51] "The Left Under the Counterrevolution," p. 40 f.

The revolutionary movement, in sum, is still incipient. There are resisters and rebels who fend off the demands and powers of the system in various settings—often unconnected and even mutually antagonistic. Then there are those who are training themselves to recognize the common context within which these diverse practices belong, a movement toward revolution, and who will undertake in time to make a common language and outlook available to these diverse actors. As this educational influence takes hold among the rebels, as consciousness is raised, the rebels form revolutionary organizations; and these organizations are presumably greatly strengthened by popular social forces compelled to consider their situation by worsening conditions and freed to understand the oppression under which they live by the undermining of integrative social morale which is the major effect of rebellious activity. Now we can speak of a "right to revolution" in its full sense. There is a general will, a revolutionary ethos, a purposive entity. Then comes the struggle for political power in the narrow sense, the ousting of those who occupy positions of command. The revolutionary victors next have to devise organizational forms for bringing the new possibilities home to every person in the society, refashioning the structures within which men work and otherwise live their lives. Given Marcuse's assumption that these possibilities coincide with the most profound, though repressed, human longings, it is then simply a matter of time until these disciplining forms dissolve. The intellectual elite whose work will have been so essential during the initial phases of the movement will not, in any case, ever come to power. Marcuse's solidarity with the rebellious young is not, of course, an irrationalist celebration of their presumed vitality and strength. If they are, in his eyes, chosen, they are called to a demanding ministry of prophecy and, quite likely, martyrdom.

But there is a certain futility in the whole design. Irrationality and corruption have been depicted as so pervasive that it would seem that the conditions upon which the temporary republic of virtue is to be built would be continually crumbling. And it is hard to see how the projected sequence of phases could ever come about. Marcuse repeatedly welcomes resistant attitudes and practices which he subsequently discovers to be incompatible with the development of a revolutionary movement. The contrast is perhaps clearest in comparing *An Essay on Liberation* (1967) with *Counter-Revolution and Revolt* (1972). That sexual libertinism is likely to be a form of that "repressive desublimation" which alleviates psychic tensions without countering domination Marcuse had argued all along. But he finds the other aspects of the so-called counterculture also increasingly disheartening. The involvement with personal liberation, the breach with established decorum of language and style, and hostility to all authority undermine consciousness and efficacy. Moreover, the authoritarianism and dogmatism of radical groups reacting against these trends lead to sterility and isolation. The politics of hope appears to require a full investment of all available energies, in order to manage these difficulties and recover ground which steadily slips away. On the other side, the established order has enormous resources to defend itself. If the internal instruments of domination are in any measure compromised, there are always external weapons and the recourse to manifestly repressive politics. Notwithstanding what might appear to be the logic of his position, Marcuse does not imagine that fascist symptoms can be welcomed as harbingers of crisis and revolution. They must be countered, even if this means alliances with liberals and retreats from revolutionary postures. The political conception outlined above comes to appear quite problematical, and the concrete political tasks are less and less comprehended by the main theoretical perspective. This offers very little help in distinguishing fascist from liberal forms of the repressive civilization and its pervasive domination.

Where does this leave Marcuse? In addition to the problem of the complex argument sketched above, there are three incompatible tendencies in his writings. One carries forward the progressive developmentalism which is a major theme in his earlier writings. Despite everything, there is said to be a cumulative movement toward revolution under way; the old theory must be adapted to discern its new form, the contemporary political confusion must be viewed from a greater distance and allowed to straighten itself out. In the second tendency Marcuse will from time to time back off from his role as a teacher of prophets and take up the posture of "third person," as "educator and intellectual" quite distant from political prac-

tice. This tendency we have earlier called "Stoic." Such a label
is something of a provocation, since the internal freedom to be
cultivated differs in content very materially from that envisioned by the ancient sages. But the break with corruption is a
common theme, as is the emphasis on discipline and form. Marcuse, for instance, both betakes himself and invites his readers
to the service of the concept, in the Hegelian sense, or to the
recreation of aesthetic form. The third tendency may be called,
in one general sense of that term, "apocalyptic." The revolutionary possibility will arise from a fortunate—or even provi-
dential—convergence of factors, provided only that the hopeful
keep the faith. In a situation of total crisis for the system—at
one point, Marcuse speaks of cataclysm—men will lack the normative clues which structure their lives, and they may be open
to new laws.

Marcuse is wrestling with a recurrent problem in Western
political thought, the politics of creating a new man. He means
to reject the most prevalent answers: a philosopher who becomes a king, a divine grace, a cyclic return or secure providen-
tial development, a triumph of reasonableness, a crucible of violence. Men must make themselves through their own actions
and there must be sense in what they do. But he sees men as
encapsulated within systematic constraint and social entities, as
crystalline forms; and it is not easy to see how such men can in-
novate and such structures change. Change itself, it seems, has
such a structural embodiment—like a Roman god. Marcuse's affinity for classical dramatic forms does not always serve him in
good stead, when it comes to the understanding of politics. His
characters are too much of a piece, and his situations tend too
much to have a single secret whose discovery reveals all. Perhaps things are more Shakespearean than that. These are coun-
tersuggestions, not arguments. We have been concerned above
all to de-totalize Marcuse, not to refute him.

Marcuse offers a diagnosis of modern civilization as corrupt tyranny. This depends, as we have seen, on a conception of
domination which renders irrelevant many of the ordinary concepts of political theory. Domination is a condition of the instinctual structure, and it is produced, under different circumstances, by many different sorts of social and political
arrangements. Correspondingly, liberation involves a revolu-

tionary reordering of human responses, although Marcuse suggests ever more strongly that in this change *prima forma,* the instinctual basis for socialism, displaces a second nature imposed by custom and coercion. The attempt to portray the structure of political acts which could mediate between these two inner conditions does not succeed. Perhaps what is needed is a political theory of diverse forms of power, a conception which does not define away the interplay between power and resistances, and a better way of acknowledging the diverse ways in which structural changes take place.

Marcuse's achievement does not require defense here. He has reopened discussion of some of the most interesting problems of political theory. Our purpose has been primarily to show that this is so. Marcuse speaks of the need to create a "mental space" within which political thinking can take place. This he has helped to do. It does not seem as though political theory today can simply explore the rights and obligations which pertain to autonomous man without sober inquiry into the moral psychology presupposed by autonomy, nor will it do any longer simply to label critics of the ways in which individuation and rationalization proceed in modern civilization, as "obscurantists," "irrationalists," and proponents of a "sweaty mechanical solidarity." Marcuse's critique, as we have tried to show, forcefully reopens these debates. Much modern political theory, certainly since the eighteenth century, has been circumscribed by a wall of presumed "facts" and has guided itself by the presumed imperatives of the factual situation. Marcuse's utopianism has helped to tear open discussion about a lot of these ostensible "givens," to compel reconsideration of the necessities supposed to sustain these facts. In particular, his radical query about a stationary alternative to the progressive state has had considerable and valuable impact. Similarly, he has emboldened the work of political theorists who now question freely the inevitability of legal-rational or bureaucratic patterns of authority or organization, as sole alternatives to the traditional or charismatic or brutal command structures.

We have been least persuaded by Marcuse's conception of revolution as the locus for meaningful political practice. But it is important to note that Marcuse has contributed importantly to a renewed willingness to relate problems of legitimacy to criteria of rationality. Editorialists for weighty newspapers rarely hesitate to welcome a coup by military men against some "demagogic" regime in Brazil or Chile or Greece which has carried on "ruinous" or "irrational" economic policies, for example. But for a long time political theorists fastidiously averted their gaze from such a superceding of consent-criteria. If nothing else, Marcuse has recalled attention to the fact that such calculations are a fairly ordinary part of political language, and that such arguments may have implications unwelcome to those who most benefit from them now. So then, we may conclude that if Marcuse has not developed an entirely adequate political theory, his work, if properly understood, can be very good for political theorists.

F. A. Hayek:
Freedom for Progress

by ANTHONY DE CRESPIGNY

Hayek's political writings have too infrequently received the careful attention that they deserve and that has been given to his work in economics. Commentators have, for the most part, been quick to praise or attack his general liberal position without bothering to concern themselves much with the numerous and sophisticated arguments used to support it. The result has been that the real importance of this branch of Hayek's work has often been obscured in the heady atmosphere which ideological responses to it, favorable or unfavorable, have generated. Moreover, the general position attributed to him is typically not that which is so lucidly presented in his writings. He has been described as an exponent of laisser-faire, as being hostile to the public provision of social services, as being indifferent to the needs of the weak, as being authoritarian and antidemocratic, and so on. Yet there is nothing in Hayek's work to endorse any such assertions, and it is difficult to understand how presumably scrupulous critics came to make them.[1]

Hayek is a liberal, but to say this is not very illuminating since there are different sorts of liberalism just as there are different conceptions of liberty. For Hayek, a man possesses "liberty" or "freedom"—he uses the words interchangeably—when

---

[1] For one example of misplaced criticism see Christian Bay's article "Hayek's Liberalism: The Constitution of Perpetual Privilege" in *The Political Science Reviewer*, 1 (Fall 1971). Bay accuses Hayek of being "a special pleader for a particular class interest," of having "an in-built preference for the demands of the strong over the needs of the weak," of being "essentially a social Darwinist," of producing a "closed system of thought," and of not being "philosophically radical." See pp. 110, 112, 115, and 123.

he is not subject to coercion by the arbitrary will of another, and liberalism is a doctrine which emphasizes the restriction to a minimum of the coercive powers of government.[2] He contrasts his own use of "freedom" with three other meanings of the term: with freedom as "the participation of men in the choice of their government, in the process of legislation, and in the control of administration" ("political freedom"); with freedom as "the extent to which a person is guided in his actions by his own considered will . . . rather than by momentary impulse or circumstance" ("inner freedom"); and with freedom as "the power to satisfy our wishes, or the extent of the choice of alternatives open to us" ("freedom as power").[3] Hayek stresses that these other "freedoms" are not conditions of the same kind as his "individual freedom" and should be kept quite distinct. Since a non-democratic order may be permissive and a democratic order restrictive, political freedom is neither a necessary nor a sufficient condition of individual freedom. And inner freedom stands opposed not to coercion by others but to moral weakness or the influence of passing emotions. As for "freedom" in the sense of "power," Hayek argues that there is a vital difference between non-interference with another's acts and a person's effective power to act. A person may be able to do what he may not lawfully do, or unable to do what nobody is trying to prevent him from doing. Indeed, Hayek goes further and asserts that it is doubtful whether we should tolerate the use of "freedom" in the sense of "power." [4]

These are strong words, particularly when one notices that the conception of freedom as power has an impressive intellectual pedigree, including such philosophers as Locke, Hume, and Dewey. Hayek's dislike for this common notion of freedom can be understood partly in terms of his desire to preserve "the original meaning of the word" and to enhance its usefulness by closely restricting its application. More important, however, is

---

[2] For Hayek, coercion occurs when an agent's actions are made to serve another's will, not for his own but for the other's purpose. Coercion implies *action* in the sense that a person who is coerced chooses to do what he does. It occurs only when one person threatens to make things unpleasant for another with the intention of thereby getting the other to act in conformity with his will.

[3] See *The Constitution of Liberty* (Chicago, 1960), pp. 13–17.

[4] *Ibid.*, p. 18.

his determination that the cardinal value of liberty should not be exploited by collectivists to justify large amounts of state intervention. If liberty is viewed as power, there is no end to the number of legislative neasures which can be justified as extending the range of choice of persons, or their effective power to do whatever they may wish. The result could be the destruction of individual liberty in the name of a spurious notion of liberty. Hayek is not denying that the limited provision by government of skills and opportunities is desirable; he is only saying that such enabling activities should not be represented as promoting freedom.

It is clear that Hayek's "liberalism" is very different from what now goes by this name in the United States. Hayek emphasizes freedom from the constraints of the state and stands in the same tradition as Madison, Tocqueville, and Acton; contemporary American liberals view freedom as participation and effective choice and are much closer to the "constructivist rationalism" of Voltaire and Rousseau. While Hayek sets strict limits to and is deeply suspicious of the powers of *all* government, American liberalism today is *étatiste* and looks to the interventions of *democratic* government for distributive justice and social progress. While Hayek, in common with Bernard Mandeville and Adam Smith, stresses the beneficial social effects of evolution and spontaneous order, American liberals seek a radical reconstruction of society on the basis of deliberate design.

Most Americans nowadays would call Hayek's position "conservative," but he resists such a description while at the same time expressing misgivings about naming himself a "liberal." These misgivings are due partly to the fact that his "liberalism" bears little resemblance to any political movement now described by that name and partly to the great difference that separates his position from what he calls "rationalistic Continental liberalism." There are a number of reasons why Hayek does not call himself a "conservative" in spite of his recognition that liberals of his kind have much to learn from some conservative thinkers. "True" conservatism, he asserts, cannot by its very nature offer an alternative to the existing direction of movement, whereas liberalism, precisely because it has guiding principles and definite objectives, knows where it wishes to go.[5] Conservatives, moreover, are fearful of change, distrustful of the new as such, "while the liberal position is based on . . . a preparedness to let change run its course even if we cannot predict where it will lead." [6] Thirdly, conservatives tend to be authoritarian and antidemocratic. Hayek refers to "the characteristic complacency of the conservative toward the action of established authority" and to "his prime concern that this authority be not weakened rather than that its power be kept within bounds." [7] In connection with the antidemocratic attitude typical of conservatives, he remarks that "it is not democracy but unlimited government that is objectionable." [8] Hayek further criticizes conservatives for their "lack of understanding of economic forces," for their "mysticism" and "obscurantism," for their "hostility to internationalism," and for their "nostalgic longing for the past." [9]

It is time to penetrate more deeply into Hayek's position and into the ideas and assumptions which underlie it. Two quotations from one of his essays express succinctly the essence of his particular brand of liberalism:

> Liberalism . . . derives from the discovery of a self-generating or spontaneous order in social affairs . . . , an order which [makes] it possible to utilize the knowledge and skill of all members of society to a much greater extent than would be possible in any order created by central direction, and [reflects] the consequent desire to make as full use of these powerful spontaneous ordering forces as possible.[10]

[5] Ibid., pp. 398–99.

[6] Ibid., p. 400.

[7] Ibid., p. 401.

[8] Ibid., p. 403. Hayek distinguishes liberalism as "a doctrine about what the law ought to be," from democracy as "a doctrine about the manner of determining what will be the law." Liberalism and democracy agree in believing that the majority should determine what is law, but they conflict where the democrat believes that the majority determines what is good law. Democracy is a method which must be judged by what it achieves whereas liberalism is a doctrine concerning the scope and purpose of government. Nevertheless, Hayek claims that there are three decisive arguments in favor of the democratic method: it is the only means of peaceful change; it is more likely to produce liberty than other forms of government; and it is the best way of raising the general level of political education.

[9] Ibid., pp. 400–10.

[10] Studies in Philosophy, Politics and Economics (London, 1967), p. 162.

And again:

> The central concept of liberalism is that under the enforcement
> of universal rules of just conduct, protecting a recognizable pri-
> vate domain of individuals, a spontaneous order of human activi-
> ties of much greater complexity will form itself than could ever
> be produced by deliberate arrangement, and that in consequence
> the coercive activities of government should be limited to the en-
> forcement of such rules. . . .[11]

Crucial to Hayek's argument is the irremediable ignorance
of individual persons concerning many of the factors on which
the attainment of their ends depends, an ignorance that increases relatively with the growth of knowledge: for the larger
the sum total of human knowledge, the smaller the share that
any one individual can absorb.[12] (As we shall see, it is on the
recognition of this inevitable ignorance that Hayek's case for individual freedom largely rests.) If we wish to make the best use
of our incomplete, dispersed knowledge and to minimize the
occasions on which we may be made to submit to another's will,
we need an impersonal mechanism to integrate our individual
actions. It is this mechanism that the spontaneous order provides, one which is not the result of deliberate action but is a
by-product of human activity. This type of order does not have a
purpose since it has not been deliberately created, and to agree
on its desirability it is unnecessary for us to agree on the concrete results it will produce.[13]

An arrangement designed to serve particular human purposes requires an organizer and is therefore more restricted in
respect of the use of knowledge than a spontaneous mechanism.
It is necessarily confined by what can be known to the organizer. But where it is a matter of employing limited resources
known to an organizer in the service of a unitary hierarchy of
ends, an arrangement will be the more successful method. On

[11] *Ibid.*

[12] *The Constitution of Liberty*, p. 26.

[13] *The Confusion of Language in Political Thought* (London, 1968), p. 11.
Hayek remarks that one of the principal sources of error in the social sciences is
the tendency to view the order of our social environment as *wholly* the product
of human design. "The insight that *not all order that results from the interplay
of human actions is the result of design* is indeed the beginning of social
theory."

the other hand, where the task involves the use of knowledge
scattered among and available only to thousands or millions of
separate individuals, the use of spontaneous ordering forces
will be more effective.[14]

To its radical or socialist critics, the prime defect of the
end-independent, spontaneous order is that it does not ensure
that for society as a whole the more important comes before the
less important. Hayek's answer is that, save in limited contexts,
we are *not* in agreement about specific ends, and we cannot
settle disputes by reference to some unitary conception of relative "merits" or "needs":

> . . . it is due to the fact that we do not enforce a unitary scale of
> concrete ends, nor attempt to secure that some particular view
> about what is more and what is less important governs the whole
> of society, that the members of . . . a free society have as good a
> chance successfully to use their individual knowledge for the
> achievement of their individual purposes as they in fact have.[15]

For an understanding of Hayek's particular brand of liberalism it is important to notice that, unlike all the major political
philosophers prior to Hegel, he does not begin with some more
or less definite conception of man, of his essential attributes and
needs. For him human nature is essentially indeterminate,
always in the process of formation, left open for unpredictable
change in many different directions. Save in physical and biological terms we cannot anticipate and limit the range of human
needs and their order of priority. Because this is so, we have no
basis on which to plan for a perfect future or to try to halt men's
development at any particular stage. If human nature is open
we cannot deduce the proper order of society from its supposed
constancies, even if we believe such a procedure to be logically
permissible. This view is nowhere stated by Hayek, but it does
appear to be presupposed by what he says.[16]

But let us return to the main argument. The difference between what is called a national or world "economy," and a firm,
a household, or a farm, illustrates Hayek's distinction between a

[14] *Ibid.*, p. 14.
[15] *Studies in Philosophy, Politics and Economics*, p. 165.
[16] For a strong attack on the fixity view of human nature, see an article by
Stuart Hampshire in *Encounter*, January 1957, p. 35.

spontaneous mechanism and an organization. The small purpose-governed organization is an "economy" properly so-called because it is a deliberate arrangement of a given stock of resources in the service of a unitary hierarchy of specific ends. On the other hand, so fundamentally different are organizations serving individual purposes from the spontaneous order of the market that Hayek thinks it highly unfortunate that the same word "economy" has come to be applied to both.[17] This confusion of terminology has obscured the vital difference between the two and has led to the view that the market ought to be made to serve a unitary scale of particular ends. But this is impossible as well as undesirable. Since the spontaneous order of the market, resulting from many interacting economies, rests on reciprocity or mutual benefits rather than on common purposes, it "cannot be judged in terms of a sum of particular results."[18] What can be said, however, is that through competition the spontaneous order tends to minimize the cost of production.

Hayek's belief in the efficiency of the impersonal mechanism should not be taken to imply any acceptance of the doctrine of laisser-faire.[19] A liberal state will do a great deal to promote competition by voiding all agreements in restraint of trade and by exposing to damages all actions designed to enforce them. And while Hayek thinks that the *coercive* powers of government should be limited to the enforcement of universal rules of just conduct—we shall come to this later—he emphasizes repeatedly the importance of the non-coercive *service* functions of government. The market mechanism does not provide, or provide adequately, for all needs; and government, to the extent that the overall level of wealth permits, should intervene in order to help those who cannot earn a minimum income

[17] Hayek proposes that the word "catalaxy" be used to describe the market order.

[18] *The Confusion of Language in Political Thought*, p. 29.

[19] In *The Road to Serfdom* Hayek writes: "There is . . . all the difference between deliberately creating a system within which competition will work as beneficially as possible, and passively accepting institutions as they are. Probably nothing has done so much harm to the liberal cause as the wooden insistence of some liberals on certain rough rules of thumb, above all the principle of *laisser-faire*." See *The Road to Serfdom* (London, 1944), p. 13. In spite of this and many other similar statements, Bay writes of "Hayek's commitment to *laisser-faire*." (See Bay, "Hayek's Liberalism," p. 110.)

through it. But there are some important provisos: namely, that government should not possess a monopoly in the provision of welfare and that it should not try to make the market itself serve some ideal of distributive justice. If government does this, it will simply reduce the total wealth in which all can share.[20]

There is no justification in Hayek's writings for asserting, as Bay and others have asserted, that he has little or no sympathy for the "underdog." The dispute between socialists and liberals like Hayek, if sufficiently explored, might well turn out to be much more about questions of *fact* than about questions of *value*. If Hayek is to be fairly criticized, he must be met on his own ground—that is, it must be shown on the basis of broad, comparative studies that he is *wrong* in contending that the creation of wealth and the long-run improvement of living standards are greatly assisted by the maintenance of a market order. There is no point in abusing his character unless at least it is clear that the dispute is not simply or primarily about matters of fact.

I shall now take up the vital question, so far merely touched on, of why it is that Hayek values individual freedom. It should be initially observed, however, that for him freedom is not the product of design: "the institutions of freedom . . . were not established because people foresaw the benefits they would bring." [21] But once limitations had been placed on the powers of government from sheer mistrust of rulers, people came to recognize the beneficial effects of freedom and sought to extend its scope. It was only then that liberalism began to emerge as a systematic doctrine.[22] What are these beneficial effects? They are described by Hayek as the attainment of material and cultural progress. But this immediately gives rise to two important questions: first, what precisely does he mean by "progress," what are its advantages and for whom?; and second, does his emphasis on the *effects* of freedom mean that for him freedom is not something valuable for its own sake? Hayek's answers to these questions are crucial since liberty and progress

---

[20] See *The Confusion of Language in Political Thought*, pp. 30–31.
[21] *The Constitution of Liberty*, p. 54.
[22] This occurred in Britain and France and mainly in the eighteenth century.

appear to be the central values in his social thought.

Hayek's notion of social progress is not that of "an advance toward a known goal" because "it is not achieved by human reason striving by known means toward a fixed aim." He continues: "It would be more correct to think of progress as a process of formation and modification of the human intellect, a process of adaptation and learning in which not only the possibilities known to us but also our values and desires continually change." [23]

Progress cannot therefore be planned and does not necessarily result in increasing levels of satisfaction or happiness. There is enjoyment to be derived from achieving one's ends and this will be more widespread in a changing than in a stationary society, but "the assured possession may give us little satisfaction." [24] This does not matter, however, since what is important is the successful striving for what at each moment appears achievable. "It is not the fruits of past success but the living in and for the future in which human intelligence proves itself. Progress is movement for movement's sake. . . ." [25]

The important aspect of progress for Hayek is the acquisition and use of new knowledge. It is by no means certain that the majority of people want all or even most of its results, but whether they do or not participation in progress is inescapable. When Hayek discusses the value of individual freedom it becomes increasingly plain that for him freedom matters primarily because of its contribution to progress understood as the cumulative growth of knowledge. "If there were omniscient men . . . there would be little case for liberty. . . . Liberty is essential in order to leave room for the unforeseeable and unpredictable." [26] Freedom for Hayek is to be valued not so much from the standpoint of the individual as from that of society: "what is important is not what freedom I personally would like to exercise but what freedom some person may need in order to do things beneficial to society." [27] Furthermore, the value of any particular freedom is not to be judged by counting heads: "the

[23] *Ibid.*, p. 40.
[24] *Ibid.*, p. 41.
[25] *Ibid.*
[26] *Ibid.*, p. 29.
[27] *Ibid.*, p. 32.

importance of freedom to do a particular thing has nothing to do
with the number of people who want to do it." [28] This is because the freedoms vital to social progress may not be widely
sought. Hayek also asserts that it is better that some should be
free than none and better that many should have full freedom
than that all should have a limited freedom.[29]

While my principal purpose is one of exposition, it is difficult at this stage to resist some comment, particularly since we
are now dealing with the core of Hayek's political philosophy.
Although he sometimes writes as if he views individual liberty
as intrinsically desirable, it seems clear that his main stress is
on liberty as an instrument of social progress. People are important as potential contributors to progress rather than as individuals with individual rights. One begins to wonder what has
become of Hayek's individualism and of his claim to be a liberal in the same tradition as Locke or von Humboldt. It certainly seems strange for a liberal individualist to argue a case
for freedom which fails to emphasize, with obvious qualifications, the undesirability of deliberately imposed obstacles to
the desires or activities, actual or possible, of individuals *qua*
individuals. A recent commentator has stated that for Hayek values other than individual liberty are justified by their contributions to liberty.[30] But it seems impossible to reconcile this interpretation with what Hayek says in the second chapter of *The
Constitution of Liberty*.

A further comment seems appropriate. It is not at all clear
that in any given society it is necessarily better that some
should be free than none. Indeed, a society where some were
free and others unfree might be markedly worse than one
where all were equally oppressed, and worse precisely because
of the effect on self-respect. Hayek could, of course, argue that
the freedom enjoyed by a section of society is of benefit to all
because it is a fertile source of material progress. But those
deprived of freedom would no doubt prefer an undiscriminating
repression, and with good reason.

Reference was made to what Hayek calls "the enforcement

[28] *Ibid.*
[29] *Ibid.*
[30] Morris M. Wilhelm, "The Political Thought of Friedrich A. Hayek,"
Political Studies, 20 (1972), 172.

of universal rules of just conduct," and we must now consider precisely what he means. This will bring us to one of the most widely-discussed elements in Hayek's thought: his conception of the rule of law.

Hayek's universal rules of just conduct are universal rules of law and are necessary for the development of a spontaneous order, one in which persons do not pursue the same particular ends or share the same values, save those reflected in the rules themselves. These rules apply to "an unknown number of future instances and equally to all persons in the objective circumstances described by the rule." They "demarcate protected individual domains . . . and lead to the formation of an . . . abstract and end-independent spontaneous order." [31] They are to be contrasted with rules of organization which are applied to particular people or in the service of the rulers' particular ends. "The rules of organization will . . . never be universal in intent or end-independent, but always subsidiary to the commands by which roles are assigned and tasks or aims prescribed." [32]

Hayek notes that the distinction between rules of organization and universal rules of conduct is roughly similar to that between public and private law.[33] Public law determines the organization of government and is deliberately made for particular purposes, whereas private case law is universally applicable, independent of particular ends, and the product of an evolutionary process. It is a mark of a "liberal" society that the private individual cannot be constrained to obey rules other than those of private and criminal law. Unfortunately for the liberal, however, the last century has seen the progressive displacement of the rules of conduct of private and criminal law by rules of organization. This development was made possible by the fact that "the same representative assemblies have been charged with the two different tasks of laying down rules of individual conduct and laying down rules and giving orders concerning the organization and conduct of government." [34] And it was made actual by

[31] *The Confusion of Language in Political Thought*, p. 15.

[32] *Ibid.*, p. 16.

[33] *Ibid.*

[34] *Studies in Philosophy, Politics and Economics*, p. 169. Hayek thinks that these two different tasks should be performed by different representative bodies.

the growing recognition that the application of uniform or equal rules to the conduct of individuals who were in fact very different in many respects, inevitably produced very different results for the different individuals; and that in order to bring about by government action a reduction in these unintended but inevitable differences in the material position of different people, it would be necessary to treat them not according to the same but according to different rules.[35]

The progressive displacement of uniform rules of individual conduct by rules of organization has had serious implications for liberty and social progress. Since the purpose underlying this development has been to achieve particular results for particular people and thereby to promote "distributive" justice, it has led increasingly to the substitution of an end-governed organization for an end-independent impersonal mechanism.[36]

The rule of law for Hayek is "not a rule of the law, but a rule concerning what the law ought to be, a meta-legal doctrine or a political ideal." [37] The doctrine is concerned not with the content of particular laws, but rather with the attributes which laws should possess if they are to be "true" laws. It is not to be confused with mere legality since the acts of a government may be legal in that they are authorized by legislation, but yet fail to satisfy the requirements of "true" law. For this reason Hayek is emphatic in rejecting the doctrines of legal positivism. Moreover, the rule of law is concerned not with all the functions of government, but only with the limitation of its *coercive* activities.

The main attributes required by Hayek's interpretation of the rule of law are those of generality, certainty, and equality. Laws must be general in nature, containing no reference to particulars of any kind and applying whenever certain abstractedly defined conditions are satisfied. This is similar to Rousseau's insistence that "the law always consider the subject in the round and actions in the abstract and never any individual man or one particular action." [38] Laws must also be known and certain. By "certainty" it is meant that people are able to predict the deci-

---

[35] *Ibid.*, p. 170.
[36] *Ibid.*
[37] *The Constitution of Liberty*, p. 206.
[38] Jean-Jacques Rousseau, *The Social Contract*, bk. II, chap. vi.

sions of the courts to a considerable extent even though complete predictability is an unattainable ideal. The third requirement is that laws should apply equally to all members of society, the rulers included. This may look like the attribute of generality, but Hayek remarks that a law "may be perfectly general in referring only to formal characteristics of the persons involved and yet make different provisions for different classes of people." [39] He recognizes that the principle of equality can only be partially applied since classification is obviously inevitable given that there are characteristics which not all people possess, such as being a veteran or a woman or above a certain age. But Hayek thinks that distinctions in the law between different classes of people will not be arbitrary provided that members and non-members alike believe them to be legitimate. If one or the other do not, then we have discrimination or privilege.

There are a number of other things which Hayek says about his uniform rules of law. First, they are for the most part negative in the sense that they tell people what *not* to do. There are exceptions, however, such as taxation, certain compulsory services, and the enforcement of voluntarily incurred obligations. Second, they merely provide a framework within which the individual can shape *his own* plans. "They are instrumental, they are means put at his disposal, and they provide part of the data which . . . he can use as the basis for his decisions." [40] Third, they are unlikely to restrict freedom seriously since they apply not only to the governed but also to those who make and enforce them. Fourth, they must be regarded as being beneficial generally rather than in their application to every individual case: "only the rule as a whole must be . . . justified, not its every application." [41] Fifth, because mutual predictabilies of behavior are so important, what they are in respect of their content is less important than that they should be enforced without exceptions. Sixth, they are not to be confused with particular commands, though laws in their ideal form might be called "once-and-for-all" commands directed at persons unknown and abstracted from all specific conditions of time and place.[42] Sev-

[39] *The Constitution of Liberty*, p. 209.
[40] *Ibid.*, p. 152.
[41] *Ibid.*, p. 159.
[42] *Ibid.*, pp. 149–50.

enth, while their purpose is to protect a man's private sphere, it
is not desirable that the specific contents of this sphere should
be permanently fixed. People themselves should play a part in
deciding what at any time should be included in their protected
private sphere.[43] Finally, it is possible to determine the justice
of a particular rule of just conduct only by reference to a whole
system of such rules. The ultimate test of the justice of rules is
"nothing else than the self-consistency of the actions which
these rules allow if applied to the circumstances of the real
world." [44]

A point which Hayek emphasizes repeatedly and which is
central to his argument is that the rule of law is not consistent
with any attempt by government to achieve distributive or social justice. A government is not justified in employing coercion
save in the enforcement of general rules, and it therefore has no
right to try to promote the substantive ideal of distributive justice. Since there are no objective criteria for determining how
much people ought to have, all decisions about the "proper"
allocation of resources are bound to be determined by the arbitrary will of the government. And this is incompatible with the
restrictions which the rule of law imposes.[45]

The rule of law is also incompatible with all measures of
economic control by government which cannot be enforced by
general rules because they are by their very nature discretionary and arbitrary. The most important of these for Hayek are
"measures designed to control the access to different trades and
occupations, the terms of sale, and the amounts to be produced
or sold." [46] Controls over prices and quantities are necessarily
arbitrary, and they make it impossible for the market to function
properly. But this does not at all mean that Hayek is an advocate of non-intervention in economic affairs. Provided it does
not invade the private sphere and claims no exclusive rights in
what it does, a government can do much to assist the spontaneous forces of a market order by providing an efficient monetary

[43] *Ibid.*, pp. 139–40.
[44] *Studies in Philosophy, Politics and Economics,* p. 166.
[45] For a discussion of this point see *The Road to Serfdom,* pp. 59–60; *The
Constitution of Liberty,* pp. 231–33; and *Studies in Philosophy, Politics and
Economics,* pp. 167–72.
[46] *The Constitution of Liberty,* p. 227.

system, by supplying useful information, by supporting education, by preventing fraud, by enforcing contracts, by protecting
property, by controlling pollution, and so on. There is, however,
a presumption against state enterprises since it is very difficult
to ensure that they enjoy no special advantages as against private business, such as subsidies or tax concessions. But if they
compete on equal terms with private enterprise there is room
for some state enterprise in a free system. Speaking generally,
the rule of law supplies the criterion which makes it possible to
distinguish those measures which are, from those which are not,
consonant with a free economy. Granted that all coercive action
by government is confined to the enforcement of general rules,
it still remains necessary to apply the sort of rules which will
enable a free system to work effectively. Measures which are
compatible with the rule of law may still have to be rejected on
grounds of expediency.

The question of the relationship between the rule of law
and individual freedom has not so far been considered.[47] It was
indicated earlier that for Hayek a person is free when he is not
subject to coercion by the arbitrary will of another. When taken
in conjunction with what he says about the rule of law, this
would appear to imply that a person is free when he obeys laws
which have the general attributes required by the rule of law.
And that this is Hayek's view seems to be confirmed when he
writes: "The conception of freedom under the law . . . rests on
the contention that when we obey laws, in the sense of general
abstract rules laid down irrespective of their application to us,
we are not subject to another man's will and are therefore
free." [48] Yet a little later Hayek tells us that "even general, abstract rules, equally applicable to all, may possibly constitute
severe restrictions on liberty." [49] Because the rules apply to all

[47] I have benefited from a careful discussion of this topic in an unpublished paper by Ronald Hamowy.—"Freedom and the Rule of Law in F. A.
Hayek".

[48] *Ibid.*, p. 153. Hayek's position is similar to that of Locke as expressed
in *The Second Treatise of Civil Government:* ". . . freedom of men under government is to have a standing rule to live by, common to every one of that society, and made by the legislative power erected in it; a liberty to follow my will
in all things, where that rule prescribes not; and not to be subject to the incon-
stant, uncertain, unknown, arbitrary will of another man . . ."

[49] *Ibid.*, p. 154.

he thinks it unlikely that they will prohibit much that anybody may reasonably wish to do. Nevertheless, the possibility remains and in the case of the universal enforcement of religious beliefs is admitted by Hayek to have been realized.

Hayek's account and defence of the rule of law are impressive in their coherence and wide-ranging character. Still, his version of the rule of law and his statements about its relation to individual liberty are not invulnerable to criticism. Given the inherent intractability of the subject-matter it would indeed be surprising if they were. The criticisms which will be summarily developed here relate to Hayek's view that the rule of law constitutes an adequate protection of individual liberty, to his use of the distinction between prohibitions and positive commands, to his approach to the problem of classification, and to his treatment of judicial or executive discretionary power. There are, of course, many other questions which might be taken up, but these appear to be among the more important ones.

The fact that Hayek's rule-of-law doctrine requires laws to be binding on legislators scarcely seems to afford an adequate protection for individual liberty. Laws which restrict trade or travel to particular foreign countries or which make it a punishable offence to drink alcoholic beverages or to engage in homosexual behavior may apply equally to all. But they may constitute serious restrictions on liberty depending on the particular interests or needs or desires of those who fall under them. Laws which apply equally to all may have very different *effects* for different people. Presumably what Hayek is really concerned to say is that there can be no freedom without the rule of law and that its application will reduce as much as is possible in human society the coercion of some by others. But if his formal restrictions on the general character of legislation do not amount to a sufficient condition of individual freedom, it may well be argued that they should be supplemented by *substantive* limitations on the power of government.

Hayek states that the sanctions of the law in a free society, especially its private law, are designed to restrain private persons from doing—rather than to constrain them to do—certain things. They are used to support prohibitions much more than positive commands. But unlike actions which are commanded, such as the payment of taxes, those which are prohibited may be avoided by the potential object of coercion. In Hayek's words: "Provided that I know beforehand that if I place myself in a particular position, I shall be coerced and provided that I can avoid putting myself in such a position, *I need never be coerced.*" [50] (My italics.) The difficulty, however, is to understand how it can be argued that prohibitions are much less coercive than commands. It is true that a prohibition leaves open a number of alternative ways of acting while a command does not. But a command may be felt to be innocuous whereas in the case of a prohibition the most eligible alternative may be regarded as much worse than the prohibited course. Whether or not a general prohibition backed by sanctions is coercive for a particular agent, and the extent to which it is, depends on weighing the importance for him of the prohibited course against his best unprohibited alternative. The prohibition is not coercive only if the difference for him is slight or non-existent.[51]

Hayek's treatment of the problem of classification seems inadequate. He recognizes that some laws will apply only to special classes of people, but argues that distinctions in the law will not be arbitrary if they are acceptable both to those who possess the properties constituting the class and to those who do not. Unanimity as to the appropriateness of a distinction is not necessary; laws referring to specific groups will not be discriminatory if they are thought to be reasonable by a *majority* of those inside and outside the groups. But this approach to the problem immediately raises the question of why, given Hayek's own views about majority decision-making, he should think that arbitrariness will be avoided in this way. "Liberalism," he writes, "accepts majority rule as a method of deciding, but not as an authority for what the decision ought to be." [52] In a particular society, a majority of women (as well as of men) might well favor or at least be indifferent about legal disabilities affecting the female sex alone, but this fact would not bear on the question of sexual discrimination.

[50] *Ibid.*, p. 142.
[51] For a discussion of this question see an essay by J. W. N. Watkins in Arthur Seldon, ed., *Agenda for a Free Society: Essays on Hayek's "The Constitution of Liberty"* (London, 1961).
[52] *The Constitution of Liberty*, p. 104.

Hayek strongly emphasizes the importance of the certainty of the law: "There is probably no single factor which has contributed more to the prosperity of the West than the relative certainty of the law. . . ." [53] At the same time, he points out that because the legislator confines himself to general rules, he can only aim to make them beneficial on the whole or in most cases. However, he adds, "it is essential that they be *always applied,* irrespective of whether or not the consequences in a particular instance seem desirable." [54] (My italics.) Against this it may be argued that while a high degree of predictability is desirable in respect of law enforcement and punishment, so also is justice in the individual case. It is precisely because the legislator is ignorant of special circumstances that it is desirable to have sufficient flexibility in the application of the law to make possible a fair degree of justice in each particular case. The discretionary power of the police, prosecutors, judges, parole officers, and the executive may do much to prevent the injustices which would necessarily result from a rigid enforcement of abstract rules of law. It need scarcely be said that discretionary power is often misused, but in America and Britain, for example, the evidence suggests that on balance its consequences are beneficent.

[53] *Ibid.,* p. 208.
[54] *Ibid.,* p. 158.

Leo Strauss:
The Recovery of Political Philosophy

by EUGENE F. MILLER

Leo Strauss's penetrating studies of the major political philosophers have won him recognition as our foremost historian of political philosophy. Seldom if ever before has one man been responsible for such cogent and illuminating interpretations of so many of the great philosophers. Strauss's studies to date cover Plato, Aristotle, Xenophon, Farabi, Maimonides, Marsilius of Padua and, among the moderns, Machiavelli, Hobbes, Spinoza, Locke, Rousseau, Burke and Nietzsche.[1] His students, following his distinctive principles of interpretation, have written on these philosophers as well as on many other important figures in Western political thought.[2] Strauss has gone beyond the study of individual philosophers to give us a critical history of political philosophy, whose division into periods corresponds to the self-consciousness of the great political philosophers themselves. He has shed new light on such fundamental problems as natural right, reason and revelation, and education in democratic society. He has presented striking interpretations of Aristophanes and Lucretius in connection with his treatment of philosophy and poetry, of Thucydides in connection with his treatment of philosophy and history, and of Max Weber in connection with his treatment of contemporary social science. We may anticipate that in the coming decades,

[1] A bibliography of Strauss's writings to 1964 is contained in Joseph Cropsey, ed., *Ancients and Moderns: Essays on the Tradition of Political Philosophy in Honor of Leo Strauss* (New York, 1964).

[2] See, for example, the various essays in Leo Strauss and Joseph Cropsey, eds., *History of Political Philosophy*, 2nd ed. (Chicago, 1972).

philosophical interpretation will be massively influenced and perhaps decisively redirected by Strauss's work.

Although Strauss's writings are devoted, by and large, to the interpretation of the great thinkers of the past, one would be quite mistaken in concluding that they are inspired by a merely historical or antiquarian interest. Strauss deplores the fact that inquiry into the history of political philosophy has replaced political philosophy itself in research and teaching. He views this substitution as evidence of the decay of political philosophy in our time. Strauss is a political philosopher and not just a historian of political philosophy. His historical studies are intended, no less than the dialogues of Plato or the treatises of Aristotle or Hobbes, to contribute to political philosophy as a nonhistorical pursuit. The "unsystematic" and "historical" form of Strauss's writings should not be allowed to obscure their philosophical intent.[3]

Near the center of a remarkable essay on Farabi's summary of the philosophy of Plato, Strauss tells us that Farabi, availing himself of the specific immunity of the commentator or the historian, chose to speak his mind concerning grave matters in his "historical" works rather than in the works that appear to set forth his own doctrines. By speaking in this manner through his exposition of Plato, Farabi reveals himself as a true Platonist:

> For Platonists are not concerned with the historical (accidental) truth, since they are exclusively interested in the philosophic (essential) truth. Only because public speech demands a mixture of seriousness and playfulness, can a true Platonist present the serious teaching, the philosophical teaching, in a historical, and hence playful, garb.[4]

Strauss is an admirer of Farabi's technique [5] and, we must suspect, a "true Platonist" in the use he makes of historical exposition.

---

[3] Cf. *The Political Philosophy of Hobbes*, trans. Elsa M. Sinclair (Chicago, 1952), p. xix; *The City and Man* (Chicago, 1964), pp. 7–8; *What Is Political Philosophy?* (Glencoe, 1959), pp. 56–59.

[4] "Farabi's *Plato*," in *Louis Ginzberg Jubilee Volume* (New York, 1945), pp. 376–77. This quotation is missing from the highly condensed version of this essay that appears as the "Introduction" to *Persecution and the Art of Writing* (Glencoe, 1952), pp. 7–21.

[5] Compare *What Is Political Philosophy?* p. 154, with "Farabi's *Plato*," p. 376.

The person who sets out to discover Strauss's own philosophical views is confronted with a task of almost overwhelming complexity. He is obligated, in the first place, to understand all that Strauss has said about the principles of philosophical speech and writing. He must then consider all that Strauss has written in light of these principles. Moreover, he must carefully compare Strauss's expositions in each case with the original sources under consideration. Such a task lies far beyond the scope of this essay, which can do no more than take a modest first step toward the interpretation of Strauss's political philosophy. Our procedure will be to examine what Strauss says in his own name about the nature of political philosophy and then to consider if his own work is addressed to the tasks of political philosophy as he defines them.

Strauss is careful to use the term "political philosophy" to designate a distinctive kind of political thought. In the title essay of *What Is Political Philosophy?* he defines political philosophy as "the attempt truly to know both the nature of political things and the right, or the good, political order." [6] This definition specifies three requirements that political thought must meet in order to qualify as political philosophy.

As "the attempt truly to know," political philosophy is set apart from all forms of political thought that are indifferent to the distinction between knowledge and opinion. This is but to say that political philosophy is a branch of philosophy, which Strauss, following the Socratic tradition, understands as the attempt to ascend from opinion to knowledge, that is, to rational knowledge that is true and final. Strauss points out that a distinction is commonly made even in political life between opinion and a certain type of knowledge. The great statesman is thought to possess more political knowledge than the man in the street. This prephilosophic political knowledge is centred, however, in a given political situation. It is concerned mainly with the particular or individual rather than the universal. Although it embodies assumptions about political life as such, these assumptions are not subjected to critical scrutiny. A philosophic or scientific quest for political knowledge emerges only when "the Here and Now ceases to be the center of reference"

[6] *What Is Political Philosophy?*, p. 12.

and assumptions about political life as such become the focus of critical inquiry.[7]

Political philosophy, then, is "the conscious, coherent and relentless effort to replace opinions about the political fundamentals by knowledge regarding them."[8] But what does political philosophy seek to know? Strauss defines philosophy itself as quest for knowledge of all things or, more precisely, quest for knowledge of the nature of all things. Philosophy seeks knowledge of "the whole," that is, the natures in their totality. Political philosophy is a branch of philosophy as thus understood. It is quest for knowledge of "the nature of political things" and their status within the whole.[9] It is no accident that Strauss speaks sometimes of "things" and at other times of "the natures of things" or of "beings." We cannot here explore this distinction, which would take us to the very core of his thought.[10] Let it suffice to say that in speaking of "political things," Strauss has in mind those things whose existence is ordinarily presupposed by political opinion. Every sane adult "knows something of taxes, police, law, jails, war, peace, armistice."[11]

Political opinion is concerned largely with political things in their particularity; political philosophy seeks knowledge of political things as such (e.g., knowledge of the nature of taxation, of police, of law, of punishment, of war, peace, and armistice). Yet the distinct political things are intelligible only with reference to the primary whole of which they are parts— namely, the political community or the whole political sphere. The political philosopher cannot be content, then, to raise such questions as "What is justice?" or "What is law?" He is forced to ask: "What is the political?" "What is the nature or what are the limits of that sphere to which political things belong?" "What is the political community?" "What is the place of the

---

[7] *What Is Political Philosophy?*, p. 16; cf. also pp. 9–17, 38–40.
[8] *What Is Political Philosophy?*, p. 12.
[9] *What Is Political Philosophy?*, pp. 10–12.
[10] A number of Strauss's statements that bear upon this issue are brought together by Victor Gourevitch in the second part of his critical study of Strauss's philosophy entitled "Philosophy and Politics," *Review of Metaphysics*, 22 (September–December 1968), 58–84, 281–328; see especially pp. 281–300. One should consider also what Strauss says in "Farabi's *Plato*," pp. 389–93, and in *Xenophon's Socrates* (Ithaca, 1972), pp. 6–17, 29–30, and especially pp. 114–23.
[11] *What Is Political Philosophy?*, p. 14; cf. *Xenophon's Socrates*, p. 71.

political community or political life within the comprehensive whole?" These questions call for an understanding of the *nature* of political things or of what it is that distinguishes political things from things that are not political. Assumptions about the nature of political things are present even in the most rudimentary knowledge of political things: "One cannot know anything about a war going on at a given time without having some notion, however dim and hazy, of war as such and its place within human life as such. One cannot see a policeman as a policeman without having made an assumption about law and government as such." [12] These assumptions or opinions about the nature of political things are made "the theme of critical and coherent analysis" by political philosophy.[13]

Quest for knowledge of the nature of political things is necessary, but not sufficient, for the existence of political philosophy. The political philosopher seeks knowledge also of "the right, or the good, political order." This concern distinguishes political philosophy, as a public-spirited and quasi-practical activity, from political theory, as a detached and purely speculative activity. Strauss shows that the question of the good society or the right political order arises inevitably within the sphere of political practice. It is not in the first instance a theoretical question but rather a question of urgent practical concern. All political action, whether aiming at preservation or change, is guided by some thought of better or worse and, implicitly at least, by some thought of the good. In questioning the opinions about the good that guide our actions, we are directed "towards such a thought of the good as is no longer questionable —towards a thought which is no longer opinion but knowledge. All political action has then in itself a directedness towards knowledge of the good: of the good life, or of the good society. For the good society is the complete political good." [14] Strauss often speaks in this context of knowledge of "the

---

[12] *What Is Political Philosophy?*, p. 16.
[13] Cf. *What Is Political Philosophy?*, pp. 12–17, 23–25, 81–84, 92–94. Strauss suggests that to understand the nature or character of the political is to understand its limits (i.e., its limits in securing the ultimate aim of happiness for which the political community itself is established). Cf. *What Is Political Philosophy?*, p. 91; Strauss and Cropsey, *History of Political Philosophy*, pp. 41, 51–52.
[14] *What Is Political Philosophy?*, p. 10.

best regime"; he means the internal ordering of a political community that determines what type of men will rule and what goals or purposes will be pursued. Regime gives a political community its identity, its distinctive character or form, and prescribes its way of life. Political experience discloses a variety of regimes, or various kinds of regimes, with conflicting purposes and conflicting views of the nature of the good or just society: "Thus the regimes themselves, and not any preoccupation of mere bystanders, force us to wonder which of the given conflicting regimes is better, and ultimately, which regime is the best regime." [15] Political philosophy raises and attempts to answer the question of the best regime. It is not willing, however, to settle this question by reference to the laws, customs, or conventions of men or even by reference to divine authority. Political philosophy is "concerned with the best or just order of society which is *by nature* best or just everywhere or always . . . ." [16]

Let us note, finally, that near the beginning of *What Is Political Philosophy?* Strauss writes that in the expression "political philosophy," the term "philosophy" indicates the manner of treatment (a treatment which goes to the roots and is comprehensive), while the term "political" indicates the subject matter and the function (the political things are dealt with in a manner that is meant to be relevant for political life).[17] Somewhat later in the book, he speaks of a "deeper meaning" of political philosophy:

> From this point of view the adjective "political" in the expression "political philosophy" designates not so much a subject matter as a manner of treatment; from this point of view, I say, "political philosophy" means primarily not the philosophic treatment of politics, but the political, or popular, treatment of philosophy, or the political introduction to philosophy—the attempt to lead

[15] *What Is Political Philosophy?*, p. 34; cf. pp. 34–36, 84–85. Cf. also *Natural Right and History* (Chicago, 1953), pp. 135–38; *The City and Man*, pp. 45–49; *Liberalism Ancient and Modern* (New York, 1968), p. 214.
[16] "Philosophy as Rigorous Science and Political Philosophy," *Interpretation*, Summer 1971, p. 1, emphasis added. The qualification "by nature" is essential to Strauss's definition. Philosophy as such is, in his view, quest for knowledge of nature (cf. *Natural Right and History*, p. 82).
[17] *What Is Political Philosophy?*, p. 10.

the qualified citizens, or rather their qualified sons, from the political life to the philosophic life.[18]

Strauss intends by these contrasting statements to raise the question of why the philosopher turns his attention to political things. The first statement suggests that political things possess a dignity that makes them worthy of philosophical attention in their own right. The second statement tends to depreciate political things by suggesting that the philosopher turns his attention to them mainly from necessity (so as to be able to prove to the citizens that philosophy is permissible, desirable, or even necessary), or from a nonpolitical motive (so as to lead the best young men to see that happiness cannot be reached by political life but only by a life devoted to contemplation, to philosophy).[19]

Strauss's account of the history of political philosophy is guided by the three criteria of authentic political philosophy that we have just examined. By applying them he is able to give very strong support to the traditional view that political philosophy emerged in the ancient world through the work of Socrates. Socrates appears to be the founder of the great tradition of political philosophy because he seems to have been the first (1) to search for genuine knowledge (2) of the nature of political things and (3) of the political order that is by nature best. Political philosophy was developed in its classical form by Plato, Xenophon, and Aristotle. Later thinkers such as the Stoics, Cicero, the Muslim and Jewish medieval political philosophers, and the Christian Scholastics adopted the classical framework.[20]

Perhaps Strauss's most significant contribution to the recovery of the great tradition of political philosophy has been his intensive study of those writers who knew Socrates himself:

[18] *What Is Political Philosophy?*, pp. 93–94; cf. *Persecution and the Art of Writing*, p. 18.

[19] Cf. *What Is Political Philosophy?*, p. 91.

[20] Cf. *Natural Right and History*, p. 120. The political thought of the poets, the historians, the rhetoricians, and, in many cases, the philosophers fails to meet one or more of Strauss's criteria of authentic political philosophy. Consider, for example, what Strauss says about Thucydides (*The City and Man*, pp. 157, 228, 236–37); the Epicureans (*Natural Right and History*, pp. 109–13, 168; *Liberalism Ancient and Modern*, p. 131); and Hippodamus (*The City and Man*, pp. 17–19).

Aristophanes, Xenophon, and Plato. Aristophanes' presentation is a poetic indictment of Socrates and philosophers generally for their indifference to political things. Plato and Xenophon appear to have written in conscious opposition to Aristophanes' presentation of Socrates. Their writings support the traditional view that Socrates was the first to direct philosophy toward the study of political things and, more broadly, human things (i.e., just things, noble things, and things good for man as man). Although Strauss deems it impossible to say which view, if either, depicts the historical Socrates, he suggests that there might be some basis in fact for both views. It is possible that the profound differences between the Aristophanean Socrates and the Platonic-Xenophontic Socrates can "be traced to a profound change in Socrates himself: to his conversion from a youthful contempt for the political or moral things, for the human things or human beings, to a mature concern with them." [21]

Judging from the writings of Plato, Xenophon, and Aristotle, Socrates was able to direct philosophy toward political and human things because of his distinctive understanding of "nature." Earlier philosophers had understood by "nature" those "first things" out of which and through which all things not of human making have come into being. In reducing things to their elements or originating causes, this approach has lost sight of what it is that makes each class of things distinctive. Socrates held that the "nature" of a thing refers primarily to "what" it is, to the form or essence that provides its specific character, and not to its material component or to the forces that produced it. In the Socratic view, the nature of a thing comes to sight most clearly at the term of the process that brings it into being, when the thing exists in its final or completed state. Moreover, the intelligible whole, the cosmos, consists of distinct kinds or classes of things, which have a natural and manifest articulation. The philosopher's quest for knowledge of the whole must attempt to understand the nature or essence of each class of things and how the "natures" are linked with one another. By recognizing the essential and irreducible differences between classes of things, this Socratic view favors the effort to understand the different kinds of political and human things on

---

[21] *Socrates and Aristophanes* (New York, 1966), p. 314.

their own terms and also to see political and human things as a distinct class by themselves within the whole. Thus Socrates raised the question "What is?" with respect to various political and human things, especially things good or bad for man, as well as the question of the nature of political and human things as such. He attempted to ascend from the awareness that is embodied in partial and conflicting opinions about such things to a complete and consistent view of their natures.[22]

Strauss shows that classical teachings about man and the political community rest upon this Socratic identification of the "nature" of a thing with its completion or perfection. The classics understood the nature of man by reference to the proper ordering of man's soul. They understood the nature of the political community by reference to the proper ordering of the community or to the best regime. In the natural order of man's being, the soul stands higher than the body. The soul of man is characterized by the capacity for speech and reason; and the good or natural life for man lies in the life of reason and reasonable action. In the political community as well, the natural order requires that reason rule the other parts. The best regime is the rule of wisdom, either by wise men directly or by the rule of wise laws that are administered by reasonable men. The classics taught that man cannot live well or reach the perfection of his nature except by living with others and cultivating justice, the social virtue par excellence. They concluded that justice or right is something natural and not merely something that depends for its being on convention or human agreement.[23]

The distinction between knowledge of the nature of political things and knowledge of the best regime plays a crucial role in Strauss's account of the classics. He argues that certain works such as Plato's *Republic*, which many recent interpreters have seen as containing proposals for political reform, were intended not as models for practice but as more or less speculative treatments of the limits of the moral-political sphere as a whole:

[22] Cf. *The City and Man*, pp. 13–29, 119–20; *Natural Right and History*, pp. 120–26.

[23] Cf. *Natural Right and History*, pp. 126–64; "Natural Law" in *The International Encyclopedia of the Social Sciences*, ed. David L. Sills (New York, 1968), XI, 80–85.

As Cicero has observed, the Republic does not bring to light the best possible regime but rather the nature of political things—the nature of the city. Socrates makes clear in the *Republic* of what character the city would have to be in order to satisfy the highest need of man. By letting us see that the city constructed in accordance with this requirement is not possible, he lets us see the essential limits, the nature, of the city.[24]

It is unnecessary to assume that Plato contradicted himself or changed his mind in order to account for differences between the *Republic* and the *Laws*. The two works are addressed to different themes of political philosophy. The *Republic* indicates the essential limits to all political action and planning and therewith the essential character or nature of the political community. It shows that the ultimate aim of political life—namely, the truly good and happy life for man—cannot be reached by political life, but only by a life devoted to contemplation, to philosophy. The *Laws* is addressed to the question of the best possible political order, "the best order of the city compatible with the nature of man." [25]

Strauss emphasizes that the classics entertained only modest expectations of improvement through political reforms. Since the conditions necessary for the actualization of the simply best regime depend on chance and are seldom if ever present, prudent men will be content to establish or improve regimes which, though best under existing circumstances and therefore just and legitimate, are, nonetheless, inferior to what is best simply. The political philosopher will try to help his fellow men, but he will not engage in revolutionary or subversive activity.[26]

Strauss draws a sharp line of demarcation between clas-

---

[24] *The City and Man*, p. 138; cf. *What Is Political Philosophy?*, pp. 92–94. The favorable observations about tyranny in Xenophon's writings serve the purpose "not of solving the problem of the best political order, but of bringing to light the nature of political things," *On Tyranny*, rev. ed. (Ithaca, 1963), pp. 102–03; cf. *What Is Political Philosophy?*, p. 99.

[25] Strauss and Cropsey, *History of Political Philosophy*, p. 52.

[26] Cf. *What Is Political Philosophy?*, p. 28: Classical political philosophy "is free from all fanaticism because it knows that evil cannot be eradicated and therefore that one's expectations from politics must be moderate." Cf. also pp. 46, 60–61, 86–88, 106–07, 119–20, 125–27; *Natural Right and History*, pp. 135–43; *Liberalism Ancient and Modern*, p. 15.

sical political philosophy, which flourished in one form or another into the middle ages, and modern political philosophy. He divides the modern tradition itself into three periods. The first "wave" of modernity lasted from the time of its founding by Machiavelli until the eighteenth century, when modernity reached its first time of crisis. Rousseau's attack on the natural right doctrines of Hobbes and Locke produced this crisis and initiated the "second wave of modernity"—a wave that culminated in the political thought of Kant and Hegel. Nietzsche's critique of German idealism produced still another crisis of modernity, "the crisis of our time," and inaugurated "the third wave of modernity," the wave that bears us along today.[27]

The moderns followed the Socratic tradition in conceiving of political philosophy as quest for knowledge of the nature of political things and of the best regime, but they disagreed fundamentally with this tradition as regards the substance and method of political philosophy: (1) The distinction between opinion and knowledge was preserved in modern political philosophy, but philosophy or science itself was redirected from the contemplation of nature to the pursuit of such knowledge as would empower man to conquer and transform nature for the relief of his estate. Scientific knowledge became the handmaiden of practice and the servant of the desires rather than the highest good to which human desire and striving could aspire.[28] (2) The moderns continued to be concerned with the nature of political things, but by denying that there are essential or qualitative differences in nature and by identifying the natural with

---

[27] *What Is Political Philosophy?*, pp. 40–55; *Natural Right and History*, pp. 252–53. Strauss once regarded Hobbes as the founder of modern political philosophy. In *The Political Philosophy of Hobbes*, he shows, in opposition to prevailing interpretations, that Hobbes's conceptions of "natural right" and "natural law" break radically with classical and medieval principles. Later, he concluded that the decisive break with classical political philosophy occurred earlier with Machiavelli. In *Thoughts on Machiavelli* (Glencoe, 1958), he shows that Machiavelli broke fundamentally with the classics and went on to develop a political philosophy that anticipated the crucial principles of the modern tradition. Cf. also "Machiavelli and Classical Literature," *Review of National Literatures*, 1 (Spring 1970), 7–25; and "Niccolo Machiavelli," in Strauss and Cropsey (eds.), *History of Political Philosophy*, pp. 271–92.

[28] Cf. *Natural Right and History*, pp. 170–77; *Liberalism Ancient and Modern*, pp. 19–20.

the subhuman or the material, they made it doubtful that political and human things enjoy a distinctive place within the whole of nature. Insofar as they agreed with the new natural science that no qualitative differences can be found in nature, the moderns abandoned the ground on which Socrates had opposed his predecessors and established political philosophy. The "first crisis of modernity" came with Rousseau's demonstration that the modern conception of nature makes it impossible any longer to understand the distinctively human in man as "natural." Thereafter the search for the humanity of man would turn from his nature to his history.[29] (3) The moderns were concerned with the best regime, but they broke with the classics regarding the nature of the best regime and the possibility of its actualization. Strauss finds in Machiavelli the principle common to all modern political philosophies: the rejection of the classical scheme as unrealistic or useless. According to Machiavelli, classical political philosophy had culminated in a utopia, "in the description of a best regime whose actualization is highly improbable," because it had taken its bearings by how man ought to live or by virtue.[30] Machiavelli and the moderns hoped to ensure the actualization of the good social order by lowering the standards of social action, that is, by defining the best regime with reference to the way men actually do live and to the objectives that all societies actually pursue. In their view, the best regime is not an aristocracy in the classical sense. It depends for its success more on the operations of its institutions than on the virtue of its rulers.[31] Much of modern political thought has a doctrinaire and revolutionary character, which Strauss traces to its expectation that the best regime can be actualized everywhere. If the best regime is always within reach, it is no longer plausible to argue that established regimes which fall short of the best are just and legitimate.[32]

The fundamental opposition of classical and modern political philosophy is the great theme of Strauss's historical studies.

[29] Cf. *Natural Right and History*, pp. 252–94.
[30] *What Is Political Philosophy?*, p. 41.
[31] Cf. *What Is Political Philosophy?*, pp. 40–53; *Thoughts on Machiavelli*, pp. 174–299.
[32] Cf. *Natural Right and History*, pp. 301–23; *What Is Political Philosophy?*, pp. 60–61, 107.

We are led inevitably to wonder where Strauss himself stands with respect to this conflict. Certainly he intends to challenge the prevailing assumption that the classical alternative has been refuted decisively by modern views of man and society. Can we conclude, then, that Strauss rejects the basic principles of modern political philosophy and embraces classical principles? There are several considerations which point toward this conclusion. What Strauss says in his own name about the nature of political philosophy coincides with the view that he attributes to the classics. He is often critical of modern viewpoints, but says little about possible defects in critical political philosophy. He finds tendencies present in modern political philosophy from the beginning that eventually would undermine it and lead to the repudiation of political philosophy as such. He argues that the classical insight into man and politics is more comprehensive than the modern, for while the classics were aware of human excellence as well as of the darker side of human nature, the moderns often forgot about the former in emphasizing the latter.

> One can safely say that there is no moral or political phenomenon that Machiavelli knew or for whose discovery he is famous that was not perfectly known to Xenophon, to say nothing of Plato or Aristotle. It is true that in Machiavelli everything appears in a new light, but this is due, not to an enlargement of the horizon, but to a narrowing of it. Many modern discoveries regarding man have this character.[33]

Strauss tells us that it is impossible to think about the fundamental and comprehensive problems of philosophy "without becoming inclined toward a solution, toward one or the other of the very few typical solutions." Allowing for the fact that there are important differences among the various statements of classical political philosophy, we may say that Strauss is inclined toward the classical solution. We must, however, keep in mind his warning that in the philosophical quest for wisdom, "the evidence of all solutions is necessarily smaller than the evidence of the problems." The philosopher ceases to be a philosopher at

[33] Strauss and Cropsey (eds.), *History of Political Philosophy*, p. 291. Cf. *Liberalism Ancient and Modern*, p. 208; *What is Political Philosophy?*, pp. 43–4.

the moment when his certainty of a solution "becomes stronger than his awareness of the problematic character of that solution." [34] The manifest collapse of modern political philosophy necessitates a return to classical political philosophy, but this return must be "tentative or experimental."

> We cannot reasonably expect that a fresh understanding of classical political philosophy will supply us with recipes for today's use. For the relative success of modern political philosophy has brought into being a kind of society wholly unknown to the classics, a kind of society to which the classical principles as stated and elaborated by the classics are not immediately applicable. Only we living today can possibly find a solution to the problems of today. But an adequate understanding of the principles as elaborated by the classics may be the indispensable starting point for an adequate analysis, to be achieved by us, of present-day society in its peculiar character, and for the wise application, to be achieved by us, of these principles to our tasks. [35]

Strauss's studies indicate that while philosophy can be of great benefit to man and the political community, it stands, nonetheless, in constant danger from very powerful opponents. Philosophy is always compelled to defend itself against actual or potential opposition from two sources: from the political community, or the citizens; and from rival claimants to wisdom or knowledge. "Political" philosophy is, in one important sense, the means by which philosophy defends itself. By considering the reasons why philosophy is endangered and the characteristic ways in which it has defended itself, we shall move closer to an understanding of Strauss's own objective.

The inherent tension and inevitable conflict between philosophy and the political community is a primary theme of Strauss's writings. Strauss appears to agree with the classics that every political community rests on particular fundamental opinions about politics, morality, and religion which citizens are ex-

---

[34] *What Is Political Philosophy?*, pp. 115–16. Philosophy, as Strauss understands it, is "zetetic," or skeptic in the original sense of the term (p. 116). It is identical with "the actual quest for truth which is animated by the conviction that that quest alone makes life worth living, and which is fortified by the distrust of man's natural propensity to rest satisfied with satisfying, if unevident or unproven, convictions" ("Farabi's *Plato*," p. 393).

[35] *The City and Man*, p. 11.

pected to accept as authoritative. Philosophy as the intransigent quest for truth tends to be at odds with the requirements of society, because it is disposed to question all opinions, including those that have the sanction of political and even divine authority. To illustrate: the political community must propagate the opinion that the established regime is best, but political philosophers are likely to see all existing regimes as inferior in principle to the simply best regime. The political community regards the traditional way of life as the right way—right because of its antiquity and perhaps also its divine origin. Yet political philosophers question the identification of the good with the ancestral or with the will of the gods, and appeal to something that is older and higher than either the founders of the community or the gods of popular religion. They look to nature for the way of life that is right or just for men and communities. The political community exalts the political life, the life of statesmen and citizens, and civic morality. Yet philosophers teach that a private life, the life devoted to the quest for knowledge, is better than political life and that the excellence of the mind is better than those virtues that have their roots in the needs of society. The political man cares for the political community and the citizens because he attaches absolute importance to man and to human things. Yet the philosopher's desire for knowledge of the eternal order leads him to depreciate the political sphere.[36]

Some modern political philosophers have believed that the tension between philosophy and society can be overcome entirely through the popularization of philosophy, or through "enlightenment." According to this view, the danger to philosophy comes not from society per se but from the falsehoods and superstitions that infect society. Once these false opinions are eradicated through relentless philosophical criticism, society will become open to the unhampered pursuit of truth. This view has been politically successful in the sense that modern societies have often claimed to rest on the true philosophical principles. "Intellectuals" now enjoy a great deal of freedom and influence. Strauss indicates, however, that the popularization (or vulgarization) of philosophy, far from reducing soci-

_____

[36] Cf. *Natural Right and History*, pp. 82–93, 206–12; *What Is Political Philosophy?*, pp. 32–33, 117–18, 125–27, 221–32; *Liberalism Ancient and Modern*, pp. viii, 14–15; and *Persecution and the Art of Writing*.

ety's inclination to tyrannize thought, has actually brought greater danger to freedom than existed in ancient societies.[37]

Strauss has given considerable attention not only to the inherent tension between philosophy and the community, but also to the philosophic response to this tension. He shows that philosophers throughout the ages have found it necessary to offer a popular or political justification of philosophy, emphasizing its benefits to the community. Furthermore, they have designed their writings in such a way as to avoid offending nonphilosophers.

How might philosophy benefit the community? Philosophers have justified their activity before the tribunal of the political community by speaking of the contribution which philosophy can make both to the community's guidance and to its defense. Strauss appears to endorse the claim that philosophical thinking about the good or just political order might help to resolve, in a thoughtful and public-spirited way, the most basic question that arises for a political community. Political life is characterized by the struggle for power between groups of men who defend their claim to rule in terms of what is good or just for the whole community. The original purpose of political philosophy was to resolve this controversy "in the spirit not of the partisan but of the good citizen, and with a view to such an order as would be most in accordance with the requirements of human excellence." [38] Political philosophers have spoken about the establishment and improvement of regimes in such a manner as to guide lawgivers and statesmen. Strauss is somewhat more emphatic in holding that political philosophy can contribute to sound practice by defending the political sphere against the intrusion of harmful threats. His studies indicate that while political philosophers have disagreed widely about the extent to which practical wisdom or prudence must be supplemented by theory in order to govern the political community successfully, they have tended to agree that theory is needed at least to defend sound practice against pernicious opinions. Strauss seems to give his endorsement to the view that "there never was and there never will be reasonable security for sound practice ex-

[37] Cf. *Persecution and the Art of Writing*, pp. 21, 56, 154–57; *What Is Political Philosophy?*, pp. 127, 132–33; *On Tyranny*, p. 26.
[38] *What Is Political Philosophy?*, p. 90.

cept after theory has overcome the powerful obstacles to sound practice which originate in theoretical misconceptions of a certain kind." [39]

The inherent tension between philosophy and the political community has led also to a distinctive mode of philosophical writing, which conceals those principles that might be offensive to established opinion. What Strauss says about esoteric writing is of crucial importance for understanding his studies in the history of political philosophy:

> In studying certain earlier thinkers, I became aware of this way of conceiving the relation between the quest for truth (philosophy or science) and society: Philosophy or science, the highest activity of man, is the attempt to replace opinions about "all things" by knowledge of "all things"; but opinion is the element of society; philosophy or science is therefore the attempt to dissolve the element in which society breathes, and thus it endangers society. Hence philosophy or science must remain the preserve of a small minority, and philosophers or scientists must respect the opinions on which society rests. To respect opinions is something entirely different from accepting them as true. Philosophers or scientists who hold this view about the relation of philosophy or science and society are driven to employ a peculiar manner of writing which would enable them to reveal what they regard as the truth to the few, without endangering the unqualified commitment of the many to the opinions on which society rests. They will distinguish between the true teaching as the esoteric teaching and the socially useful teaching as the exoteric teaching; whereas the exoteric teaching is meant to be easily accessible to every reader, the esoteric teaching discloses itself only to the very careful and well-trained readers after long and concentrated study. [40]

Esoteric writing had to be rediscovered because the need for it had been forgotten in contemporary liberal societies, where absolute freedom of expression is supposedly guaranteed and where dissimulation is regarded as altogether vicious. Strauss shows that an accurate interpretation of the history of political

[39] *What Is Political Philosophy?*, p. 105; cf. pp. 86, 92–94, 126–27, 180; *Liberalism Ancient and Modern*, pp. 205–06; *The City and Man*, pp. 25–27; *Natural Right and History*, pp. 262–63; *Persecution and the Art of Writing*, pp. 154–56, 190–98.
[40] *What Is Political Philosophy?*, pp. 221–22.

philosophy depends on a recognition of the fact that most of the great political philosophers practised esotericism in some degree. Esoteric writing allows the philosopher to engage in philosophical discourse and to introduce qualified young men to philosophy while at the same time protecting society from any harmful or corrosive effects of his thought and protecting himself from those who would be offended by his questioning of the established political, religious, and moral opinions.[41]

The political community and the sphere of opinion to which it belongs is not the only source of opposition to political philosophy. Strauss shows that political philosophy is opposed also by various rival claimants to knowledge or wisdom. In the ancient world, for example, the classical political philosophers were required to defend their enterprise against the poets, the rhetoricians and Sophists, and apolitical philosophers such as the Epicureans. The spread of revealed religion brought yet another challenge to political philosophy. In the ancient world, political philosophy had often been attacked as irreligious, but since ancient religions were subordinate to civil authority, we may subsume these attacks under the conflict between philosophy and the political community. Judaism, Christianity, and Islam claimed, however, to be ultimately independent of merely secular authority; and they claimed also that revelation was the final arbiter in those areas where it came into conflict with reason or went beyond reason. In those times when revealed religion was a powerful force, philosophers were compelled to avoid an open denial of its authority. Today, philosophy or science does not usually regard revealed religion as a serious antagonist, but Strauss himself believes that the challenge posed by revelation to reason or philosophy is, intrinsically, of the utmost importance. The conflict between philosophy and revealed religion goes deeper, for example, than the conflict between classical and modern political philosophy. The issue raised by the conflicting and irreconcilable claims of Athens and Jerusalem, of philosophy and revelation, is, in Strauss's view, the most fundamental issue that confronts man.[42]

[41] See *Persecution and the Art of Writing*, along with Strauss's restatement of the thesis of this book in *What Is Political Philosophy?*, pp. 221–32.

[42] Cf. *Persecution and the Art of Writing*, pp. 107, 142–43; *Natural Right and History*, pp. 74–76; *Thoughts on Machiavelli*, pp. 51, 133. Strauss draws a sharp distinction between political theology and political philosophy: "By polit-

In the course of its long history, political philosophy was able to survive and even to flourish in the face of strong opposition from the political sphere and from rival claimants to wisdom. Strauss contends, however, that political philosophy is today "in a state of decay and perhaps of putrefaction, if it has not vanished altogether." [43] But how can political philosophy have declined in a time when religion no longer stands as a potent rival and in countries where freedom of thought and expression is supposedly guaranteed? Strauss traces this decline to opposition from within philosophy or theory itself. The combined influence of two powerful theoretical movements, which Strauss calls "positivism" and "historicism," has almost succeeded in destroying the very possibility of political philosophy and, as a result, has produced "the crisis of our time." We must turn our attention now to Strauss's account of this crisis.

In Strauss's view, the "crisis of our time" or "crisis of the West" has both a theoretical and a practical side. The theoretical side of this crisis consists in the virtual destruction of political philosophy by the most influential movements of thought in our time—positivism and historicism. The political side is to be found in the fact that the West has become uncertain of its purpose.

Positivism is described by Strauss as "the view according to which only scientific knowledge, as defined by modern natural science, is genuine knowledge." [44] This view of knowledge has discredited political philosophy as quest for knowledge of the good or just political order, and directed efforts instead toward the construction of a social or political science that resembles modern natural science. Although important forerunners of

---

ical theology we understand political teachings which are based on divine revelation. Political philosophy is limited to what is accessible to the unassisted human mind" (*What Is Political Philosophy?*, p. 13). Strauss treats the problem of reason and revelation in essays, contained in his various works, on Islamic, Jewish, and Christian writers. See also his "Preface to the English Translation" of *Spinoza's Critique of Religion*, trans. E. M. Sinclair (New York, 1965), pp. 1–31; and *Jerusalem and Athens* (New York, 1967). The "Preface" is reprinted in *Liberalism Ancient and Modern*, pp. 244–59; an adaptation of "Jerusalem and Athens" appears in *Commentary*, 43 (June 1967), 45–57.

[43] *What Is Political Philosophy?*, p. 17.

[44] "The Crisis of Political Philosophy," in *The Predicament of Modern Politics*, ed. Harold J. Spaeth (Detroit, 1964), p. 91.

contemporary positivism, such as Hume and Comte, did not hesitate to claim knowledge of the good society, twentieth-century positivism has insisted that genuine knowledge of the good life for man and society is unattainable. In the social sciences, positivists have typically made a fundamental distinction between facts and values. They have gone on to argue that factual knowledge lies within the reach of social science, but not knowledge of values. Social science can never validate or invalidate value judgments; and it must strive insofar as possible to avoid them. Political philosophy is a futile enterprise, according to positivism, because it proceeds on the erroneous assumption that knowledge of values is possible.[45]

Strauss uses the term "historicism" to refer to a complex movement of modern thought whose leading representatives are Hegel, Nietzsche, and Heidegger. What Strauss calls "theoretical" or "contemplative" historicism made its appearance in "the second wave of modernity." Its leading exponent was Hegel. Theoretical historicism identifies the task of science as the contemplation of the historical process—a process that has developed rationally and is completed in the essential respects. It replaces political philosophy in the Socratic sense with philosophy of history: "Hegel's demand that political philosophy refrain from construing a state as it ought to be, or from teaching the state how it should be, and that it try to understand the present and actual state as something essentially rational, amounts to a rejection of the *raison d'être* of classical political philosophy." [46]

"Radical" or "existentialist" historicism appeared in "the third wave of modernity." Nietzsche is its father, and Heidegger is its most powerful spokesman in the twentieth century. Radical historicism agrees with Hegel that man must be understood in light of his history, but it denies that the historical process is fundamentally progressive or rational. Man cannot transcend this process nor can he understand it, for all interpretations of the past are colored by the transitory perspective or world view of the present. Radical historicism agrees with positivism in rejecting the very possibility of political philosophy. Man cannot hope to gain knowledge of the good that

[45] Cf. *What Is Political Philosophy?*, pp. 18–26.
[46] *What Is Political Philosophy?*, p. 88.

holds true for all times and places. Indeed, radical historicism "casts a doubt on the very questions of the nature of political things and of the best, or the just, political order" by insisting that philosophy itself and its universal questions, including the questions raised by political philosophy, "are 'historically conditioned,' i.e., essentially related to a specific 'historic' type, e.g., to Western man or to the Greeks and their intellectual heirs." [47] Radical historicism goes on, however, to reject the positivist account of knowledge as well as the accounts of traditional philosophy. It holds that positivism is deluded in its belief that science can discover objective knowledge of the factual world; for "all principles of understanding and of action are historical, i.e., have no ground other than groundless human decision or fateful dispensation: science, far from being the only kind of genuine knowledge, is ultimately no more than one form among many of viewing the world, all these forms having the same dignity." [48]

Strauss views the political crisis of our time as a consequence of the destruction of political philosophy by positivism and historicism.[49] He would not contend that political society necessarily requires political philosophy as a condition of its viability, but he does insist that a political society must believe in the truth of the purpose or end to which it is committed. The universalistic purpose that has guided Western societies since the seventeenth century is derived from modern political philosophy—specifically, from modern conceptions of natural rights and liberal democracy. Through the influence of modern political philosophy, Western man came to expect a world community, "a universal league of free and equal nations, each nation consisting of free and equal men and women." [50] Universal peace and prosperity would be assured through enlightenment,

[47] *What Is Political Philosophy?*, pp. 57, 60; cf. p. 26.
[48] "Philosophy as Rigorous Science and Political Philosophy," p. 1; cf. *Natural Right and History*, pp. 9–34; *What Is Political Philosophy?*, pp. 56–77, 246; "The Crisis of Political Philosophy," pp. 91–92; "Relativism," in *Relativism and the Study of Man*, Helmut Schoeck and James W. Wiggins (Princeton, 1961), pp. 135–57.
[49] Strauss discusses this political crisis in *The City and Man*, pp. 1–12; "The Crisis of Our Time," in Spaeth, *The Predicament of Modern Politics*, pp. 41–54; "Relativism," pp. 135–45; and *Liberalism Ancient and Modern*, pp. v–ix, 3–25, 203–72.
[50] *The City and Man*, p. 4.

or the instruction of men about their natural rights and the institutions needed to safeguard them, and through the application of modern science and its technology for man's comfortable preservation. When the truth of these central tenets of modern political philosophy became questionable, so too did the Western political societies that were founded upon them.

The guiding purpose of the West was rendered questionable, first of all, by contemporary political experience. While communism was seen at first by many Westerners as a movement parallel to liberalism—a movement with "the same goal of a universal prosperous society of free and equal men and women"—experience would show that communism stands in fact for tyrannical rule and, therefore, that its victory would not produce the kind of universal society which the West desired. The most urgent task for the West became the preservation of particular liberal democracies, not the establishment of a global society. Moreover, "the same experience which has made the West doubtful of the viability of a world-society has made it doubtful of the belief that affluence is the sufficient and even necessary condition of happiness and justice: affluence does not cure the deepest evils." [51] Finally, the crises of modern life have cast doubt on the belief that the quality of life is necessarily improved by the progress of modern science.

Although political experience has caused the West to doubt its purpose, a more profound reason for the West's self-doubt lies in the fact that belief in the truth of its purpose has been shaken by those theoretical movements that brought political philosophy itself into question. Positivism and historicism teach that no principles about the good life for man and society can be generally true or valid. Far from being self-evidently true, "the teaching originated by modern political philosophy in favor of the universal and prosperous society has admittedly become an ideology—a teaching not superior in truth and justice to any other among the innumerable ideologies." [52] Once realizing that liberal democracy is only an ideology, with no claim to truth, Western man finds it impossible to believe wholeheartedly in its principles. Moreover, he is told that he

[51] *The City and Man*, p. 6.
[52] *The City and Man*, pp. 6–7; cf. *Natural Right and History*, pp. 1–8.

cannot possibly show, by reason or experience, that any political order is good or just. The practical consequence of positivism and historicism is either nihilism—"a state of indifference to any goal, or of aimlessness and drifting"—or a fanatical obscurantism that tries to overcome inner doubts about the truth and rightness of one's cause by blind and passionate commitment to it.[53]

We have taken notice of Strauss's conviction that political philosophy is compelled at all times to give both a political, or popular, and a theoretical defense of itself. It must show, before the tribunal of the political community, that it contributes to the community's well-being. It must also defend itself against attacks by rival claimants to knowledge. In this time of unprecedented danger for political philosophy, Strauss's writings are intended to fulfill these vital tasks. We shall see that Strauss provides a direct, theoretical justification for political philosophy by his critiques of positivism and historicism. Moreover, the defense he gives of liberal democracy is, at the same time, an indirect political justification for political philosophy, for it demonstrates to everyone how political philosophy can combat the dangers to liberal democracy that arise from prevailing theoretical movements.[54]

Strauss's treatment of liberal democracy is fundamentally different from that of positivistic political science, which he indicts for its blindness to the dangers that threaten liberal democracy from without and from within. The external danger to liberal democracy has come from regimes that Strauss identifies as forms of tyranny. Because of its refusal to recognize essential or qualitative differences between regimes, positivistic political

[53] *What Is Political Philosophy?*, pp. 18–19; *The Political Philosophy of Hobbes*, p. xix; *Natural Right and History*, pp. 4–6, and also p. 42, where Strauss defines nihilism as "the view that every preference, however evil, base, or insane, has to be judged before the tribunal of reason to be as legitimate as any other preference."

[54] Vital to an understanding of Strauss's purpose are his statements about natural and artificial obstacles to philosophy (*Persecution and the Art of Writing*, pp. 154–58); about "philosophic politics" (*What Is Political Philosophy?*, pp. 63–64, 92–94, 126–27); and about argumentation (*What Is Political Philosophy?*, p. 93; *The City and Man*, pp. 53–54; *Persecution and the Art of Writing*, pp. 186, 189; *On Tyranny*, pp. 25–26, 74; and "The Crisis of Our Time," p. 42).

science fails to see contemporary tyrannies for what they are, that is, as regimes that are different in kind, and not just in degree, from liberal democracy. Moreover, positivism can find no rational basis for thinking that liberal democracy is better than tyranny. Strauss argues, however, that liberal democracy, while not the best regime imaginable, is the best regime possible today. Strauss's defense of liberal democracy is complicated by the fact that he is critical of those currents of modern political philosophy that gave rise to it. He concedes that liberal democracy is closer in some matters of principle to its rivals than to the classical position that he favors.[55] Still, he maintains that it would not be difficult to show "that liberal or constitutional democracy comes closer to what the classics demanded than any alternative that is viable in our age." [56] Specifically, liberal democracy can be defended on the classical principle that the rule of wise laws, administered by prudent men, is superior to such forms of absolute rule as can be expected in practice. Moreover, philosophy has a better chance to survive under liberal democracy than under the modern forms of tyranny.[57]

Strauss identifies the primary internal danger to liberal democracy as its steady decline into permissive egalitarianism. He points out that the founders of liberal democracy had believed that the success of their project would require the people and their leaders to respect human excellence and also to possess a measure of virtue and self-restraint. Yet under positivist and historicist influence, contemporary liberalism "has abandoned its absolutist basis and is trying to become entirely relativistic." [58] The abandonment of all standards of excellence has led to a degraded and permissive form of liberal democracy, or to what often is called "mass democracy." Positivistic political

---

[55] Cf. *What Is Political Philosophy?*, p. 55.

[56] *What Is Political Philosophy?*, p. 113; cf. pp. 36–38, 95, 306; cf. also *The City and Man*, pp. 35–41; *Liberalism Ancient and Modern*, pp. 15–25, 214–15, 220–23, 270; "Science and Humanism," in *The State of the Social Sciences*, ed. Leonard D. White (Chicago, 1956), pp. 415–25.

[57] Cf. *What Is Political Philosophy?*, pp. 132–33; *Liberalism Ancient and Modern*, p. 24. Cf. also Strauss's defense of liberal democracy as offering the best practicable solution today to "the Jewish problem" (*Liberalism Ancient and Modern*, pp. 224–31).

[58] "Relativism," p. 140.

science reflects and at the same time strengthens the most dangerous proclivities of contemporary democracy:

> By teaching in effect the equality of literally all desires, it teaches in effect that there is nothing of which a man ought to be ashamed; by destroying the possibility of self-contempt, it destroys with the best of intentions the possibility of self-respect. By teaching the equality of all values, by denying that there are things which are intrinsically high and others which are intrinsically low as well as by denying that there is an essential difference between men and brutes, it unwittingly contributes to the victory of the gutter.[59]

Strauss speaks as a friend of liberal democracy and of human excellence when he reminds us that education toward virtue is indispensable to liberal democracy at its highest.[60]

Let us now turn to Strauss's defense of political philosophy against positivism and historicism. This defense is the heart of his response to the crisis of our time, for as we have seen, he interprets the political element of that crisis—the crisis of liberal democracy—as a consequence of the destruction of political philosophy.

Strauss replies to positivism's attack on political philosophy by rejecting its distinction between facts and values and, more broadly, by denying that its attempt to break entirely with "prescientific" or "commonsense" understanding can succeed. In opposing the demand for a "value-free" social science, Strauss argues that evaluation is indispensable to an adequate understanding of social or political things. He shows, for example, that Max Weber, who insisted on the principle that social science must remain value-free, was unable in his own research to adhere to this principle. Positivistic social science cannot, in practice, avoid value judgments. The only question, then, is whether evaluations will be made intelligently or unintelligently. Positivism assumes that human reason is incapable of resolving the conflicts between different values or value systems, but in Strauss's view, positivism has never provided the kind of philosophical analysis that would be necessary to

---

[59] *Liberalism Ancient and Modern*, p. 222.
[60] Cf. *Liberalism Ancient and Modern*, pp. 2–25, 63–64; *What Is Political Philosophy?*, p. 38.

uphold this assumption. Weber, for example, merely took for
granted the impotence of reason to know the good without attempting seriously to prove the point.[61]

Strauss suggests that there is a basis in experience for the
belief that we can know what is right or good for man. He calls
our attention to "those simple experiences regarding right and
wrong which are at the bottom of the philosophic contention
that there is a natural right." [62] He has in mind our sense that
some actions are inexcusably unjust and also "the phenomenon
of admiration of human excellence," which includes "the immediate pleasure which we experience when we observe signs
of human nobility." [63] Strauss would deny that positivism has
given an adequate account of these experiences.

Strauss's critique of positivism calls to mind the position of

---

[61] Cf. What Is Political Philosophy?, pp. 18–26; Natural Right and History, pp. 35–80; Liberalism Ancient and Modern, pp. 203–23.

[62] Natural Right and History, pp. 31–32, 100, 105; What Is Political Philosophy?, p. 23. The epigraphs to Natural Right and History, which are taken
from the Bible, give examples of the sort of phenomena regarding justice or
right that are known to the prephilosophic consciousness and that underlie the
philosophic contention that there is a natural right. The passages are Nathan's
parable of King David about the rich man's slaughter of the lamb of the poor
man (II Samuel 12) and the story of King Ahab's desire for Naboth's vineyard,
which culminates in Jezebel's successful plot to destroy Naboth (I Kings 21). Cf.
What Is Political Philosophy?, p. 23, regarding the latter passage. In Natural
Right and History, Strauss writes: "There is no relation of man to man in which
man is absolutely free to act as he pleases or as it suits him. And all men are
somehov. aware of this fact. Every ideology is an attempt to justify before one's
self or others such courses of action as are somehow felt to be in need of justification, i.e., as are not obviously right. . . . By virtue of his rationality, man
has a latitude of alternatives such as no other earthly being has. The sense of
this latitude, of this freedom, is accompanied by a sense that the full and unrestrained exercise of that freedom is not right. Man's freedom is accompanied by
a sacred awe, by a kind of divination that not everything is permitted. We may
call this awe-inspired fear 'man's natural conscience.' Restraint is therefore as
natural or as primeval as freedom." (pp. 129–30). In What Is Political Philosophy?, Strauss criticizes Hobbes and Hegel for "starting from the untrue assumption that man as man is thinkable as a being that lacks awareness of sacred restraints or as a being that is guided by nothing but a desire for recognition." (p.
111).

[63] Natural Right and History, p. 128; What Is Political Philosophy?,
p. 122. In both of these locations, Strauss makes statements about admiration for
"the well-ordered soul" that are of the utmost importance for the present topic.

Edmund Husserl and the phenomenological movement.[64] Strauss points out that positivism's exclusion of value judgments from "scientific" understanding is part of its broader tendency to doubt the reliability of prescientific understanding as such. This tendency, which is present in modern science generally, produces an understanding of things that is radically different from the "natural" or "commonsense" understanding. Yet the problematical character of the scientific understanding of man and the world compels us to turn again to prescientific understanding in order to find our bearings. Strauss holds that in science as well as in common life, there is an inescapable reliance on the commonsense understanding of the world.[65] He thus agrees with phenomenology in redirecting philosophical or scientific inquiry toward the analysis of the natural understanding of the world, or the world of common sense.

Nevertheless, there are two important ways in which Strauss's position differs from that of phenomenology. First, he doubts that we can arrive at the natural or prescientific world by considering the phenomena of the contemporary world, for our world is already a product of science or is profoundly affected by the existence of science: "To grasp the natural world as a world that is radically prescientific or prephilosophic, one has to go back behind the first emergence of science or philosophy." [66] The information that classical philosophy supplies about its origins enables us to reconstruct the essential character of "the natural world," especially when this information is supplemented by consideration of the most elementary premises of the Bible. Strauss's studies in classical political philosophy and its origins are directed toward the recovery of the natural or commonsense understanding of the political world. The classical political philosophers, writing before the establishment of a tradition of political philosophy, were able to see the political world of citizens and statesmen with a freshness and directness that could not be equaled by later political thought:

[64] After receiving a degree at Hamburg, Strauss went to the University of Freiburg in 1922 to see and hear Husserl. Cf. Jacob Klein and Leo Strauss, "A Giving of Accounts," *The College* (a publication of St. John's College, Annapolis, Md.), April 1970, p. 2.

[65] Cf. *The City and Man*, pp. 8–12.

[66] *Natural Right and History*, p. 79.

"In all later epochs, the philosophers' study of political things was mediated by a tradition of political philosophy which acted like a screen between the philosopher and political things, regardless of whether the individual philosopher cherished or rejected that tradition." [67] The recovery of the political world as known to prephilosophic opinion (or what phenomenologists might call "the life world") is vital, Strauss believes, because the awareness of this world is an indispensable basis or matrix for all social science.[68] A second way in which Strauss departs from phenomenology is by conceiving of philosophical inquiry as dialectical in the Socratic sense. Philosophy begins from the fundamental awareness that is already present in our opinions about things, but it seeks to transcend the sphere of opinion in order to know "essences," "natures," or "beings" that subsist in a world beyond subjective consciousness.

Although he is probably known best among social scientists for his critique of positivism, Strauss himself does not regard positivism as his primary opponent. In his view, positivism cannot support its principles against the critique made against them by historicism. Historicism is the most potent theoretical force in our time. It is "the serious antagonist of political philosophy." [69] Strauss's defense of political philosophy has been framed, therefore, with historicism chiefly in mind.

Strauss defends political philosophy against historicism in both its theoretical and radical forms. Theoretical historicism, as developed by Hegel and restated in this century by such Hegelians as Alexandre Kojeve, holds that political philosophy in the Socratic sense has been superseded by a philosophy of history that contemplates the historical process as a rational and completed whole. According to theoretical historicism, political philosophy as *quest* for knowledge of the good political or social order can be replaced by political science as *possession* of such knowledge, for the good political or social order is now visible as the one emerging with the culmination of history. In opposition to this view, Strauss denies that the good political order can

[67] *What Is Political Philosophy?*, p. 27.

[68] Cf. *Natural Right and History*, pp. 78–80; *The City and Man*, pp. 8–12; *What Is Political Philosophy?*, pp. 73–94; *Liberalism Ancient and Modern*, pp. 203–23.

[69] *What Is Political Philosophy?*, p. 26.

be identified as the one that succeeds in history. In particular, he argues that the universal and homogeneous state applauded by Kojeve is one in which man would lose his humanity. If this state were established, the very survival of human excellence would depend on its overthrow or decay, that is, on the possibility that history had not actually come to an end. Philosophy of history has not given a definitive answer to the question of the best regime. It has not eliminated the need for political philosophy.[70] More broadly, Strauss doubts that "history" can be regarded as an intelligible field or world. Philosophy is concerned with the natural or cosmic whole, which will never be fully accessible to the human mind. Philosophy must forever remain what it was for Socrates—the quest for wisdom, arising from the awareness of one's ignorance about the most important questions. It cannot be superseded by wisdom simply, or by the possession of complete or absolute knowledge.[71]

Strauss replies to theoretical historicism by arguing that we know *less* than it claims. He replies to radical historicism by arguing that we can know *more* than it claims, that is, that while knowledge of the whole is inaccessible to us, some measure of knowledge or truth is within our reach. It is possible here only to point to the central thread of Strauss's complex and subtle reply to radical historicism. He argues that what we know of history, and especially of the history of political philosophy, fails to support the radical historicist's claim that we can have no insight into what is permanent or eternal. History seems rather to prove that all human thought is concerned with the same fundamental problems or questions, including the questions that are raised explicitly by political philosophy. The historicist is not justified in concluding that human thought is simply bound to historically changing horizons. The persistence of fundamental questions is evidence for an absolute horizon or a

---

[70] The English translation of Strauss's debate with Kojeve is contained in the revised and enlarged edition of *On Tyranny*. Strauss's reply to Kojeve appears also in *What Is Political Philosophy?*, pp. 95–133. Cf. *Natural Right and History*, pp. 9–34; *What Is Political Philosophy?*, pp. 56–77; and "Relativism," pp. 147–48.

[71] Cf. *What Is Political Philosophy?*, pp. 38–40, 60; *Natural Right and History*, pp. 125–26; *Liberalism Ancient and Modern*, pp. 6–8, 33–34; *The City and Man*, pp. 20–21.

natural horizon of human thought, an unchanging framework within which thought takes place and of which the mind always has some awareness. Man's opinions (e.g., his opinions about justice or the good life) are best understood as faltering attempts to answer the fundamental questions.[72] To see a fundamental question as a question—to raise explicitly a question such as "What is justice?"—is already to possess some "understanding of the nature of the subject matter with which the question is concerned." [73] Radical historicism is wrong, then, in holding that the very questions of philosophy are relative to particular epochs or dependent on presuppositions that are historically contingent. Nothing more than the persistence of the fundamental questions is needed to establish the possibility of philosophy in the Socratic sense.[74] Moreover, a genuine awareness of the fundamental questions and the importance of answering them provides the answer to the question of the best life for man:

> Philosophy, being knowledge of our ignorance regarding the most important things, is impossible without some knowledge regarding the most important things. By realizing that we are ignorant of the most important things, we realize at the same time that the most important thing for us, or the one thing needful, is quest for knowledge of the most important things, or philosophy. In other words, we realize that only by philosophizing can man's soul become well-ordered.[75]

It is important to recognize that Strauss's entire account of the history of political philosophy is framed as a reply to radical historicism. This fact is easy to overlook because Strauss chooses to remain silent, for the most part, about the identity of the contemporary thinker whom he intends above all to answer. That thinker is Martin Heidegger. In one of his infrequent references to Heidegger, Strauss observes that one

---

[72] Cf. *Natural Right and History*, pp. 9–36, 81, 100–01; *What Is Political Philosophy?*, pp. 56–77; *The City and Man*, p. 35.

[73] *What Is Political Philosophy?*, p. 11.

[74] Cf. *Natural Right and History*, p. 32; *The City and Man*, pp. 20–21.

[75] *What Is Political Philosophy?*, pp. 121–22; cf. *Natural Right and History*, pp. 36, 156; *On Tyranny*, pp. 104–06; *Liberalism Ancient and Modern*, p. 13; *The City and Man*, p. 29.

has to go back to Hegel until one finds another professor of philosophy who affected in a comparable manner the thought of Germany, nay, of Europe. But Hegel had some contemporaries whose power equalled his or at any rate whom one could compare to him without being manifestly foolish. Heidegger surpasses all his contemporaries by far.[76]

Strauss's historical studies contain a twofold answer to Heidegger and radical historicism. First, Strauss argues that the roots of historicism lie not in a unique "experience of history," as historicists claim, but in the crisis of modern political philosophy which made it doubtful that man's humanness can be understood by reference to nature. Modern man's "discovery of history" turns out to be "an artificial and makeshift solution to a problem that could arise only on the basis of very questionable premises." [77] Second, Strauss's interpretation of Socratic philosophy, especially as developed by Plato, corrects Heidegger's interpretation of the classics and, at the same time, provides a powerful alternative to Heidegger's identification of being and time and his denial of the intelligibility of being.

Let us return, finally, to the question of how Strauss's studies in the history of political philosophy can serve a philo-

[76] *What Is Political Philosophy?*, p. 246. In speaking of his studies at Freiburg, Strauss observes that "one of the unknown young men in Husserl's entourage was Heidegger. I attended his lecture course from time to time without understanding a word, but sensed that he dealt with something of the utmost importance to man as man. I understood something on one occasion: when he interpreted the beginning of the *Metaphysics* [of Aristotle]. I had never heard nor seen such a thing—such a thorough and intensive interpretation of a philosophic text. On my way home I visited [Franz] Rosenzweig and said to him that compared to Heidegger, Max Weber, till then regarded by me as the incarnation of the spirit of science and scholarship, was an orphan child." ("A Giving of Accounts," p. 3)

[77] *Natural Right and History*, p. 33. *Natural Right and History* is designed to show that historicism was produced by a crisis in modern political philosophy and that the thought of Hobbes, Locke, Rousseau, and Burke prepared for its emergence. Strauss's early study of Hobbes had emphasized those aspects of Hobbes's thought that would prepare for and influence Hegel (cf. *The Political Philosophy of Hobbes*, pp. 57–58, 76–110, 122–23, 167–70). Machiavelli prepared for the philosophy of history by lowering the standard of the good society to ensure its actualization (cf. *On Tyranny*, pp. 110–11; *What Is Political Philosophy?*, pp. 40–55, 111, 131–32). Cf. also *Liberalism Ancient and Modern*, pp. 240–41, regarding Spinoza.

sophical purpose. Strauss conceives of political philosophy as "an essentially non-historical pursuit," but he holds that the history of thought "takes on philosophic significance for men living in an age of intellectual decline." [78] At the heart of this decline is the fact that political philosophy—the branch of philosophy that raises the most urgent question, the question of the best life for man and society—has been discredited by the combined influence of positivism and historicism. The decline of our age is largely obscured, however, by the pervasive belief that we live in a time of intellectual progress. Even positivism and historicism, which are symptoms as well as causes of our decline, represent themselves as unqualifiedly superior to the thought of the past.

Historical inquiry provides a way by which political philosophy can, in its time of greatest crisis, defend itself against its powerful adversaries. First, historical inquiry can show us the nature and limitations of political philosophy's theoretical opponents. We cannot simply take for granted the accounts that positivism and historicism give of themselves, for neither movement possesses an adequate understanding of its own presuppositions. Such an understanding can be gained from inquiry into the history of political philosophy. Positivism presupposes that man and society must be understood in terms of the methodology of modern science and the account that modern science gives of nature. Strauss illuminates the sources and implications of this presupposition by his studies of the early modern political philosophers. These studies lead to the conclusion that man and society cannot possibly be understood on the basis of modern science alone. Strauss's "nonhistoricist understanding of historicism" shows that this theoretical movement represents the ultimate outcome of the crisis of modern political philosophy and not the discovery of some hitherto unknown phenomena.

Strauss regards inquiry into the history of political philosophy as indispensable in framing a critique of positivism and historicism. He deems such inquiry to be indispensable also to the recovery of a genuine understanding of what political philoso-

[78] *The Political Philosophy of Hobbes*, p. xix; "On Collingwood's Philosophy of History," *Review of Metaphysics*, 5 (June 1952), 585.

phy is. Men today usually see the thought of the past through lenses provided by positivism and historicism. Through these lenses, earlier political thought appears either as something akin to folklore or as an ideology that reflects the world view of a specific historical epoch. Positivism and historicism try to understand the thought of the past better than it understood itself, that is, in terms of principles that allegedly were unknown to or concealed from the earlier thinkers. As a result, they have failed to understand the great thinkers of the past at all. Strauss attempts to understand the great writings in political philosophy as their authors meant them to be understood. The incentive for his meticulous studies of earlier writings is the expectation that there is something of utmost importance to be learned from them: "Studying the thinkers of the past becomes essential for men living in an age of intellectual decline because it is the only practicable way in which they can recover a proper understanding of the fundamental problems." [79] Historical inquiry helps us to understand the fundamental problems of political philosophy and the typical alternative solutions to these problems. Yet historical inquiry is not sufficient to tell us which of these solutions is true. We are compelled to judge among the teachings of the great political philosophers. Strauss bids us try ourselves to be political philosophers.[80]

[79] "On Collingwood's Philosophy of History," p. 585; cf. *Persecution and the Art of Writing*, pp. 15, 55–60, 154–62; *Thoughts on Machiavelli*, p. 14.
[80] Cf. *Liberalism Ancient and Modern*, p. 7; *The City and Man*, p. 11.

Eric Voegelin:
The In-Between of Human Life

by DANTE GERMINO

As an even cursory examination of his list of publications will indicate, Eric Voegelin's scholarly interests have been richly interdisciplinary, ranging over the fields of philosophy, political science, economics, sociology, theology, philosophy of history, archaeology, linguistics, and comparative religion. There is an inner coherence found in all of his work, which results from Voegelin's lifelong search for what Aristotle, in the *Nicomachean Ethics*, called *philosophia peri ta anthropina*, or the "philosophy of man." Voegelin's disregard for the conventional boundaries between disciplines and his creative attempt to recapture for our times the wholeness of vision characteristic of Greek philosophy have encountered predictable reactions of hostility and suspicion among scholars wedded to current academic structures and approaches. Yet Voegelin is such a careful, rigorous, and philosophically sophisticated thinker that even those who oppose him can ill afford to neglect his work.

To read Voegelin requires us to reorient ourselves to much of the inherited symbolism of our political language, both practical and "scientific." An embattled thinker, he rejects completely any attempt to confine political science to an analysis of political "behavior" or to the confines of a particular *Weltanschauung*. For Voegelin, a "philosophy of man" is something altogether distinct from an expression of one's merely personal standpoint or value system. The dichotomy between empirical statements on the one hand, and value judgments on the other is rejected by him as epistemologically untenable.

True enough, he argues, the philosopher begins his reflections with his own life experiences (what other standpoint could he possibly adopt?). Only a little inner reflection is required, however, to surmise that man is not sufficient unto himself alone, but is conscious of participating in an order extending both in time and space. He is not simply a "self" in the abstract, but is also a concrete person existing in a specific culture and an heir to a collective memory or consciousness. All authentic philosophizing then, is "empirically" based, and may be characterized as "a result in the life history of the philosopher, and beyond that in the history of the community whose language symbols he shares, and beyond that in the history of the cosmos." [1]

The aim of a philosophy of man, then, is to be empirical *in the full sense*. It will explore man's participation in a *multidimensional* reality and will articulate concepts appropriate to the illumination of that experience, insofar as it can be known. If it does its work properly, such a philosophy will be not just another world view, but a carefully articulated, critically self-reflective characterization of the experience of man's participation in the drama of his existence. The perspective of the philosopher will remain partial, of course, for there is no way to get "outside Being," and he must take his point of departure from the experience of participation itself. Nevertheless, within the limits inherent in his humanity, the philosopher can articulate a vision of political reality which is not simply private, but which illumines the mystery of existence for everyone who will take the trouble to reenact within his own psyche the experience of participation to which the philosopher's symbols refer. So bold a claim for philosophy sounds arrogant in our day, when the tentative hypothesis and an attitude of positivistic self-denial toward metaphysical questions often rule the intellectual roost. And yet Voegelin's cautious confidence in the possibility of ontological inquiry may well be far more modest than the real arrogance of a good many practitioners of behavioral social science, who in effect mask an implicit and seemingly unexamined metaphysic under the cover of allegedly value-free research.

[1] "Zur Theorie des Bewusstseins," in *Anamnesis* (Munich, 1966), p. 57. See my article, *"Eric Voegelin's Anamnesis"* in *The Southern Review,* Winter 1971, pp. 68–88, for comments on the volume as a whole; this issue also contains other articles on Voegelin, together with his own essay, hitherto unpublished, on William James's *Turn of the Screw.*

According to Voegelin, the "problems of human order in society and history originate in the order of the consciousness. The philosophy of the consciousness is therefore the core of a philosophy of politics." [2] As early as 1943, in his essay "Toward a Theory of Consciousness," Voegelin sought to transcend both idealism and materialism in his search for an adequate epistemology. In opposition to idealism, Voegelin maintained that consciousness is not coterminous with Being but is rather a process within it. "In our finite being," he wrote, "we stand always inside Being." In opposition to materialism, he rejects the view that ultimate reality is an "object" of human experience which stands over against man conceived as the possessor of a "subjective" consciousness; the philosopher becomes aware of Being as the ground of all existing things and the source of their "ontic coherence" through a process of meditation, as a result of which he may succeed in bracketing out all that partakes of created existence, experiencing, in a fleeting moment of intuition, the enveloping Ground itself. In this sense, authentic mysticism, as discussed in a famous chapter of William James's *Varieties of Religious Experience* (1902), and as exemplified in the treatise *The Cloud of Unknowing*, by an anonymous English mystic of the fourteenth century, goes hand in hand with philosophy.

The defect of both idealism and materialism, Voegelin concluded, is that each mistakes the part for the whole and seeks to reduce the "entirety of Being to the rank of a particular segment or dimension" of it. Materialism fails to account for the reality of the consciousness but regards it as a reflection of an external material process; idealism, on the other hand, fails to see that the illumination consciousness gives us of reality "from within," as it were, "does not penetrate either the created being of nature or the ground of Being as such. The being of nature remains an external world in the dual sense of something outside the consciousness and something external to itself." For ontological inquiry, then, "neither an idealistic nor a materialistic metaphysics is tenable." [3]

Voegelin has recently returned to the problem of articulating an adequate philosophy of the consciousness—the "core of any valid philosophy of politics"—in his important essay

---

[2] *Anamnesis*, p. vii.
[3] *Ibid.*, p. 57.

"Equivalences of Experience and Symbolization in History." [4] In this essay, Voegelin reiterates his earlier warning that there can be no "absolute statements for a philosophy of consciousness." Consciousness is not a "datum of experience"; rather, "all philosophizing regarding consciousness is a result in the consciousness of the one who is philosophizing and presupposes this consciousness with its structure." (*Anamnesis*, p. 57.) Voegelin is even more emphatic in his paper on "Equivalences" in rejecting the possibility of setting forth a "foolproof," "objectively true," or "value-free" philosophical "system." "Ultimate doctrines, systems, and values are phantasmata engendered by deformed existence," he vigorously observes. What is "constant" in the history of mankind are not the *symbols* in which men express their experiences, but "the structure of existence itself." This structure is the proper object of philosophical inquiry. And although no fixed propositions valid for all time about consciousness can be advanced, it is possible to articulate such propositions about the structure of existence.

Human existence, Voegelin informs us, "has the structure of the In-Between of the Platonic *metaxy*, and if anything is constant in this history of mankind it is the language of tension between life and death, immortality and mortality, perfection and imperfection, time and timelessness. . . ." [5] This primordially experienced structure of existence as a field of tension between contrary poles is for Voegelin the basis for a series of propositions concerning the nature of man's participation in reality:

(1) Man participates in the process of reality.
(2) Man is conscious of reality as a process, of himself as being part of reality, and of his consciousness as a mode of participation in its process.
(3) While consciously participating, man is able to engender symbols which express his experience of reality. . . .
(4) Man knows the symbols engendered to be part of the reality they symbolize: the symbols consciousness, experience, and symbolization denote the area where the process of reality becomes luminous to itself. [6]

[4] *Order and History*, vol. iv (Baton Rouge, 1974).
[5] "Equivalences of Experience and Symbolization in History," p. 7.
[6] *Ibid.*, p. 8.

To these positive propositions about the process of reality, Voegelin informs us, there are three "corollaries of a cautionary nature":

(1) Reality is not a given that can be observed from a vantage point outside itself but embraces the consciousness in which it becomes luminous.

(2) The experience of reality cannot be total but has the character of a perspective.

(3) The knowledge of reality conveyed by the symbols can never be the final possession of truth, for the luminous perspectives that we call experiences, as well as the symbols engendered by them, are part of reality in process.[7]

Man's "existence in the In-Between," then, is "not an object of sense perception." This does not mean that the propositions of a self-reflective philosophy of man cannot be tested objectively. The validity of such propositions "can and must be tested by placing the propositions in the historical field of experiences and their symbolizations, i.e. in the dimension of existence itself." The "validating question," Voegelin maintains, "will have to be: Do we have to ignore and eclipse a major part of the historical field . . . or are the propositions recognizably equivalent to the symbols created by our predecessors in the search for truth about human existence?"[8] If the answer to the first question is "yes" and to the second "no," then we are not on the trail of the *philosophia peri ta anthropina* but of the "deformed existence" of "ideological doctrinaires."

An important refinement of Voegelin's philosophy of consciousness may be discerned in his discussion (in the essay on "Equivalences") of the "depth of the psyche." In his search for what is constant and invariable in the structure of existence, the philosopher is driven to ever deeper experiential levels: from the level of symbols (such as "participation," the "identity and non-identity of the knower and the known," the "process of reality," and the "In-Between" [*metaxy*] of man's existence), we descend to the symbol-engendering experience of participation itself. However, we cannot halt our inquiry with the experience of participation itself, because "the constant experience,

[7] *Ibid.*
[8] *Ibid.*, p. 10.

once identified, would have to become articulate," and once it was articulated it would claim to be *the* true philosophical system. Consequently, to avoid a derailment into fundamentalism or dogmatism, the philosopher discerns yet another level, which is "deeper than the level of equivalent experiences which engender equivalent symbols."[9] Voegelin calls this deeper level the "depth of the psyche." As a result of this analysis, Voegelin offers three interchangeable propositions regarding the depth of the psyche:

> There is a psyche deeper than consciousness, and there is a reality deeper than reality experienced, but there is no consciousness deeper than consciousness.

> Or:

> We experience psyche as consciousness that can descend into the depth of its own reality, and the depth of the psyche as reality that can rise to consciousness, but we do not experience a content of the depth other than the content that has entered consciousness.

> Or:

> We consciously experience psyche as a reality extending beyond consciousness. The area "beyond" is of the same nature as the reality of consciousness. Moreover, the two areas are a continuum of psychic reality in which man can move by the actions and passions symbolized as "descent" and "ascent."[10]

The descent into the depth of the psyche by the philosopher occurs at different periods in history in response to a crisis of the mind and spirit. Such crises occur when traditional symbols are losing their credibility and when more recently articulated symbols convey a distorted or "deformed" sense of reality. A descent into the depth will be required, then, when "night is sinking on the symbols that have had their day," and the philos-

---

[9] *Ibid.*, p. 13. That is to say: no one philosopher can claim to present a "definitive account" of the ultimate source of the experience of participation itself. The experience of the depth is elusive and has on principle the character of ineffability; it is impossible to render in conceptual language.

[10] *Ibid.*, pp. 15–16. Subsequently Voegelin remarks that although there is a depth below consciousness, "there is no depth below depth in infinite regress." *Ibid.*, p. 19.

opher must "return to the night of the depth that is luminous with truth to the man who is willing to seek it." Like a diver, the philosopher can "drag up from the depth a truth about reality that hitherto has not been an articulate insight." The "return from the depth with a truth newly experienced" may be characterized as a "*renovatio* in the double sense of a renewal of truth and a renewal of man." The "luminous depth" thus yields symbols to the open-souled representatives of mankind that are at once the "equivalences" of symbols articulated by their predecessors and that may incorporate an "advance" in man's self-understanding by virtue of the greater degree of "differentiation" relative to the previous symbols. But the truth emerging from the process of noetic (philosophical) exploration of the depth "is not entirely new"; it is not "a truth about a reality hitherto unknown, but a differentiated and therefore superior insight into the same reality that has been compactly symbolized by the old truth." [11]

When the philosopher descends for a fleeting moment into the depth of the psyche, he becomes aware of his consubstantiality with both his fellow men and with cosmos. Following Plato's *Timaeus*, we may say that "the reality of the Cosmos in depth is the anima mundi" or world-soul. The *anima mundi* is the symbol which indicates the philosopher's trust (*pistis*) in the "underlying oneness of reality, its coherence, lastingness, constancy of structure, order, and intelligibility." It is this very faith and trust of the philosopher which guides his descent into a depth that yields no certainties of the order of those experienced in sensory reality, and which "will inspire the creation of images which express the ordered wholeness sensed in the depth." [12]

For Eric Voegelin, philosophy is bound by history, and we must understand his own philosophy of consciousness not as an abstract piece of speculation but as the result of sustained empirical inquiry into the process by which man experiences the process of reality moving through him in time. This "moving presence" of reality is what we mean philosophically by his-

[11] *Ibid.*, p. 15.
[12] *Ibid.*, pp. 17–18.

tory, which leaves in its wake "a trail of equivalent symbols in time and space." [13] The depth of the consciousness, therefore, may not legitimately be construed as an "Absolute, removed from the historical field." [14]

Voegelin's insistence on the historical character of human truth does not lead him into a conformist "historicism," which preaches "adjustment" to whatever institutions and doctrines prevail at a given moment. Rather, he employs the term "history" differently from its conventional meaning: history "is not an unbroken stream of existence in truth, but is interrupted by periods, or is shot through with levels, of deformed existence." [15]

Voegelin's philosophy of history centers around the concept of the "leap in being" which results in the vision of a community of mankind open to the experience of the world-transcendent God. The "leap in being," he informs us, is the "epochal event that breaks the compactness of the early cosmological myth and establishes the order of man in his immediacy under God. . . ." [16] The "initial leap in being, the break with the order of the myth, occurs in a plurality of parallel instances, in Israel and Hellas, in China and India. . . ." [17] The break with the compact world of cosmological mythical symbols of order as represented in the ancient Near Eastern empires produced Buddhism in India and Confucianism and other schools in China, but it is only in the West, with the Israelite and Christian experiences of revelation and the articulation of philosophy in Greece, that there occurred a radical break with the compactness of the "closed society" (as understood by Henri Bergson). The "history of mankind" is thus "an open society—Bergson's, not Popper's—comprehending both truth and untruth in tension." [18]

[13] *Ibid.*, p. 23.
[14] *Ibid.*, p. 21.
[15] *Ibid.*, p. 4.
[16] *Order and History*, vol. *II, The World of Polis* (Baton Rouge, 1957),
p. 1.
[17] *Ibid.*, p. 3.
[18] "Immortality: Experience and Symbol," *Harvard Theological Review*, 40 (July 1967), 235–79 at 239.

In Voegelin's important article "The Gospel and Culture," [19] we find the most sustained discussion by him to date of
the character of human existence as a field of forces in tension
between such poles as openness and closure, love of God and
love of self, attunement and revolt, the life of reason and irrational obsession, and so forth. What the "leap in being" (experienced initially by the great-souled representatives of mankind
in Israel and Hellas) accomplished was to reveal the "height" of
man's existential possibilities. In the process of doing so, however, the "counterpull" of opposing forces experienced in the
psyche was not abolished. In this mortal life man walks a tight-
rope, suspended between nothingness and paradise. [20]

Human existence, Voegelin maintains, is "a disturbing
movement in the In-Between of ignorance and knowledge, of
time and timelessness, of imperfection and perfection, of hope
and fulfillment, and ultimately of life and death. From the experience of this movement, from the anxiety of losing the right direction in this In-Between of darkness and light arises the inquiry concerning the meaning of life." [21] Adopting Plato's
language of "pulling" (helkein) and "counterpulling" (anthelkein),[22] as well as parallel symbolism from the Bible, Voegelin
finds that existence is a "mystery." Man experiences in the
depth of his psyche the "pull" of the "golden cord of reason and
right judgment," as related in Plato's myth of the puppet player
in the Laws; at the same time, man is also aware of the "counterpull" of the iron cords of appetite in which he becomes prey
to hubris and existential revolt. In order to follow the golden
cord of logos, which would bring him closer to attunement with
the divine ground of Being, he must constantly struggle against
the counterpulls of self-seeking, self-indulgence, self-glorifica-
tion, and lust for power, which draw him nearer to a kind of life
in subservience to material temptations that better deserves the
name of spiritual death. Why, one asks, are the forces of counterpull so strong? Why is the struggle to overcome these im-

[19] "The Gospel and Culture," in *Jesus and Man's Hope* (Pittsburgh,
1971), II, 59–101.
[20] See in this connection Gerhard Niemeyer's book of the same title, *Between Nothingness and Paradise* (Baton Rouge, 1971).
[21] "The Gospel and Culture," p. 63.
[22] *Republic* 494E, *Phaedrus* 238A, *Laws*, pp. 644–45.

pulses so arduous and why are our victories over them so precarious? To this question, neither philosophy nor revelation can provide a definitive answer: this is part of the mystery of existence and the good man can only live in trust and hope of deliverance beyond time and the world. For the more developed is our awareness of existence as a condition of tension between the pull of the divine ground and the counterpull of rebelliousness and idolatry, between life and death of the spirit, the more puzzling becomes the character of the condition itself. Having recourse to Plato's parable of the Cave in the *Republic*, we may ask:

> Why is the prisoner fettered in the Cave in the first place? Why must the force that binds him become a counterforce that turns him around? Why must the man who ascended to the light return to the Cave to suffer death at the hands of those who did not leave it? Why does not everybody leave, so that the Cave as an establishment of existence be abandoned? [23]

To these questions Plato gave the answer (in the myth of man as a puppet made by the gods) that we are, insofar as is in our power, to follow the golden cord of the *logos*. This is the "saving tale," the way of salvation. And that is all that we may say about the matter. "Rebellious questioners," observes Voegelin, "who want to complain about the structure of existence," wherein the Cave continues to exert its counterpull even after the saving tale has been discovered, are offered essentially the same answer by Plato as that given by the prophet Jeremiah:

> Behold! What I have built I will pull down;
> and what I have planted I will tear up—
> and you seek great things for yourself?
> Seek them not!
> For behold! I will bring evil upon all flesh—
> says Yahweh—
> But your life will I give you, as a prize of war,
> in every place where you go.[24]

The lesson of existence is that "life is given as a prize of war. Who wants to save his life in it will lose it. The Saving

[23] "The Gospel and Culture," p. 73.
[24] Voegelin's translation of Jeremiah 45: 4–5 in *Ibid.*, p. 74.

Tale is not a recipe for the abolition of the *anthelkein* (counter-pull) in existence but the confirmation of life through death in this war. The death of Socrates which, just as the death of Jesus, could have been physically avoided—is representative because it authenticates the truth of reality." [25] We are in the end left with nothing but the process of "knowing questioning" toward the ground, as well as with symbols articulated as a reminder of the possibilities of the search:

> There is no In-Between other than the *metaxy* experienced in a man's existential tension toward the divine ground of being; there is no question of life and death other than the question aroused by pull and counterpull; there is no Saving Tale other than the tale of the divine pull to be followed by man; and there is no cognitive articulation of existence other than the noetic consciousness in which the movement becomes luminous to itself.[26]

Voegelin's characterization of existence as irremediably confined to the field between the forces of divine pull and of demonic counterpull leads him to make some observations on the task of political philosophy. While we may speak of an "advance" in the relative differentiation of symbols reflecting man's condition as we move from the cosmological myth to Platonic and Aristotelian philosophy and then to Judeo-Christian religiousness, it cannot be overemphasized that while we have gained a more adequate understanding and illumination of our condition, *nothing has changed with respect to the structure of existence* as a field of tension between contrary poles:

> The symbolization of participating existence . . . evolves historically from the more compact form of the comological myth to the more differentiated forms of philosophy, prophecy, and the Gospel, but the differentiating insight, far from abolishing the *Metaxy* of existence, brings it to fully articulate knowledge. [The experience of a Beyond—*epekeina*—of existence transcending the realm of the In-Between, or of a] consciousness of the Beyond of Consciousness . . . is the area of reality which articulates itself through the symbols of mythical imagination. . . . The Saving Tale can be differentiated beyond classical philosophy, as has historically happened through Christ and the Gospel, but there is

[25] *Ibid.*
[26] *Ibid.*, p. 75.

no alternative to the symbolization of the In-Between of existence and its divine Beyond by mythical imagination. The speculative systems of the Comtean, Hegelian, and Marxian type, favored today as alternatives, are not "science" but deformations of
the life of reason through the magic practice of self-divination
and self-salvation.[27]

Voegelin, then, takes his stand with premodern philosophy
and revelation in opposition to secular symbolisms of the modern era. He does this, however, not out of some idiosyncratic
"preference" for the old or venerable, but because he finds that
philosophy and revelation illumine, while modern thought
(elsewhere characterized as "gnosticism")[28] obscures the structure of human existence as the In-Between.

Before proceeding, it may be worthwhile to recall that, unlike many political philosophers, Voegelin actually began his career as a student of political institutions and that he immersed
himself in philosophical problems only after it became clear
that we could not understand occurrences at the "practical" or
phenomenal political level until we viewed them in the context
of a greater order of things, or, to be more precise, employing
the symbolism of philosophy, in the context of mankind's experience of the order of being. When he began his career in the
1930s, Voegelin was confronted with the breakdown of seemingly well-constructed post-World War I constitutions and with
their replacement by totalitarian or autocratic political regimes.
These momentous developments led him to the conclusion that
the viability of "political" institutions (understood in terms of
the narrower, more conventional view of the "political" sphere)
depended upon the self-interpretations which undergird these
societies, and that if such interpretations go to pieces then their
institutions do so as well. This discovery (or rediscovery) made
Voegelin conclude that the conventional understanding of politics and political activity needed to be expanded from preoccupation with participation by candidates and voters in elections to a concern with mankind's participation in the drama of
history. The political philosopher is needed to sketch in the
contours of the larger scheme of things on the canvas of man's

[27] *Ibid.*, p. 76.
[28] *The New Science of Politics* (Chicago, 1952).

total experience, so that the political scientist will not continue to keep his gaze riveted only on the lower portion of that canvas. This conception of political activity as multidimensional led Voegelin to argue, in effect, that the philosopher is just as politically active as the man who runs for office.[29]

Voegelin's language, then, is often different from that of the mainstream of contemporary political discourse; it sounds awkward to our ears. But very possibly we need to develop our ability to listen to the philosopher's language. We shall then understand what Voegelin attempted to point out in his chapter on "Representation" in the *New Science of Politics:* namely, that a society is not only represented in the elemental sense (through the selection of governmental officials), but also in the existential and transcendental meanings of the term. At the existential level an ordered society is animated by a civil theology which provides the substantive principles which tend to guide the decisions of the representative and the represented. Finally, there is the dimension of transcendental representation, wherein sages, prophets, saints, and philosophers attempt to "speak truth to power" and to supplement, and if possible to correct, the distortions of the moral insights and implicit ontological assumptions of the prevailing civil theology. Looking at politics in this fashion means that one is enabled to understand how it is possible for a ruling group which is representative in the elementary sense (of having been elected or appointed to positions of power) at the same time to be unrepresentative in terms of one or both of the other two meanings of representation (existential and transcendental). It is well to bear in mind, then, that for Voegelin the present task of philosophy is to *extend* (or re-extend) the reach of contemporary political science rather than to *oppose* it with something heterogeneous.

In 1965, Eric Voegelin read a paper entitled "What Is Political Reality?" to the German Political Science Association. This paper was subsequently expanded into an article three or four times the length of the original paper (a frequent practice of Voegelin's) and published in his book *Anamnesis.* In this article, Voegelin defines political science as the "noetic interpre-

---

[29] Gregor Sebba made this point in a letter to the author of 28 December 1972.

tation of man, society, and history" which emerges out of the soil of "non-noetic" interpretations and exists in tension with them.[30] Political science is concerned with the elaboration of symbols which assist men in gaining a more differentiated and self-critical understanding of political reality. Political science may therefore also be called "political philosophy" or the "philosophy of order." Voegelin defines the philosophy of order as "the process in which we as men find the order of our existence in the order of consciousness." [31]

Political reality is obviously a part of reality as a whole. Concerning reality as a whole, Voegelin says that it is "not a thing, over against which man stands, but the all-encompassing Real [*das umgreifende Reale*] in and through which the participating individual himself is real." Reality as a whole may be subdivided into distinguishable "things" (God, men, etc.); these "things" are real in the same sense as the "participation of the things in each other within the all-encompassing Real." In men this participation has the "character of consciousness, and we may speak of consciousness as the sensorium of human participation in reality." [32]

Now consciousness, as we have previously seen, is not the whole, but a process within the whole. The whole (*das umgreifende Reale*) cannot be known as such by man, although its character can be intimated through myth and philosophical analogy. Political reality is that aspect of reality as a whole which concerns man's continuing attempt to order his existence in the light of his understanding of its structure. In one sense, then, Voegelin regards "political reality" as a sharply delimited sphere; it is emphatically not equivalent to reality as a whole but is rather confined to a specific "area" between the existential poles illumined by the consciousness and by the exploration of its "depth." In another sense, however, Voegelin's concept of "political reality" is extremely comprehensive, for by this symbol he designates the totality of relations and possibilities within human existence. The important thing to note is that for Voegelin existence as such has ineluctable limits, and the alleged attempt of modern philosophy to change the struc-

[30] *Anamnesis*, pp. 283–354 at 284.
[31] *Ibid.*, p. 11.
[32] *Ibid.*, p. 304.

ture of existence has resulted not in its illumination but in its "deformation."

Political reality (as distinguishable from "all-encompassing reality"), then, has to do with the specifically human realm of being (*Seinsbereich Mensch*); and it can be divided into three dimensions for purposes of analysis in political philosophy: those of man, society, and history. The cataclysmic disorders of the modern age are due primarily to the "eclipse" of political reality at the hands of ideological doctrinaires. These doctrinaires invert the order of man, society, and history (in which political philosophy—or the noetic interpretation of society—is grounded in philosophical anthropology) and construct so-called philosophies of history which reduce the human person to a means of "history" or "society" conceived of as realities superior to man. According to Voegelin, in Comtean "sociology" and Hegelian or Marxist "historicism," we witness the replacement of political reality with bogus "second reality" constructions. The sequence of an authentic philosophy of politics— man, society, history—is reversed, so that in modern political theory we encounter instead the sequence history, society, man.[33] In the process of this ideological deformation of reality, we come dangerously close to what C. S. Lewis once termed the "abolition of man."

In another important paper, "On Hegel: A Study in Sorcery,"[34] Voegelin further explains what he means by the "eclipse of reality" accomplished in modern political thought. In his view, the symbolisms which "express reality as experienced by a man whose soul is open toward the divine ground of the cosmos and his existence" are three in number: myth, philosophy, and revelation. This is the threefold path to reality which has emerged from humanity's millennial struggle to make sense of existence. These paradigmatic symbolisms, which on principle cannot be improved upon, have been replaced in modern thought by other symbolisms, such as science, progress, world-spirit, Marxian dialectics, and the Nietzschean "death of God."

A key figure in this tragic story, according to Voegelin, has

---

[33] *Ibid.*, p. 350.
[34] *Order and History*, vol. IV, *op. cit.*

been Hegel. Hegel's symbolism of *Geist, Idee, Gedanke,* etc. was "the instrument for eclipsing the reality of Myth, Philosophy, and Revelation." [35] In particular, Voegelin insists, Hegel has been prodigiously successful in accomplishing the "demythologization" of modern philosophy (or what is called "philosophy"). The revolt against the myth can only end in the eclipse of reality, however, because the "experience of participation in a divinely ordered cosmos extending beyond man can be expressed only by means of the myth; it cannot be transformed into processes of thought within consciousness. . . ." [36] It is true, of course, that with the "differentiation of noetic consciousness through the philosophers", the "old myth" presupposing a more compact experience of the cosmos was shown to be inadequate. "When consciousness becomes noetically luminous, a new myth is required." Such a "new myth" adequate to the advance made by noetic thought may be found in the dialogues of Plato and in the Christian gospels. The relationship between consciousness and its beyond can be expressed only by means of the myth and not by speculative *gnosis.* Hegel and other modern philosophers, however, fallaciously attempt to "absorb the beyond of consciousness into consciousness itself." [37]

Bearing in mind Voegelin's characterization of political reality, what view does he take of the place of politics in human life? This question does not fully make sense in his thought because he does not distinguish between the "political," "economic," "social," "cultural," "religious," or other spheres of human life. He would, I think, regard such distinctions as abstract and artificial. For Voegelin, political activity, properly understood, is *coterminous with human life.* This most emphatically does *not* mean, however, that Voegelin is a political messianist who places no limits upon what man may attempt through collective political action. On the contrary, his entire political philosophy is concerned with elaborating an adequate symbolism to express the experience of the human condition as one of limit, in the sphere of the In-Between. In a sense Voegelin attempts to return to the Greek conception of politics as

[35] *Ibid.,* p. 29.
[36] *Ibid.,* p. 30.
[37] *Ibid.*

embracing all human activity and as concerned with the "highest good" for man. This is an orientation quite different from the conception of politics in much of liberal thought, where we are dealing primarily with the public sphere and the activity of government. Voegelin sees politics as the attempt to experience the source of human order and to create structures within the flux of temporality which reflect that experience. Man's cultural, philosophical, and religious experience is the soil from which governmental institutions and policies spring.

The term "state" for Voegelin is not a proper concept of political science, but a symbol which emerged at one specific point in modern history (namely, with Jean Bodin in the sixteenth century and his attempt to find a *via media* between conflicting religious positions). The nation-state itself is not an "intelligible unit of study" from the perspective of a philosophy of order and history. Rather, as Arnold Toynbee pointed out, nation-states do not have histories; only civilizations have. Therefore England, for example, "has no history." [38] The question then about the proper relation between the "state" and "other human associations" is therefore meaningless from a philosophical point of view. In its place we should use the symbol "society" or "political community." Societies are capable of an enormous variety of internal articulation, and it is not the philosopher's task to offer a blueprint precisely delimiting the activity of the government (not "the state") as opposed to other institutions in society. However, the existence of philosophy and revelation themselves presuppose that government may not legitimately control the whole lives of men; government exists to serve man rather than the reverse.

Hence the quality of political discourse depends on what it starts from. Logical operations achieve valid results only if they are grounded in man's experience of himself as an existent among other existents endowed with the capacity to make this existence luminous to itself.[39] If the logic of political discourse

[38] For further comments on Voegelin's philosophy of history as developed in the first three volumes of *Order and History*, see my book *Beyond Ideology* (New York, 1967), chap. 8.

[39] See Voegelin's essay "On Debate and Existence," *The Intercollegiate Review*, 3 (March–April 1967), 143–52, and the discussion of this essay in Germino, *Beyond Ideology*, pp. 163–67.

proceeds from fallacious second-reality constructions, then the results, no matter how impressively "consistent," will lead those who follow it in the direction of an antihuman ideologization of politics. In addition, it should be noted that Voegelin follows Aristotle in insisting that the dianoetic virtues in which the philosopher excels must be complemented by the practical virtues, above all *phronesis*, the practical virtue of prudence. Beyond this, Voegelin observes that the practicing politician will need strong doses of the "existential virtue" of "common sense," understood after the manner of Thomas Reid as the sense "common to all men with whom we can transact business or call to account for their conduct." [40] Like Camus (whom he admires), Voegelin would argue that the greatest political crimes are those of "logic" rather than passion. Airtight logical consistency, therefore, is more the mark of ideology than of an adequate philosophy of politics, whose symbolization must be appropriate to the complex and multifaceted "process of reality."

It is indeed part of current ideology that it not merely makes a parade of logical consistency, but also presses the positivist distinction between fact and value. But the "ought" for Voegelin is not a "value"; it is rather the "experienced tension between the order of being and the conduct of man." Such a tension generates the sort of moral vision which Voegelin believes has considerable, if limited, relevance for political action. This is a much wider conception of what animates political striving than can be conveyed in the terminology of "value-judgments." Voegelin regards the very term itself, together with the distinction between "facts" and "values," as results of the corruption of the contemporary philosophical vocabulary by positivism. Noetic symbolization is, of course, only one mode of

---

[40] See Voegelin's discussion of common sense in *Anamnesis*, p. 352 ff. He there indicates the great importance of developing a noetic basis for the virtue of common sense by relating it to a philosophy of order. For Voegelin, common sense is not full rationality, but only a minimal grade of the same. Nonetheless, academic "political science", in an unprofitable chase for methodological "purity," cannot dispense with commonsense propositions—especially in dealing with issues of contemporary foreign and domestic policy. Thus, common sense is a "pragmatic factor" of great significance for "political order and stability," according to Voegelin.

self-interpretation in the social field, and it must compete with non-noetic thought for influence upon men. There has never existed a society whose entire self-interpretation was noetic. The philosopher, however, can exert a leavening influence on society and can assist those with eyes to see and ears to hear to gain their bearings in an age of "diremption and boredom." There are two passages from the previously cited essay on Hegel which seem to express Voegelin's teaching regarding the relationship between philosophy and politics particularly well:

> Nobody can heal the spiritual disorder of an "age." A philosopher can do no more than work himself free from the rubble of idols which, under the name of an "age," threatens to cripple and bury him; and he can hope that the example of his effort will be of help to others who find themselves in the same situation and experience the same desire to gain their humanity under God.[41]

> The philosopher can clarify the structure and process of consciousness; he can draw more clearly the line between the reality of consciousness and the reality of which it is conscious; but he can neither expand man's consciousness into the reality in which it is an event, nor contract reality into the event of consciousness.[42]

I have confined myself in this essay to an exposition of Eric Voegelin's political philosophy, and I have concentrated in particular on his most recent writings. It would be possible, of course, to offer a critique of his thought, but I have deemed it more important here to present his thought, insofar as possible, unencumbered by my own evaluation. Those readers who are interested in my evaluations might wish to consult my *Modern Western Political Thought: Machiavelli to Marx*,[43] wherein I dissent from Voegelin's interpretation of modernity as in essence "gnostic," as well by implication at least from his interpretation of a number of modern political theorists, especially Hegel. In a recent essay, "Bergson, Popper, and Voegelin on the Open Society," I have also criticized some aspects (mainly the excessive emphasis upon the "counterpull" or "mundane reality") of his conception of the open society. None-

---

[41] "On Hegel," p. 28.
[42] *Ibid.*, p. 29.
[43] Chicago, 1972.

theless, despite reservations about particular aspects of his thought, I remain as convinced today as I was ten years ago when I first began to write about Voegelin, that with him we are in the presence of one of the most creative, sensitive, erudite, and profound philosophical minds of our century. He has played a leading role in the revival of political theory in our time.

As Voegelin said of his enterprise some years ago, his work was essentially "an anamnetic venture," an exercise in recollection of what has been discovered but what is perpetually in danger of being forgotten. Our task, he writes, is to recover "the flow" of the "presence" of Being moved through time.[44] And he tells us that T. S. Eliot has "caught the essence of such a venture" in the following lines:

> And what there is to conquer
> By strength and submission, has already been discovered
> Once or twice, or several times, by men whom one cannot hope
> To emulate—but there is no competition—
> There is only the fight to recover what has been lost
> And found again and again; and now, under conditions
> That seem unpropitious.[45]

Only, as Voegelin adds, "perhaps the conditions are less unpropitious than they seemed to the poet when he wrote these lines" a generation ago.[46]

[44] "Immortality," p. 264.
[45] From "East Coker" in *Four Quartets*, copyright 1943, by T. S. Eliot, copyright 1971, by Esme Valerie Eliot. Reprinted by permission of Harcourt Brace Jovanovich, Inc. Quoted in "Immortality," p. 264.
[46] "Immortality," p. 264.

Michael Oakeshott:
The Boundless Sea of Politics

by KENNETH R. MINOGUE

The structure of a philosophical argument can often best be explored in terms of an image: caves, ships of state, Great Beasts, states of nature, and similar pictures abound in the writings of political philosophers. It has been an important part of Michael Oakeshott's philosophical style to invent or extend a number of such striking images; and this is why we may best begin by quoting a passage so well known that its chilling quality has seldom been properly appreciated.

> In political activity, then, men sail a boundless and bottomless sea; there is neither harbour for shelter nor floor for anchorage, neither starting-place nor appointed destination. The enterprise is to keep afloat on an even keel; the sea is both friend and enemy; and the seamanship consists in using the resources of a traditional manner of behaviour in order to make a friend of every hostile occasion.[1]

Those who first heard these words, as part of Oakeshott's Inaugural Lecture at the London School of Economics in 1951, connected them with his criticism of rationalism and with the light that Oakeshott might be expected to throw upon the problems of the time. They expected from a political philosopher a discussion of some rational principle (such as liberty, justice, or equality) which, although suitably remote from practical life, could still conceivably be used as a star to steer the ship of state by. This element of remotely practical guidance had been provided by Plato in the *Republic*, and had formed the common specification of the task of a political philosopher ever since. Expectations of this sort were dashed by a speaker who apolo-

---

[1] *Rationalism in Politics* (London, 1962), p. 127.

gised for his scepticism and went on to give an account of political activity as "the pursuit of intimations." Speaker and audience were at cross-purposes, and subsequent criticism took the form of complaining that Oakeshott had provided no criterion of rational political judgement. Dissatisfaction, indeed, went further than this: it reflected a clear sense of desperation at the fact that the practical question: What is to be done? had been ignored in favour of an academic preoccupation with what actually happens.

It is true, of course, that since most readers of philosophy are practical people, there will always be some tension between a philosopher and his audience. Few are the philosophies which no one has tried to turn into gospels. In the case of Leo Strauss, this tension between the city and the academy has been set up as the key that will unlock the meaning of philosophers. But the situation of Oakeshott is specific both to his philosophy and to the dominant expectations of liberally minded men at the end of the Second World War. Two of these expectations are particularly significant. The first is that good politics is the application of rational principles to public affairs. The second is that the only alternatives to the application of abstract rational principles are prejudice, caprice, superstition, and force—all the evils of an irrationality which had recently been dramatised in the Nazi regime in Germany. Oakeshott's assertion that the boundless ocean contained "neither harbour for shelter not floor for anchorage, neither starting-place nor appointed destination" swept aside rational principles, and the dismay it occasioned was the fear that seizes people who have just been told their most trusted advisers are charlatans.

Yet the actual doctrine outlined in the Inaugural Lecture was hardly a novelty in the middle of the twentieth century, even in liberal circles.[2] Across the channel, something not al-

[2] Indeed, in a note attached to the published version of the Inaugural Lecture (*Rationalism in Politics*, p. 136), Oakeshott refers to John Stuart Mill's abandonment of general principle as a guide to political activity in favour of "a theory of human progress" and a "philosophy of history," and then adds: "The view I have expressed in this essay may be taken to represent a further stage in this intellectual pilgrimage, a stage reached when neither 'principle' (on account of what it turns out to be: a mere index of concrete behaviour) nor any general theory about the character and direction of social change seem to supply an adequate reference for explanation or for practical conduct."

together dissimilar was then enjoying a vogue under the name of Existentialism, and was generating literary imaginings about the absurdity of human existence and man's lonely freedom in a hostile universe. Moreover, Oakeshott's remarks about the boundless sea of politics states one of the possible answers to a question as old as philosophy itself: How are we to explain the fact that social customs, moral standards, and political practices vary according to time and place? Are such things merely matters of fashion, like skirt-lengths, or do they register the confusions of imperfect humanity in comprehending some stable set of values, such as the laws of nature, the commands of God, or the rational structure of the universe? Plato is the master of those who have given the latter answer, but it has never been enough to convince a long line of sceptics, of whom Oakeshott is merely the latest.

The point at issue is obviously both complicated and far-reaching. It raises both theoretical and practical questions— such as the way in which the sexes ought to behave towards each other. When, for example, Luciana gives advice to Adriana in the *Comedy of Errors,*

> There's nothing situate under heaven's eye
> But hath his bound, in earth; in sea, in sky:
> The beasts, the fishes, and the winged fowls,
> Are their males' subjects, and at their controls.
> Men, more divine, the masters of all these,
> Lords of the wide world, and wild watery seas,
> Indu'd with intellectual sense and souls,
> Of more pre-eminence than fish and fowls
> Are masters to their females and their lords:
> Then, let your will attend on their accords.[3]

is she pointing to an order of things which embraces the universe and from which only human blindness and the Fall of Man can separate our wills? Or is she merely scattering a few persuasive analogies in order to persuade Adriana to take up an attitude of which she approves? It has certainly been very commonly felt that right human decisions may be based upon Nature, the commands of God, rational principles, or some other foundation independent of the variable passions of human be-

[3] *Comedy of Errors,* II, i, 16–25.

ings. But even Aristotle, from whom some of these arguments about Nature derive, recognised that, as a supplement to the rigours of deductive logic, there had to exist another sort of reasoning by which human beings could arrive at suitable decisions in assemblies, law courts, and the public judgements of men, for in these areas, no decisive considerations could be discovered. In the *Rhetoric*, he theorised a mode of human rationality that Plato had taken to be fundamentally nothing more than confusion, a mode of thought which, lacking the hardness of *episteme* (knowledge), had been consigned (even though on occasions with regret) to the second-rate world of *doxa* (opinion). Aristotle had recognised clearly that, at least at the lower levels of abstraction, moral and political actions are categorically indeterminate. For the sheer abstractedness of rational principles prohibited them from being able to determine the actual details of their laws, norms, and values: such details as the exact penalty required for a crime, the wording of a law, the arrangements for enforcement, and so on. These matters, at least, could come from nothing else but current human practice and belief.

Michael Oakeshott is pre-eminent amongst modern political philosophers in carrying his doubts about rational foundations to the furthest corners of the human understanding. It might be thought (and indeed Oakeshott has himself admitted the possibility) that an argument concluding that men are adrift on a boundless ocean and that keeping afloat is the best option open to them, would be a depressing one, but there are two reasons why this is not so. Firstly, Oakeshott, for all the literary brilliance of much of his work, is a philosopher, and therefore he is not concerned to create pictures as objects of emotion. The kind of nihilism that dilates upon the absurdity of human life, the death of God, or the indifference of the universe, belongs to the world of literary imagination—a kind of diffused intellectuality whose design is to create striking images rather than valid arguments. It is perhaps relevant to note that there is little in these pictures which had not been explored by the Stoics and Epicureans of the ancient world. But the main point is that philosophy does indeed leave everything as it was, and hence whatever resources men have found to guide them in past times cannot be swept away merely because they have become objects of philosophical understanding. Secondly, Oakeshott's scepticism has been thoroughgoing. He has pushed on beyond merely doubting the validity of those objective values thought to sustain human decency and arrived at the further conclusion that, even if they had been valid, they could not have done the work actually assigned to them. As foundations, rational principles won't hold up the building. And hence, instead of being tempted to respond to the logic of his position by a species of romantic despair, Oakeshott has rather been impressed and fascinated by the human creativity which, in laws, religions, political doctrines, myths, narratives, and affirmations, has made out of unpromising materials a world in which men can live a decently human life.

That the world men live in is through and through a thing of their own creation is the main understanding Oakeshott has taken from the tradition of German idealism. One crude but efficient way of outlining what this means is by contrasting it with the central tenets of British empiricism, which (especially since Locke) has been preoccupied with the problem of our knowledge of the external world. The result has been an account of knowledge by which a true proposition was one that *corresponded* with an objective feature of the material world. Knowledge was the discovery of previously unnoticed features of an outside world, and human understanding, a more or less passive register of what is simply lying about waiting to be observed. Perhaps the central feature of this very plausible tradition of thought is the status it gives to judgements that can be tested according to their correspondence with a reality independent of human thought. Scientific judgements can be tested against "facts" or, perhaps more fundamentally, against sense data; history against the evidence of records; practical judgements against consequences—only evaluative judgements, seeming to have no relevant court of appeal, had become a kind of intellectual red-light district. German philosophy from Kant onwards modified this account of human knowledge by emphasizing the active contribution of the human mind to the world it understands and, in the case of idealism, this apparently reliable "outside" world was swallowed up altogether by the active powers of the mind. Oakeshott has taken from this tradition the element of scepticism never far below its surface, and only held at bay by an apparatus of beliefs about an ultimate reality which notionally guaranteed the final reliability of truth.

All human experience (Oakeshott argued in *Experience and Its Modes*) [4] involves judgement, and human understanding is a continuum rising from the barest apprehension of sensations to the most fully articulated human understanding. What for various purposes we distinguish as "sensation" necessarily involves some minimal element of identification as being a "this" rather than a "that," and to render such experiences intelligible is a process by which an isolated and barely characterised element of experience is brought progressively into a closer connection with an already existing body of thoughts. Such an increase of intelligibility is the creation of a coherence between the new sensation and the already existing world of experience. There can be no question of outside or primitive elements of reality by which we may check our judgements, for that "outside" is itself simply an abstracted part of the single world of experience within which we live.

So far as Oakeshott is concerned, then, human life is lived out amongst abstractions, and abstraction is to be found not merely in general ideas but in *any* manner of apprehending things short of philosophy itself.[5] We live amongst abstractions because that is what living involves: a response merely to selective fragments of a larger whole which is available to us only in the temporary and exceptional circumstances of philosophical contemplation. Most human experience—and certainly all poli-

---

[4] Cambridge, 1933; reprinted in 1966.

[5] Such, at least, is the view taken in *Experience and Its Modes*. But even in that work, Oakeshott carefully insists upon the oddity of philosophy as a form of knowledge: "There is perhaps something decadent, something even depraved, in an attempt to achieve a completely coherent world of experience; for such a pursuit requires us to renounce for the time being everything which can be called good or evil, everything which can be valued or rejected as valueless. And no matter how far we go with it, we shall not easily forget the sweet delight which lies in the empty kisses of abstraction." (p. 356) The development of Oakeshott's thought has been to explore the conditional validities of non-philosophical manners of thinking, and to insist upon the peculiar status and the limitation of philosophy itself. The cave itself is a fascinating place, and there is no outside sunshine.

tics—is practical: it is "the production and prevention of change." [6] But there are times when our involvement in the abstractions which constitute "practice" lessens, whereupon other "modes of experience" (as Oakeshott calls them) may appear. One such mode he calls "poetry." [7] It is the contemplation of images severed from their place in the world of practice, and thus reconstituted into something we may contemplate with delight. Another mode, that of science, results from "the pursuit of a homogeneous world of quantitative experience." [8]

Another distinguishable mode of experience is history, the attempt to understand the world in terms of interlocking contingencies. For purposes of understanding Oakeshott's political philosophy, this mode is the most important of all. Although all of these modes are forms of human judgement, they are all in Oakeshott's terms "arrests of experience" because they all depend upon a constitutive abstraction, and none of them can provide that element of completeness which makes philosophy the only finally satisfactory form of understanding. Indeed, even the expression "political philosophy" cannot describe a fully concrete form of understanding, for to the extent that philosophising continues to recognise the abstractions of politics, it remains in some degree "arrested." A common metaphor that Oakeshott uses for the engagement of understanding is that of ascent, and this may serve to remind us of its Platonic affinities. But these affinities must not be allowed to conceal from us a fundamental difference: that Oakeshott takes the ascent of understanding to be irreversible. The philosopher may well have a far more profound understanding of politics than a practising politician, but it is a type of understanding which cannot replace that of the politician. Plato, of course, believed that the philosopher, dazzled by the sunlight, would take a little time to adjust once more to the dimness of the cave, and that he would indeed appear disoriented to the practised troglodytes, for they were adept in finding their way about in a world of shadows. Nonetheless, the idea of a philosopher king envisages the rele-

[6] *Ibid.*, p. 256.

[7] Poetry was passed by as a mode in *Experience and Its Modes*, but is discussed in "The Voice of Poetry in the Conversation of Mankind," *Rationalism in Politics*, p. 197.

[8] *Experience and Its Modes*, p. 244.

vance of philosophical understanding to the practical business of running a state. Few things are more central to Oakeshott's political philosophy than his denial of this possibility. His celebrated criticism of "rationalism" revolves around the sharp break between the abstractions of understanding and the very different abstraction of the phenomena being understood.

It is typical of Oakeshott's approach to political ideas that he should locate rationalism firmly within its setting in intellectual history. That setting is the much-discussed appearance of individualism at the beginning of the modern era. The significant feature of individualism so far as Oakeshott's account is concerned was that, as it developed, increasing numbers of men were faced with tasks for which their background had not prepared them. For instance, they needed to know the practices of etiquette at court, how to manage an estate or govern a principality, and how to manage commercial transactions. Previously, men had often needed to study the grammars of foreign tongues if they went abroad; now they needed "grammars" for many other things, for in one respect or another they were often "abroad." The result was the rapid growth of a literature of manuals which met this demand for good advice.

In politics, Machiavelli, Bentham, and Marx have all been interpreted by Oakeshott as writers who responded to different versions of this need. Such manuals were generally written by knowledgeable men who reflected upon their own practices, and then wrote them down in the form of principles and precepts. This literature was, Oakeshott argues, simply an abridgement of current practices, a crib for the ignorant, and usually also impatient, parvenu. The early exponents of this literature, such as Machiavelli and Castiglione, were generally aware of its character and alert to its limitations. Machiavelli, Oakeshott notes, offered not only the precepts contained in the *Prince* but also his own services as an adviser in actual political crises. But in the course of the seventeenth century, in the hands of thinkers like Bacon and Descartes, the rationalising of practices became bolder and more ambitious. Men came to believe that if the body of knowledge applied to an activity were powerful enough, then the hit and miss of the human condition might be replaced by reliability. Human hopes and dreams notoriously outpace achievement, but the rationalists of the seventeenth century did more than hope. They produced a variety of ambitious "methods." The tail of abridgement came to wag the dog of practice. By the time we reach Bentham, for example, we find the view that the rationalised code of law which he seeks to substitute for the tangled common laws of England is superior to that from which it fundamentally derives.

Rationalism thus became the prevalent modern attitude to the growth of knowledge. It led to an urgent search for principles of action that would remove the ills and miseries from which mankind so commonly suffered. Oakeshott was, of course, particularly concerned with its eruption into politics, where it became the progenitor of an endless series of doctrines which promised to abolish privilege, end war, achieve social justice, turn men into brothers, and replace conflict with co-operation. But rationalism came to raise men's hopes across the whole range of human activity, not stopping short even of those areas of personal interaction which had previously been thought wholly dependent upon personal talent: manuals were offered to teach people how to win friends and influence people, or how to be sexually dynamic. Oakeshott dates the appearance of fully fledged rationalism from the seventeenth century, the same period that has been chronicled as the time when Europeans abandoned the delusory practices of magic in favour of a more rational and scientific attitude to the problems of life. There is more than a hint in Oakeshott's writings that what actually happened was that rationalism transformed the scientist into the magus.[9]

The fact that modern technology was indeed greatly increasing human control over the resources of the earth served to reinforce the hopes the doctrine encouraged, and these hopes made rationalism not merely an error but a misfortune. For the failure of each grandiose project (such as the "war to end all wars") did not at all discourage the vogue for rationalism. It merely led people to conclude that they had not yet worked out the project that would have the desired effect. So far as Oakeshott is polemically attacking a political attitude, his main objection to rationalism is that it generates catastrophes of quite

---

[9] Cf. *Rationalism in Politics*, p. 93: "the instrumental mind may be regarded as, in some respects, the relic of a belief in magic."

stupendous magnitude. He is certainly not arguing that the abandonment of rationalism will produce a perfect world, for he appears to have abundant faith in mankind's capacity for committing blunders whatever beliefs happen to be current. But to abandon an illusion is usually some degree of improvement.

Rationalism is, then, "a belief about the nature and scope of rational understanding which, on the one hand, confines it to the promulgation of abstract general propositions and, on the other hand, extends its relevance to the whole of human life." [10] Rationalists, that is to say, refuse to admit rationality in human behaviour unless there has been a deliberate and self-conscious application of principles. Habit and custom, all the practices we have merely inherited, are thereby consigned to the all-embracing category of irrationalities. The intolerant notion that no one but the intellectually athletic rationalist is fully awake was Oakeshott's main target. His argument was in essence the extremely simple distinction between two types of knowledge required in the successful carrying out of a practice: one intellectual and therefore susceptible of statement in terms of principles; the other practical and beyond possibility of formulation. This distinction points to the fact that practical activities require a skill, talent, knack, or feel for situations which cannot be learned from books. The argument looks like an appeal to intuitions, and therefore somewhat obscurantist. Critics were quick to make just this attack upon Oakeshott's characterisation of human activities as traditional. But the argument is in fact about the logic of abstract principles. If such principles are actually "applied" to a situation, they must be joined to other propositions which identify some feature of an actual situation with some general idea contained in the abstract principle. A political theorist like Machiavelli can give his ruler advice about how to deal with riots, rebellions, and revolutions, and he can stiffen his instruction by the use of examples which will help his pupil to identify what he is faced with. But he cannot, in his manual, help his pupil judge whether the noisy crowd surging through the streets is a bread riot or a collection of sporting partisans. In 1853 in Paris, soldiers expecting revolution intervened in a tur-

---

[10] "Scientific Politics," *The Cambridge Journal*, 1, no. 6 (March, 1948), 349. Here Oakeshott discusses Hans J. Morgenthau's *Scientific Man versus Power Politics*.

bulence which turned out to be merely the enthusiasm aroused by the American chess genius Paul Morphy who had just won eight games blindfolded at the Café de la Régence.[11]

Many regimes have fallen because rulers did not take some little local difficulty seriously enough—or responded with excessive force to something that had begun quite innocently. Human actions take place at particular times and places, sometimes with protagonists ill or confused, and responses (as Keynes has reminded us) are often based on theories that are inappropriate to the new situation. Experience constantly surprises us, and perhaps it is the frequently unpleasant nature of the surprises which tempts men to dream of a totally predictable and manageable world. The composer of manuals, then, is quite incapable of supplying more than a few rough props to help the practitioner, and the closer he gets to describing an actual situation, the further he must move from his rational principles. But even as an umbrella of abstractions the principles are defective, for they are mere summaries of earlier practice; and the great sportsman, politician, or architect is likely to be the man whose brilliance leads him to defy some of the currently accepted principles of the game.

It is clear, therefore, that there are many occasions when we recognise in practice the limitations of rationalism. We know perfectly well that to have mastered the rules of a game, or read a book of instruction, is very different from knowing how to play properly. Yet we are often sympathetic towards bookish politics. Why is this so?

> Each man engaged in a certain kind of activity selects a particular question and engages himself to answer this question. He has before him a particular project: to determine the weight of the moon, to bake a sponge cake, to paint a portrait, to disclose the mediations which comprise the story of the Peninsula War, to come to an agreement with a foreign power, to educate his son—or whatever it may be. And, with the normal neglect with which a man engaged upon a particular task treats what is not immediately before him, he supposes that his activity springs from and is governed solely by his project. No man engaged in a particular task has in the forefront of his attention the whole context

[11] Ernest Jones, *Essays in Applied Psycho-Analysis* (London, 1951), I, 185.

and implications of that engagement. Activity is broken up into actions, and actions come to have a false appearance of independence. And, further, this abstraction of view is normally increased when what we observe is somebody else's activity. Every trade but our own seems to be comprised wholly of tricks and abridgements. There is, then, no mystery how it can come to be supposed that an activity may spring from an independently determined purpose to be pursued; the mistake arises from endowing a whole activity with the character of a single action when it is abstracted from the activity to which it belongs, from endowing, for example, the activity of cooking with the character of making a particular pie when the maker is assumed not to be a cook.[12]

The rationalist in the kitchen is, then, a stranger amongst strange things, and the logical form of the strangeness is abstraction. To perform an activity in this manual-dominated fashion is to have a narrow and rigid view of the elements of one's situation, and it is commonly associated with a certain nervousness about whether the thing will come out right. Mastery of a skill is relaxing, if only because it is not so completely involved in a single wished-for outcome; it is much more open to experiment because it is less involved in clear specifications of end. Had the Chinese in the story who found the pig roasted because his house had burned down been a rationalist, he would have lamented the loss of livestock rather than invented roast pork.

Such are the considerations, reminiscent of Socrates' discussions of skill, with which Oakeshott is concerned in his articles on rationalism; but his development of them brings him close to the work of Gilbert Ryle and Richard Peters, who were at the same time involved in extensive criticism of the survivals of faculty psychology, which gave plausibility to some features of rationalism. Ryle's criticism of the idea of the mind as a "ghost in the machine" may be compared with Oakeshott's rejection of the notion that "a man's mind can be separated from its contents and activities," and his consequent rejection of the supposition that "the human mind must contain in its composition a native faculty of 'Reason,' a light whose brightness is dimmed only by education, a piece of mistake-proof apparatus,

[12] *Rationalism in Politics*, p. 98.

an oracle whose magic word is truth." [13] Will, reason, passion, and similar abstract terms are useful in pointing to some features of our mental life, but they cannot be combined to compose a satisfactory account of human activity. To understand a thing concretely cannot in Oakeshott's terms be done by adding together the abstractions. That merely leads to mechanising even the ghost in the machine.

The theme that something more is always happening in human behaviour than the participants imagine is also taken up in the essay on "rational conduct." The argument here is attached to an extended discussion of the attempt made in the 1880s to invent a rational garment for young ladies riding bicycles. The solution arrived at was bloomers, and the problem is why the inventors did not press on to shorts, which conform even better to the terms of reference set for rational dress. The solution, of course, is to be found in what now would be called the "social context": considerations of propriety were no doubt at work, and hence the inventors of bloomers had solved the problem which actually faced them though not quite the problem they deliberately set themselves. Oakeshott's emphasis on tradition in these arguments is that of a historian who looks to the tangled web of human acts and contrivances and understands them as having a pattern, indeed a special sort of rationality, of their own. In human affairs, pure accident and pure reason are equally absent. This pattern of argument becomes entirely explicit in the essay on "Political Education," where a pragmatic or "empirical" kind of politics as pure response to circumstance, and an "ideological" account of politics as the application of a body of knowledge, are both set aside as accounts not of politics itself, but of fragmentary elements of it. To have shown two sides of a coin is not to have described the whole penny. The problem is to give an account of politics as a "concrete, self-moved activity," and both the rejected views fail because they replace the activity itself by "what is never more than an abstract moment in any manner of being active." [14]

---

[13] *Ibid.*, p. 86. On the similarity between some of Oakeshott's arguments and the attitude of contemporary linguistic philosophers, see H. W. Greenleaf, "Idealism, Modern Philosophy and Politics," in *Politics and Experience: Essays Presented to Michael Oakeshott on the Occasion of His Retirement*, Preston King and B. Parekh, eds. (Cambridge, 1968), p. 93.

[14] *Rationalism in Politics*, p. 115.

Oakeshott's solution is to take politics as a traditional activity, the point of the word "traditional" being to emphasize that it can only be understood in historical terms. This means that not only the shifts and dodges of the politician, but also his principles and the very ends he seeks to achieve must be understood as arising from his inheritance: if this were not so, the actual ends of politics would be inexplicable entities *ex machina*, attached to political life by some transcendental thread. The ends of politicians, whether presented as absolute values or rational principles, are derivations from experience, however often they may be conceived by apologists as if they had the delusory grandeur of an independent existence. This view of ends is to be found throughout Oakeshott's account of human activities, for he takes "ends" and "means" alike, as abstractions from the concrete choices of a tradition of human activity; and this is true whether we are considering cooking, politics, chess, science, or anything else. Rationalism appears once more as the mistake of regarding one aspect of an activity ("the means") as if it were the whole.

To interpret a political action as *either* an implication or an impulse is therefore rejected as mistaken—indeed as the very same mistake. How then may politics be more satisfactorily characterised? Oakeshott offers the famous formula of "the pursuit of an intimation."

> The arrangements which constitute a society capable of political activity, whether they are customs or institutions or laws or diplomatic decisions, are at once coherent and incoherent; they compose a pattern and at the same time intimate a sympathy for what does not fully appear. Political activity is the exploration of that sympathy; and consequently, relevant political reasoning will be the convincing exposure of a sympathy, present but not yet followed up, and the convincing demonstration that now is the appropriate moment for recognizing it.[15]

Oakeshott's favourite example of this is the enfranchisement of women in the early years of the twentieth century, when social custom and property law had changed to the point where political enfranchisement appeared as the clearing up of an anomaly. Arguments that purported to derive female enfranchisement from the rights of women might well look more im-

---

[15] *Ibid.*, p. 124.

pressive and give the act a metaphysical status, but since the rational structure that purported to do so was logically a mere house of cards, such arguments could only be regarded as a confused manner of pointing to the one relevant reason: that in terms of the usages of European society at the time, failure to allow women the vote was anomalous. Another example used by Oakeshott is the way in which a lawyer would contest the rightness of a scale of damages in the law courts. He would certainly not be able to deduce his suggested revision from the abstract idea of justice, but would have to present a contingent argument in terms of the scales of damages currently being awarded in plausibly similar cases. One might, again, take the creation of the welfare state in Britain after 1945, where the legislation was justified in terms of principles like "social justice," yet the actual legislation is inexplicable except as an activity of developing and extending welfare legislation that had been coming onto the statute books since at least 1909. In this case, the experience of warfare provided the administrative apparatus for centralised running of social services, and circumstances such as the unemployment of the depression years made the development of *this* kind of state activity (rather than other possible kinds) attractive.

Political activity, therefore, is not succumbing to an impulse, nor is it drawing an implication: it is the pursuit of an intimation. In terms of the dialectical argument Oakeshott used to establish them, intimations appear as a kind of *via media* between the extremes of logical implication and inexplicable accident. The response of contemporary critics, however, was to refuse recognition to this middle way, and to assimilate an intimation to an impulse. The common view was that Oakeshott believed in "a select and privileged class of governors whose intimations are the ones that matter . . . ." [16] This line of thought (for which Oakeshott's writings give no real warrant) was plausible because Oakeshott himself could superficially be assimilated to Edmund Burke: "We are afraid to put men to live and trade each on his own private stock of reason; because we suspect that this stock in each man is small, and that the indi-

---

[16] Colin Falck, "Romanticism in Politics," *New Left Review*, January–February 1963, p. 69.

viduals would do better to avail themselves of the general bank and capital of nations and ages." [17]

It was certainly true that most of the trees felled by Oakeshott's dialectical axe were progressive and socialist doctrines; though some were not. Oakeshott had also written an essay exploring conservatism as a disposition, an essay whose evident sympathy made it tempting to write Oakeshott off as a conservative apologist. But all such interpretations in terms of practical political commitment are beside the point of an argument (such as that in the essay on political education) which seeks to *explain* political activity. Moreover, that argument is, in essence, simple to the point of banality: that to understand men as free-floating agents who embrace projects they have rationally chosen and impose these projects upon the world, is superficial; on a wider view, we should see them as creatures embedded in the traditions of their society, to which they owe not only their skills, but also such ideas as occur to them about how those skills might be used. In other words, the common logical distinction between facts and values is likely to suggest to us a view of human behaviour which is historically false. Something like this view is insisted upon in Marxist writings,[18] and it has become a sociological commonplace, yet in Oakeshott's hands, the doctrine has been an object of suspicion. Why is this so?

The main reason is that whilst there is general agreement that men are the creatures of their social context, there is no agreement upon *how* they are so. Marxism is a doctrine of social determination in which human action and behaviour are to be understood in relation to grand theoretical structures with names like "capitalism" and "feudalism." These structures are often thought to "govern" human thought and action in just the same sense as a scientific law "governs" an instance. In a posi-

---

[17] *Reflections on the Revolution in France*, Everyman ed., p. 84.

[18] Nor has this similarity gone unnoticed: "This insistence on knowing our traditions seems to me right and impossible to dispute. Oakeshott is in fact very close here to the foundation of any serious socialist thinking. Emphasizing the concrete and the historical, he is opposed to the politics of the slogan and the empty framework of liberal (or any other) values; and his claim that we can only know where to go next on the basis of a thorough understanding of where we have come from is a profoundly Marxist idea." Falck, "Romanticism in Politics," p. 68. Whether Oakeshott does actually say this is, of course, another question; but there certainly are affinities.

tivist environment, only an explanation of this kind is regarded as a proper explanation: just as politics is interpreted as either implication or impulse, so whatever has not been exhibited as law-governed must be regarded as mysterious and unintelligible. The traditional manner of posing a related problem such as free-will versus determinism, involves the same assumption. But as we have seen, Oakeshott regards both forks of such dilemmas as being abstractions from the concrete whole of human behaviour. His problem is to show not only that politics is the pursuit of intimations, but also to exhibit such behaviour as having a rationality distinctively its own.

What is it that happens when we understand a concrete event, whether it be a plane crash, a political crisis, a murder, or a revolution? The attempt at such understanding is made by historians, detectives, judges, journalists, gossips, and investigatory tribunals. Starting from the event to be explained, inquiries of this kind build up a set of other events that are relevant and illuminating. All these events may be called "contingencies" because, however they look to God, they all appear to the inquirers as things that might not have happened, but which actually did happen; hence in all but trivial details none of them can be deduced, and all of them must be established from evidence as having happened. Why did the 3.45 express crash into the goods train? Because the signals had not been changed. Why had they not been changed? Because the signalman had left the box. Why had he left the box? He was seen to have drunk seven pints of beer earlier in the day . . . . The sequence of interlocking contingencies thus built up makes the event *intelligible*, and the process of inquiry is a continuous asking of questions until all the gaps (or unintelligibilities) have been filled by eliciting further events. We need not imagine that there is any finality about this intelligibility: in history, one generation of historians has often found things puzzling that seemed clear enough to their predecessors. Thus, things that at first had the mysterious status of accidents may be shown as emerging from earlier events in an intelligible way.

The problem, however, is to explain how one contingent event may cast light upon another. One common solution has been to assimilate this kind of explanation to that of science by inserting between one contingency and the next an implicit general law, which would convert a narrative of contingencies into a structure of rational implications. How do we get from a drunken signalman to an unchanged signal, it may be asked, except in terms of some implicit general law relating drunkenness and carelessness? Oakeshott would deny this. For what we are connecting is *this* particular drunken signalman in *this* particular box on *this* particular occasion—the complicated components of a concrete event—and to move into an abstraction like drunkenness would immediately be to abandon *this* sequence of events, in favour of hypothetical abstract relations. It is no doubt possible (though probably unprofitable) to develop a general theory of drunken signalmen to be applied to the case, but that would be to attempt a scientific explanation of the case, and would be recognisably different from the kind of intelligibility that a narrative of events can give to a puzzle presented in terms of the actions of people recognized as free and rational agents. In any case, the banality and implausibility of many of the general laws suggested for making the spark of implication jump the gap between two contingencies casts considerable doubt on the worthwhileness of the whole enterprise. It seems likely that this attempt to force all explanation into the same mould derives from a dogma to the effect that whatever has not been subsumed under an abstract law has been left unexplained.

Oakshott is, then, at one with those philosophers of history who regard historical explanation as having its own distinct formal characteristics not to be identified with those of science. These philosophers are concerned particularly to emphasize the narrative element in history. As Oakeshott sees it, a historian deals with events in rather the way a man puts a jigsaw puzzle together: when the events have been correctly assembled, they fit together without the need of anything additional. And whether this account of historical explanation is valid or not, it makes clear that two common criticisms of Oakeshott's work are based upon a misunderstanding. Those who think that "tradition" is but a mask for the unexamined preferences of rulers base their view upon the argument that anything except the explicit application of rational principles must be totally capricious. Similarly, those who have taken the whole argument as conservative apologetics have misconstrued the mode of most of

Oakeshott's argument. For to say that political projects emerge from a tradition is to point to the only possible source of understanding of such events: the character and antecedents of the agents. Such an argument may indeed cast doubt upon any form of justification that pleads historical rationalities, but it in no way forecloses the character or the extent of what politicians may do. It is certainly not an argument against any specific change, however ambitious in scale.

There is, then, in Oakeshott's political philosophy a disposition to try and bring to birth a third way of understanding between two unsatisfactorily abstract extremes; it is, however, a synthesis rather than the *via media* we suggested earlier, and it may be illuminated by the *schema* Oakeshott used in supplying a historical location for Hobbes's *Leviathan:*

> The singularities of political philosophies (like most singularities) are not unique, but follow one of three main patterns which philosophical reflection about politics has impressed upon the intellectual history of Europe. These I call traditions because it belongs to the nature of a tradition to tolerate and unite an internal variety, not insisting upon conformity to a single character, and because, further, it has the ability to change without losing its identity. The first of these traditions is distinguished by the master-conceptions of Reason and Nature. It is coeval with our civilization; it has an unbroken history into the modern world; and it has survived by a matchless power of adaptability all the changes in European consciousness. The master-conceptions of the second are Will and Artifice. It too springs from the soil of Greece, and has drawn inspiration from many sources, not least from Israel and Islam. The third tradition is of later birth, not appearing until the eighteenth century. The cosmology it reflects in its still unsettled surface is the world seen on the analogy of human history. Its master-conception is the Rational Will, and its followers may be excused the belief that in it the truths of the first two traditions are fulfilled and their errors find a happy release. The masterpiece of political philosophy has for its context, not only the history of political philosophy as the elucidation of the predicament and deliverance of mankind, but also, normally, a particular tradition in that history; generally speaking it is the supreme expression of its own tradition. And, as Plato's *Republic* might be chosen as the representative of the first tradition, and

Hegel's *Philosophie des Rechts* of the third, so the *Leviathan* is the head and crown of the second.[19]

In these grander terms, Oakeshott's concern with rationalism appears as a footnote in a vastly wider scheme, even though his arguments on the subject may in some respects be taken as that "revelation of the universal predicament in the local and transitory mischief" which he has suggested as characterising a masterpiece of political philosophy.[20] The error of rationalism had already been neatly if indirectly skewered in *Experience and Its Modes:* "To turn philosophy into a way of life is at once to have abandoned life and philosophy." [21] But to elicit from the historical experience of modern European states the postulates by which they might be philosophically understood was a far more daunting task. It is a task that was not adumbrated in *Experience and Its Modes*, but it has come to be Oakeshott's dominant theme of recent decades.

The problem arises from the very concept of a state as a *civil* association. Oakeshott argues convincingly that the expression "nation-state" has a false currency by appearing to be a solution to part of the problem. Such an expression suggests that the character of the civil association called a "state" rests upon the historical or (in some less persuasive views) natural unity of something called a "nation." But the history of modern Europe is a history of boundaries and frontiers being adjusted according to the highly unstable contingencies of warfare and negotiation, and all European states contain miscellaneous populations whose "nationhood" is an aspiration and not a fact. There is, in other words, nothing in Europe that could plausibly be passed off as a nation-state. This is even more obviously true of the imitations of European statehood which have sprung up in other parts of the world. Alternatively, it has been widely believed that a European state in some sense rests upon a form of association called "society." But whatever the acceptability of this belief, it clearly does not describe the basis of the kind of civil association that has actually featured in European history.

[19] Introduction to *Leviathan* by Thomas Hobbes (Oxford, 1946), pp. xi–xii.

[20] *Ibid.*

[21] P. 355.

It is evident that the modern state is a political entity which neither corresponds to anything in nature, nor yet was ever designed. Aristotle had difficulty in deciding whether the polis ought to be regarded as a thing given in nature or constructed by man, but he lacked any convincing alternative. In modern times, however, the development of historical studies has allowed us to take seriously things which are clearly part of a world of human meanings (and therefore not natural), yet were never rationally designed for any particular purpose. In many ways, this is the specification of the subject matter of the social sciences, and it has preoccupied both Hayek and Popper: the former talking of "the result of human action but not of human design" and the other of "the unintended consequences of human actions." [22]

One feature of this cluster of problems has exercised a continual fascination over Oakeshott in the last two decades. This is a tension that runs through European political thought from its very beginnings up to the present moment, between the state construed as an association of human beings joined together in respect only of subscribing to a system of laws which are the conditions of choosing, and the state taken to be a body of associates united in the pursuit of some common purpose. One writer whom Oakeshott regards as having written acutely on this theme is Montesquieu, for the latter's celebrated distinction between monarchies and republics seems to be concerned with this problem. The *république* of Montesquieu describes men as bound together in what lawyers would call a "corporative aggregate". Although the republic will have laws for reasons of convenience, "the most important instrument of control will be the initiation of successive generations into the 'mystery' of the common purpose being pursued—what Montesquieu called *l'éducation.*" [23] The view of the office of government appropriate to such a state has been called by Oakeshott "teleocratic" because it is management of the common business (and in such a state there is little else) in terms of a

----

[22] See, for example, F. A. Hayek's collection of essays, *Studies in Philosophy, Politics and Economics* (London, 1967).

[23] This quotation comes from the manuscript of an essay "Some Reflections on the Character of Modern European States," which forms part of a new volume *On Human Conduct* (Oxford, 1975).

communal end. Montesquieu, writing in the first half of the eighteenth century, took the view that no such states existed in modern Europe, but that some Greek cities and early republican Rome could be understood in terms of his construction. The *monarchie*, by contrast, is a mode of association in which a plurality of individuals is joined solely in terms of rules of conduct: law in monarchic associations "is a system of conditions, indifferent to the satisfaction of wants and reflecting no common purpose, to be subscribed to and used by persons in making their own choices of what to do or say in contingent situations, and the associates are joined solely in recognition of the authority of these conditions." [24]

Human behaviour is always conditional: upon the characteristics of individuals, upon material possibilities, and upon the behaviour of other people. In a *monarchie* (or in what Oakeshott, in specifying the appropriate view of the office of government corresponding to it, calls a "nomocracy") individuals must subscribe to the abstract conditions specified by the authority of law, and it is this subscription alone that constitutes their association. It leaves them completely free to choose whatever purposes may occur to them, either individually or in combination. This is a profound distinction which we cannot here explore, but which Oakeshott considers in depth in *On Human Conduct*. It is worth noting, however, as characteristic of his thought that every new development in his political philosophy is partnered by a new theory of what it is to enquire into these matters.

We began with Oakeshott's image of the boundless sea of politics; it is appropriate to end with another central image. Human intercourse is often construed by Oakeshott as a conversation, and this is an image of great range in the understanding of his thought. For it takes almost the opposite view of human existence from that suggested by John Stuart Mill's hope that as time goes on men will come to agree upon more and more things. Oakeshott does not believe that the point of the conversation is to elicit truth, though at times it will doubtless do so. Indeed, the whole point of the conversation is that it doesn't have a point, and therefore many things may find a place in it which would be expelled as irrelevant in a seminar or a debate

[24] *Ibid.*

in a legislative assembly. "It is with conversation as with gambling, its significance lies neither in winning nor in losing, but in wagering." [25]

Now this is an image of the human condition in which tolerance and good manners become central virtues, partly because these are the conditions of any conversation, and partly because the image itself insists upon an element of scepticism which would make it mere boorishness for any one of the "voices" in the conversation to become a monopolist. A tendency towards monologue is certainly a standing risk, for there is an ancient tradition that would accord philosophy (which Oakeshott takes to be not so much an independent voice as the impulse to study the quality and style of each voice) a special status; and "In recent centuries the conversation, both in public and within ourselves, has become boring because it has been engrossed by two voices, the voice of practical activity and the voice of 'science': to know and to contrive are our pre-eminent occupations." [26] Oakeshott's philosophical impetus derives from a profound conviction that the conversation has fallen into disarray; that some of the voices (such as poetry) can only get a hearing by pretending to be what they are not (science or politics, for example); and that some conversationalists are bullying the rest. It is this condition of things that partly explains Oakeshott's impact upon the world of professional students of politics.

He has been widely distrusted as a dealer in mysteries, and what is even worse, in well-bred mysteries. For he writes as a confidently civilised man of the world contemplating graceless *parvenus* endlessly active in trying to improve themselves. He has presented skill as a matter of "connoisseurship." Instead of asserting ponderous relational propositions in philosophical language, he has made deft use (and occasionally overuse) of the gentlemanly term "appropriate." In talking of the hereditary prince, Oakeshott recognised him as a man "who knows how to behave," taking this knowledge as if it were obvious to anyone with eyes to see, rather than a debatable matter of competing values. So far as the string of essays on rationalism are con-

[25] *Rationalism in Politics*, p. 198.
[26] *Ibid.*, p. 202.

cerned, we may add to these considerations a relevant cultural circumstance: in much political writing in the twentieth century, it has been the practice for writer and reader to engage in what it is not too much to call a "conspiracy of self-congratulation," in which the writer flatters the reader by taking for granted his commitment to social compassion and civilised values. In dealing with what were regarded as the great issues of the moment, even philosophers have been accustomed to give us the benefit of their opinions—a practice no doubt encouraged by the circumstances of war, but not entirely limited to issues arising from it.[27]

Oakeshott austerely eschewed such devices. He did not wring his hands at the horrors of war, the sufferings of humanity, or the evil of aggressors. Instead of congratulation or hopeful political advice, his readers learned that the very navigational instruments they cherished in finding their way about the boundless ocean of politics were largely valueless (and certainly valueless for navigation) and that only a nerveless poltroon would worry about such things. They were denied their "fix" of abstract uplift. They gained the impression (in fact a false one) that their circumstances were being interpreted as hopeless, and that going out to buy a book in order to learn how to improve (exactly the kind of move the reader of such essays would habitually make when desperate) was worse than useless. To a British audience exhausted by war, living on optimism and a few ounces of meat per week, what could be more infuriating?

Oakeshott appeared, furthermore, to be vulnerable in more professional ways. Possessed of a witty and brilliant style, he could be dismissed as a literary essayist rather than a rigorous philosopher. He certainly wasted little time in the boiler-room philosophical work of analysing concepts; he tended to eschew footnotes, "for a philosophy, if it is to stand at all, must stand absolutely upon its own feet, and anything which tends to obscure this fact must be regarded with suspicion." [28] And he had an obvious distaste for the parade of flashy technicalities which is the mechanical sign of professional competence in modern aca-

[27] Cf. "We should listen to philosophers only when they talk philosophy." *Experience and Its Modes*, p. 355.
[28] *Ibid.*, p. 7.

demic circles. Academic controversy in philosophy tends to issue in the slow revolving of questions which come and go, so that each contributor takes up a position to be opposed and thus leaves dangling some gauge or problem to which the next contributor can attach himself. But Oakeshott has preferred, whatever the scale in which he is working, to present a finished essay in which the surface is smooth at all points, and initial entry must first be made by a somewhat blundering assault upon the central ideas of the argument. "Guarded by the armour of his definitions," as one critic wrote, "it seems that Professor Oakeshott cannot be confronted on his own terms with any hope of success." [29] The work of a radical individualist (and one with no taste for surrounding himself with disciples), Oakeshott's work has often seemed to inhabit a different universe from that of his professional colleagues.

The notion of Oakeshott as arrogantly conservative is a reflection of the intense and utilitarian world of the twentieth century rather than a genuine understanding of his views. For it runs quite counter to such obvious features of his thought as his addiction to, almost his cult of, the comfortably shabby rather than the pretentiously high-flown, his insistence that no literature can (for obvious logical reasons) consist entirely of masterpieces, and his strongly argued view that "the pursuit of perfection as the crow flies" [30] will produce not perfection but hysteria. In many ways, the practical consequences of the argument on rationalism were simple and almost relaxing: an unwise intoxication with reason and science, construed as magical powers, had led Europeans to treat many of their most valuable resources (traditions, customs, amusements, relaxed acceptances) as valueless. Having gone whoring after perfection, Europeans were neglecting the pleasures of their own backyards. Yet instead of accepting Oakeshott's invitation to cease from rationalist striving, many people behaved as if they had broken their compass. One reason for this response may well be Oakeshott's romantic individualism. He writes as if everybody took the weight of his own individuality and accepted the burden of its cultivation without complaint or regret: he presents a world

[29] John Sanderson, "Definitionism in Politics," *Durham University Journal*, March 1965, p. 108.
[30] *Rationalism in Politics*, p. 59.

which may contain distress, grief, pain, and frustration, but in which guilt, anxiety, perhaps even shame are unknown. Thomas Hobbes, of whose thought Oakeshott has been incomparably the most imaginative reader in recent times, took refuge from some elements of his understanding of human nature in contemplating the memory of his friend Sydney Godolphin, and Oakeshott has himself placed peculiar stress upon the philosophical importance of this admiration:

> Let us suppose a man of the character Hobbes supposed all men to be: a man unavoidably his own best friend and (on account of his weakness) subject to the fear of finding himself shamed and dishonoured and even killed. But let us also suppose that the preponderant passion of this man remains pride rather than fear; that he is a man who would find greater shame in the meanness of settling for mere survival than in suffering the dishonour of being recognised a failure; a man whose disposition is to overcome fear not by reason (that is, by seeking a secure condition of external human circumstances) but by his own courage; a man not at all without imperfections and not deceived about himself, but who is proud enough to be spared the sorrow of his imperfections and the illusion of his achievements; not exactly a hero, too negligent for that, but perhaps with a touch of careless heroism about him; a man, in short, who (in Montaigne's phrase) 'knows how to belong to himself,' and who, if fortune turned out so, would feel no shame in the epitaph:
> Par delicatesse
> J'ai perdu ma vie.[31]

This is a view of individuality perhaps to be found in the earlier centuries of the modern era, but now remote from us. Oakeshott's individualist has a thoroughness which derives from the consistency of his passions rather than from the standards of professional competence; and Oakeshott is likely to mislead imitators because the deliberate absence of a scaffolding of technical apparatus makes it seem that the building must be made of air. Those who have taken him to be an essayist rather than a philosopher are, however, beside the mark. As has been pointed out before,[32] his style is integral to his thought. It

[31] *Ibid.*, pp. 289–90.
[32] Cf. H. W. Greenleaf's illuminating monograph, *Oakeshott's Philosophical Politics* (London, 1966), p. 88.

reflects a very precise sense of the complexity of things, allowing Oakeshott to register lightly what in other philosophers requires a ponderous dialectical apparatus. A profound understanding of human experience is built up into an interlocking structure which neither rests upon fundamentals nor culminates in an Absolute, for "the determination not to be satisfied with anything inconsequent, the refusal to relieve one element of experience at the expense of another, are the motives of all philosophical thinking." [33]

[33] Oakeshott, Introduction to *Leviathan*, p. xv.

Karl Popper:
Politics Without Essences

by ANTHONY QUINTON

The three great exponents of classic liberalism—Locke, Bentham, and John Stuart Mill—make up a dialectical sequence. Locke based his advocacy of minimal government, charged with the negative task of protecting life, liberty, and possessions of individuals, on the premise that men have certain axiomatic natural rights. He conceived these principles of natural rights as the self-evident objects of a kind of intellectual intuition analogous to that which supplies the foundations of mathematics. The necessity, and also the narrowly drawn limits, of government he took to be deducible from these principles in conjunction with the fact of human moral imperfection. Since men claim these rights for themselves while self-interestedly failing at times to respect them as they apply to others, one of them has to be given up so that the remainder may be effectively maintained. The exception that has to be foregone is complex and procedural: the executive power of the law of nature, which concerns the ascertainment of natural laws, their application to particular cases, and the enforcement of their applications through sanctions. For Locke the right to the greatest possible freedom is second in importance only to the right to life. That there is such a right is a basic, intuitive moral truth.

For Bentham and James Mill, liberty and such associated liberal preferences as equality and democracy are not axiomatically good. Their justification, to the extent that they are justified, is derived from the degree to which their assurance contributes to the general happiness. On this view the principle of utility alone is self-evident. In fact, as far as liberty and democracy are concerned, Bentham and James Mill thought that they were to a very large extent justified by considerations of utility. Bentham believed that happiness would be maximised by allowing men a very large freedom of choice in their actions since men are, by and large, the best judges of what will make them individually happy. James Mill favoured democracy as the form of government most likely to serve the common interest since it is the only one in which the rulers have a reliable motive—the desire to retain their power—for seeking the happiness of all. The two were less explicit about equality. But as extreme environmentalists they rejected all notions that some men were innately superior to others. There is at least an egalitarian flavour to Bentham's elusive formula "each to count for one and none for more than one." Furthermore, some measure of equality in the distribution of the conditions of happiness is implied by the project of maximising utility. The allocation of an instrumental good to some man who has one already will generally produce less utility than its allocation to someone who has none at all.

John Stuart Mill inherited a commitment to the principle of utility from Bentham and his father, but qualified their concrete development of it in a number of ways. In the first place, he had a somewhat more complicated conception of utility than their narrowly hedonistic idea of it. His view is expressed in his unsatisfactory argument for the superiority of the "higher pleasures" in his *Utilitarianism* and, more significantly, in the important, if fleeting, reference to "the permanent interests of man as a progressive being" in his essay *On Liberty*. Secondly, his endorsement of liberty is so unqualified as to go beyond the reach of utilitarian justification and almost to reinstate it as a natural right in the manner of Locke. On the other hand, he did not have his father's breezy confidence in democracy. He saw it as likely to install the tyranny of the majority, to enforce the general pursuit of mediocre ends, and to inhibit individual freedom. He favoured its administration in comparatively small doses as a way of educating the mass of mankind in political responsibility and public spirit. Finally, while passionately committed to liberty in its intellectual, political, and personal aspects, he came to question the desirability of unrestricted economic freedom and, in the later editions of his *Principles of Political Economy,* argued for redistributive taxation.

Since the time of John Stuart Mill there has been no comparably original, sensitive, and systematic defence of the whole range of liberal ideals. His complex and imperfectly utilitarian arguments for liberty, equality, and democracy, in which the dangers of each for the others are acknowledged, has remained the authoritative presentation of the liberal creed. There has been a direct tradition stemming from him in which the moderately socialistic features of his later thinking have been further developed, as in the welfare-state liberalism of such theorists as Leonard Hobhouse, prepared, as Mill was not, for the risk to liberty involved in state education. There has also been a more rigidly libertarian current of thought, whose most distinguished contemporary exponent is F. A. Hayek, which, from its distrust of state power, supports an extreme individualism even at the cost of massive inequality. But until the publication of Karl Popper's *Open Society*[1] there has been no large-scale reformulation of liberal doctrine that has presented it in a significantly novel way.

In the preface to his book Popper describes it as "a critical introduction to the philosophy of politics and history" and the dedication of its companion volume, *The Poverty of Historicism*,[2] is to "the countless men and women of all creeds or nations or races who fell victims to the fascist and communist belief in the Inexorable Laws of Historical Destiny." Popper's immediate enemy, then, is modern totalitarianism in its fascist and communist forms. But his main attack on it is not carried out by direct advocacy of its liberal and democratic opponent. Democrats and liberals reject totalitarianism partly because of its authoritarian nature and partly because of its all-embracing scope. Popper's primary target is a thesis in the philosophy of history, not in the philosophy of politics: the doctrine of historicism. This doctrine holds that the proper goal and most fruitful achievement of social and historical inquiry is the substantiation of a general law of the historical development of society. Historicists believe that with such laws the next stage of social development can be prophesied and that the content of this prophecy is the only rational determinant of correct political action: action, that is to say, which is appropriate to the inevitable

[1] *The Open Society and Its Enemies* (London, 1945).
[2] London, 1957.

historical future. His main argument, then, is that totalitarian politics rests for its support—at least to the extent that it claims intellectual respectability, to be more than a collection of ideological prejudices—on historicism.

At the same time, like the classic liberals, Popper defends liberty, democracy, and equality directly, on moral grounds. His primary argument against historicism is designed to show that the ideals of liberalism are not impossible, that there is no discoverable historical necessity which rules them out altogether. Having defended the idea that liberal ideals can be realised, he goes on to argue that they should be. The basis of his argument here is utility, not self-evident natural rights. He rejects the general essentialist doctrine of intellectual intuition for a number of reasons. He goes on to argue, more specifically, that absolute principles of liberty and democracy are invalid because logically paradoxical. His utilitarianism differs, however, in two major respects from that of either Bentham or John Stuart Mill. In the first place, largely on the basis of a theory of rational social action of an anti-utopian or gradualist character, he formulates his principle of utility in a negative way, as *eliminate suffering*, and not in a positive way as *maximise happiness*. Secondly, he does not regard his principle as a truth or item of possible knowledge but as a demand or, more mildly, proposal.

There are, then, two principal strands to Popper's overall argument: one methodological, designed to refute the allegedly historicist foundation of the totalitarian rejection of liberal democracy; the other ethical, in which a moral point of view is proposed entailing the desirability of the liberal-democratic programme, whose possibility has been established by the critique of historicism. The particular, gradualist, or piecemeal version of democratic liberalism that Popper supports is defended on broadly methodological grounds. We do not possess the kind of social knowledge required for the overall reconstruction of society; rational social action is not directed to ultimate, utopian ends. But there is much more to his position that is relevant to political theory than these main themes. First of all there is his argument that absolute principles in politics— of freedom, tolerance, democracy, and sovereignty—are logically defective. Furthermore, there are a large number of partic-

ular discussions of political interest: about nationalism, about
the prospects of preventing international conflict, about laissez-
faire and interventionism, and about the attractions of totalitarianism in a time of disturbing social change. In what follows I
shall first examine Popper's critiques of historicism and utopianism, then his moral defence of liberal democracy and his
contention that absolute political principles involve logical
paradoxes, and finally some of the specific issues that are
comparatively independent of his main argument.

Popper's more direct arguments against historicism are to
be found in *The Poverty of Historicism*. There is, first, a short
"formal" refutation in the preface. The course of history is affected by the growth of knowledge; we cannot predict the future growth of knowledge; therefore, we cannot predict the future course of history. This argument carries less than complete
conviction since the knowledge that affects history may not be
the same as the knowledge that cannot be predicted. The
knowledge that directly affects history is applied, technological
knowledge. We may be able to predict *that* a certain technological problem will be solved—for example, that of finding a military use for atomic forces—a considerable time before we know
how to solve it. Popper's point, however, in holding future
knowledge to be unpredictable, is not the simple, verbal one
that future knowledge that is known now is not purely future
knowledge.

More convincing, at least in being less elusive, are his detailed arguments attributing methodological confusions to historicists. The two great models of systematic predictability by
analogy with which historicists advance their claims are both
bad guides. The solar system, far from being a standard instance
of a law-governed system, is a rare and unrepresentative case. A
small number of variables is involved, and the system as a
whole is very little affected by extraneous factors. The supposed "law" of evolution, on the other hand, is not a law at all.
At best it is a trend. More correctly it is a unique historical
reconstruction in which the laws proper of genetics, amongst
other things, are invoked to order a mass of data about organic
species and their environments. It affords no ground for rational
extrapolation into the unknown future. Such a "law of evolu-

tion" as Spencer's famous formula about differentiation and integration is too vague and elastic to make possible any definite predictions at all.

Popper does not discuss the analogy which seems to have weighed heavily with such ardent historicists as Spengler and Toynbee. This analogy discerns a parallel between a society or a civilisation and a living organism. Every organism has a characteristic life-span which divides into a regular sequence of developmental stages. Certainly the analogy is very loose. A man is a single, continuously identifiable material object. A society or civilisation is not; and, indeed, the identification of any such entity as an individual is highly problematic. Toynbee's apparented and affiliated societies merge into one another in a way for which there is no parallel in the relations of human parents and children. Popper's anti-inductivism prevents him from criticising historicism on the grounds of the small number of instances of the development of single societies on which it rests. The developmental pattern of human aging is highly reliable predictively. It is a paradigm of the inevitable. Knowledge of it could be used rationally in prediction long before there was any knowledge of the laws explaining the passage from one of Shakespeare's ages of man to the next. It follows that the predictive employment of recurrent patterns of development is not irrational as such. So, it would seem, the historicist project is not doomed from the outset. Historicist theories must stand or fall by their ordinary empirical merits, by their ability to withstand our most resolute efforts to falsify them, as Popper has taught us. Their falsification is a task for historians rather than philosophers.

But, despite their frequent dramatic suggestiveness, such theories do not do very well. Marx's predictions for the comparatively immediate future have been uniformly false. The misery of the industrial proletariat has not increased; the proletariat has not become the immense majority of the population; revolution has not come in industrial but in peasant societies. If we assume, as there is good reason to do, that no historicist theory is well enough confirmed to base confident rational predictions on, the question arises of the extent to which totalitarian political doctrines depend on them. Popper does not try to substantiate the proposition that totalitarianism rests on historicism di-

rectly, but connects the two through three great philosophers
—Plato, Hegel, and Marx—whom he holds to be, first, historicists, and, secondly, the crucial theorists who provide foundations for totalitarianism. Let us examine these two claims.

Popper's characterisation of Plato as a historicist is based
on an interpretation of the theory of forms and on the doctrine
of a regular pattern of political degeneration set out in the
eighth book of the Republic. Plato's forms, according to Popper,
are at once the paradigms of their kinds and the creative origi-
nals of their particular instances. If this is correct, then the first
is the best: the most primitive form of state or society is the one
which most closely resembles the ideal exemplar. The first and
best society, for Plato, is one in which the wisest and most god-
like of men is king. It is followed by a heroic or feudal timocracy; then by plutocratic timocracy, which gives way to lawless
mob-democracy and, finally, to tyranny.

I think that Popper has shown beyond doubt that there is a
historicist strain in Plato. He connects Plato's law of political
degeneration in a biographically convincing way with the despair inspired in Plato, as it had been in Heraclitus, by the
anarchically democratic disturbances of the age. Does he also
show Plato to have been a totalitarian? There can be no question that he irreversibly corrects the idea that the Republic is
the ideal training-manual for high-minded and public-spirited
administrators, Jowett's bible for a higher civil service, selected
by examinations. Plato's ideal state is one in which political
power is monopolised by a rigidly closed class of rulers and is
thus a particularly virulent form of authoritarianism. Numerous
typical features of modern totalitarianism are present in Plato's
construction. The ruling class has the discipline, esprit de
corps, and selfless dedication of the parties founded by Hitler
and Lenin. Lying is laid down as an indispensable technique of
government. Popper's argument that Plato is a racialist leaves a
gap yawning between Plato's proposals for the deliberate
breeding of rulers and the genocidal atrocities of Hitlerism.
There is little of the emphasis on terror in Plato that there is in
the theory and practice of Lenin and Hitler. Finally, the ruled,
although wholly without political power, do seem in Plato, if
only by default, to be left pretty much to their own fleshly devices. There is no suggestion of the kind central to modern to-

talitarianism that all the citizens should be wholly made over into cogs in the machinery of state.

But, if Plato is rather an extreme authoritarian than a totalitarian proper, the question still arises of the extent to which his political doctrines, which, however they are to be described, are radically opposed to democratic liberalism, depend on the strain of historicism in Plato's thought. Now although, as I have agreed, this strain is undoubtedly present, it does not seem to be the main source of Plato's authoritarian politics. The historicist strain is entirely *congruous* with Plato's politics, but what the politics actually follows from are the premises that rationality and knowledge are the proper qualifications for political power and that these intellectual virtues are substantially present in, and dominate the personalities of, only a small minority of mankind. Together with the functional principle that each man should do what he is most fitted for, these premises about the nature of reason and human inequality entail that the ideal form of government is the dictatorship of an intellectual elite.

There is no need to argue the claim that Hegel and Marx are historicists, or the claim that their historicism is fundamental to their political doctrines. What is open to question is Popper's view that they are both totalitarians and, what is more, the originating theorists of fascism and communism respectively. Although, as has been pointed out, Popper's discussion of Hegel is somewhat intemperate, there is plenty of substance in the charges he brings, not least against Hegel's polluting effect on the language and argumentative procedures of German philosophy. As far as his formal recommendations about government are concerned Hegel can most accurately be described as an authoritarian of a constitutionalist kind. Although his legislature has a representative element, the representation is functional rather than democratic. The legislature has limited powers. The real ruler is the bureaucracy, unified in the person of the sovereign.

As Popper sees, however, the formal constitutional apparatus is not the substance of Hegel's political doctrine. He lists six Hegelian theses which are all typical features of fascism: (i) nationalism, as expressed in the views that the nation is the collectivity to which the individual must subordinate himself and that the aim of a nation must be to be the dominant one of the epoch; (ii) states are natural enemies which assert themselves in war; (iii) the interest of the state is the highest morality; (iv) glorification of war; (v) the creative role of world-historical great men; and (vi) the elevation of dangerous heroism above bourgeois mediocrity. Even if none of the institutions typical of fascism are proposed by Hegel—the party, the police working through terror, the propaganda ministry working through lies— his belligerent, nationalistic collectivism, in which the individual has value only through his service to the state, anticipates the frame of mind, the prevailing mood, of twentieth-century fascism. Hegel is a much less *respectable* figure than his strictly constitutional recommendations suggest or than his current apologists try to make out.

All the same this is at most a matter of broad temperamental affinity; fascism is more a lunatic continuation of Hegel's politics than a direct realisation of it. Hegel is more the theorist of Wilhelmine than of Hitlerian Germany. There is a marked lack of connection between Hegel and the later development of fascism. Hitler's personal disdain for precise theoretical commitments has often been pointed out. The little bit of Alfred Rosenberg's *Myth of the Twentieth Century* that Hitler actually read he condemned as "too abstract." The most solid element in his personal ideology was the maniacal drivel about racial purity which supplied his movement with an identifiable opponent and a solution to the pseudo-problem of the root of the world-wide conspiracy to drag Germany down.

Finally, in so far as there is a correspondence between the morally objectionable "background material" of Hegel's politics and fascism, it does not extend to Hegel's historicism. For Hitler, Germany's struggle for world domination was a heroic risk, not a foreordained necessity, more a Kierkegaardian leap than an irresistible dialectical transition.

But, despite all these reservations, there is an underlying respect in which Hegel's social theory prepared the way for modern totalitarianism. For it was Hegel who produced the most massively systematic and influential critique of individualism, and fascism is simply the most radical assault on the moral ultimacy of the individual. Popper himself is prepared to accept collectivism in one of its methodological senses, namely as a theory about the proper character of explanations in the social sciences. He sides with Marx against Mill in rejecting the idea that all the laws of the social sciences should be deduced from a universal psychology of human nature. But this, he insists, has no implication of *moral* collectivism, the theory that the ultimate criterion of value is the welfare of the collective.

It may at first seem frivolous to question the connection between Marx and Russian communism. But anyone who denies that Marx was a totalitarian, as a close study of Marx's early writings gives one every reason to do, does implicitly question that connection. Marx's own writings contain hardly any totalitarian elements. Marx's ideal society is, indeed, anarchistic: the state has withered away. The vast totalitarian apparatus of Soviet Russia and its colonial dependencies was entirely created by Lenin and perfected by Stalin. The idea of an elite party of dedicated revolutionaries is a Leninist invention. The only explicitly totalitarian element in Marx is largely verbal; the word "dictatorship" in the phrase "the dictatorship of the proletariat." Marx himself was a libertarian—an angry and acrimonious one no doubt—and the possessor of a cantankerously authoritarian personality. Accuracy, as much as devotional zeal, would justify the description of the Russian state religion by its priesthood as Marxism-Leninism rather than Marxism. This is not to say that the Marxist element of the compound, and, in particular, Marxian historicism, is not a crucial ingredient of the whole. But as originally formulated by Marx, although utopian and violent, it was not totalitarian. What Marxian historicism actually predicts, wrongly as usual, as the outcome of proletarian revolution is a social condition in which men, wholly liberated from economic necessity and the oppressive institutions that necessity has hitherto required, pursue their varied forms of self-realisation in equal and total freedom.

It must, then, be concluded that the connection which Popper seeks to establish between historicism and totalitarianism by way of Plato, Hegel, and Marx is rather tenuous. Plato and Hegel were both moral collectivists and the political doctrines they derived from their collectivism were both strongly authoritarian and contained various totalitarian features: in Plato, rule by a caste and a fairly rudimentary racialism; in Hegel, aggressive nationalism. But Plato was not much of a historicist, and although Hegel was, in neither case is their near-totalitarian politics very closely connected with their historicism. Marx, although very much a historicist, was not a totalitarian at all.

A final point before leaving the subject of historicism is that while at most associated with, and nowhere essential to, totalitarianism, it has been, at least until the present century, at least as closely associated with liberalism. Condorcet is only the most systematic of the many liberal thinkers who have supposed that liberal democracy was inevitably destined to triumph by some law of progress. This is implied by a sentence that Popper italicises in his favourite quotation from H. A. L. Fisher: "the fact of progress is written plain and large on the page of history; but progress is not a law of nature." The error that Fisher is correcting here is that of *liberal* optimism. It is natural that anyone who wants some large historical change to come about should keep his spirits up by finding reasons for thinking that it must do so. The desire for change is the fundamental thing; the historicism is only a reassuring addition. The need for such reassurance is not confined to totalitarians.

"Utopianism" is one of those polemical words which writers hasten to mobilise for meanings of their own. In its most usual sense it refers to the indifference to the practicability of their proposals that is characteristic of the devisers of utopias or ideal societies. In common speech, to call a scheme "utopian" is to object either that it is absolutely impossible to realise or that it cannot be realised without unacceptable costs. Thus to show that some ideal is not utopian is to show that it can in fact be realised, at an acceptable cost, and that can best be done by specifying the steps leading from the present state of affairs to the projected one, tracing out the side-effects of each stage.

The claim of Marx and Engels that their socialism is free from the utopian character of all previous socialism rests on a curious intensification of the procedure of setting out the steps of the realisation of the ideal. They contend, not merely that capitalism *can*, but that it *must*, give way to socialism. The energies squandered by utopian socialists on the detail of the desired end are in Marxism devoted to demonstrating its inevitability, to such an extent that the end in question was hardly described by them in a positive way at all.

Popper's conception of utopianism is something different again. He uses it to cover any large-scale project of social reconstruction, more specifically, the view that rational political action should always be guided by an ultimate end which takes the form of a fully worked-out plan of an ideal social order. Such a "holistic" conception of social engineering he regards as disastrously misguided, and he puts forward in its place a conception of piecemeal social engineering, in which reform is directed towards the elimination of the most pressing present evils.

His underlying argument for this conclusion is that our knowledge of the workings of society is altogether inadequate to the tasks which utopian social engineering imposes on it. The social sciences aim to discover the unintended consequences of human action. These are always manifold and, inevitably, more or less surprising. He also assumes, in effect, that most or significantly many of the consequences will be undesired as well as unintended, being more fearful of bad effects than hopeful of happy accidents. For Popper, rational action must always take account of the imperfections of our knowledge. All programmes of change should advance in small steps so that unexpected ill effects can be corrected as soon as they arise and before they do too much damage.

A second argument for piecemeal reform is that there is likely to be much more agreement about the desirability of removing specific present evils than about a remote, complex ideal. Thus the latter's realisation will have to be achieved in the face of opposition and can be pursued resolutely only by authoritarian means. Generally, as he argues, the exponents of large-scale *social* revolution recognise that violence is indispensable for the securing of their ends.

A further consideration is that a programme of utopian social engineering will take a long time to carry through. Might not the ideal come to seem less attractive with the passage of time? There is injustice in imposing the burdens of change on those who have to live through the process of radical reform and delivering all its alleged benefits to those who experience its fulfilment.

In his essay "Utopia and Violence" in *Conjectures and*

Refutations [3] Popper develops further his point about the minimisation of disagreement. Not only will there be more disagreement about comprehensive ideal schemes than about present evils whose elimination is desirable, but the disagreement will be more intense, even religious, in character, thus increasing the likelihood of violent persecution of dissenters.

Popper's arguments for gradualism in social reform are in close correspondence with his ideas about the nature and growth of scientific knowledge. Science, in his view, is gradualist in two respects. It progresses not by the discovery of large, definitive truths but by approximation to truth, by the development of theories of increasing verisimilitude. Secondly, it advances cumulatively by the steady amendment of its tradition of beliefs and methods. However, Popper is less averse to revolutions in thought than in society. No blood is spilt in intellectual revolutions.

There is plenty of empirical confirmation for his scepticism about utopian social engineering. Revolutions, notoriously, produce results that bear little relation to the intentions of their initiators. It is, all the same, possible to admit the substance of this point and still favour large-scale revolutions founded on utopian myths. Sorel contended that gradual reform never really achieves anything, in the long run. Small concessions by the privileged to the oppressed are in due course counteracted, once they have served their purpose of palliating discontent.

But on closer inspection Sorel's argument seems doubly defective. Although relatively peaceful and gradual processes of social reform have not eliminated differences of power and wealth altogether from social relations, and do not seem likely to do so, they have got rid of some particularly extreme varieties of inequality: those embodied in the relation of master and slave or lord and serf. Furthermore, slavery and serfdom have not been removed by violent revolution. To the extent that they have been resuscitated in this century it has been in just those countries where violent revolutionary change has taken place.

Popper is insistent that the obsession of philosophers with

[3] London, 1963.

close examination of the meanings of words is misguided and fruitless. Certainly he regards it as a moral obligation to use language clearly, but he holds that no amount of antecedent explicit defining of terms can eliminate confusion and misunderstanding. Definitions can only be as precise as the defining terms that they employ. For effective communication what can be done is to convey what one has to say in such a fashion that it does not depend on any special interpretation of the words one uses. It is consistent with this, therefore, that he should spend little time on the task of precisely articulating the terms which express the liberal values that he endorses.

In the case of liberty, for example, he is prepared to condemn as a distortion what he sees as Hegel's identification of liberty with self-obliterating service to the state. On the other hand, he does not work with a strictly negative conception of freedom, in which it is seen as the absence of deliberate restraints on action. "A certain amount of state control," he writes, "in education, for instance, is necessary, if the young are to be protected from a neglect which would make them unable to defend their freedom, and the state should see that all educational facilities are available to everybody." [4]

Again, Popper's conception of equality seems to be much more political and legal than economic. In pointing out that most of the specific proposals for institutional reform listed in the *Communist Manifesto* have in fact been carried out, at least in the advanced Western democracies, he comments in a parenthesis about the proposal for the abolition of all right of inheritance: "Largely realized by heavy death duties. Whether more would be desirable is at least doubtful." [5] He favours intervention by the state to prevent the excesses of unrestrained laissez-faire capitalism, but he defends this as required for the protection of the "economic freedom" of the workers rather than as a means for eliminating economic inequality.

For him the important point about democracy is that it is that method of government in which the public can change its rulers without recourse to violence. More positively, he approves it as the institutional scheme which allows conflicts in

[4] *The Open Society and Its Enemies*, rev. 5th ed. (London, 1966), I, 111.
[5] *Ibid.*, II, 141.

society to be resolved by rational argument and persuasion rather than by violent coercion. If an anti-democrat were to argue that in practice rational argument does not play a large and decisive role in democratic politics, Popper would no doubt reply that democracy, according to him, only *allows* for it. He has not claimed that democracy ensures it. He might go on to claim that authoritarian government excludes it.

Popper does not directly confront the problem posed by Mill and Tocqueville of the possible degeneration of democracy into majority tyranny. In an essay on the subject in *Conjectures and Refutations* he is critical of public opinion, however, if it is regarded as the ultimate seat of political authority. Public opinion is never as unanimous as its singular name might suggest; since it is anonymous it is irresponsible; the majority is not always right, it may be neither well-intentioned nor prudent. His endorsement of democracy is consistently minimal: it is the least evil form which that necessary evil the state can take. "Only democracy provides an institutional framework that permits reform without violence, and so the use of reason in political matters." [6]

In particular, Popper expressly abjures the claim that democracy will necessarily choose the best policies. Its virtue, for him, is that it is the style of government which will most probably and most rapidly correct bad ones. He is hostile generally to any inference from the indubitable fact of natural human inequalities to the conclusion that some elite should be authoritatively empowered to rule. The reason for this is his conviction that knowledge is at once imperfect and social. The truly intellectually superior man is he who knows how little he knows rather than the sage gifted with esoteric insight; a Socratic fallibilist, not a Platonic shaman. Anyone, however specially gifted, may err, and the only way in which sound knowledge may grow is through the social give and take of unrestricted critical discussion. Popper goes on to draw the rather large conclusion that "institutions for the selection of the outstanding can hardly be devised." Virtuoso rulers will naturally select obedient drudges as their successors. This may be appropriate for a society dedicated to the Platonic programme of arresting all change, but not

[6] *Ibid.*, I, 4.

for anyone who believes that there are defects in society which can and should be eliminated.

With regard to the prime liberal ideals, then, Popper is a consistent pluralist. Neither liberty nor democracy is an absolute good; indeed he argues that attempts to formulate unlimited principles of freedom, tolerance, or democracy are logically paradoxical. Freedom, if it is to be fairly distributed and even worth having, requires a measure of intervention by the state and thus at least local or partial limitation of freedom.

Before going on to consider this thesis of the paradoxical nature of absolute political principles, brief mention should be made of what Popper has to say about the nature and functions of the state. His distaste for essentialism, and for the obsession that flows from it with definitions and the meaning of words, rules out his giving an account of the "essential nature" of the state. But he is prepared to answer the questions: "What do we demand from a state? What do we propose to consider as the legitimate aim of state activity? Why do we prefer living in a well-ordered state to living without a state, i.e. in anarchy?" [7] The answer he gives is that he wants protection for his freedom and other people's freedom, or again, protection against aggression from other men. He goes on: "I am perfectly ready to see my own freedom of action somewhat curtailed by the state, provided I can obtain protection of that freedom which remains." [8]

The prominence of Popper's references to freedom in this passage suggests that its equal distribution and protection is the main service he demands from the state and, also, that he equates the protection of freedom with security against aggression. But only if the concept of freedom is taken so widely as to embrace all sorts of things that it would be more natural to call by other names can freedom be regarded as the prime victim of aggression. Locke's other two values, life and property, are just as much the object of aggressive violence as freedom. Security of life and property are just as much ingredients of the well-ordered state that Popper demands as "freedom" in any ordinary sense of the word. Indeed, security, for other things besides freedom, seems to be more fundamental than freedom itself.

[7] *Ibid.*, I, 109.
[8] *Ibid.*, I, 110.

The potential for conflict between the requirements of freedom and security is not really dispelled by Popper's assertion that "there is no freedom that is not secured by the state; and conversely, only a state that is controlled by free citizens can offer them any reasonable security at all." [9] Popper here tends to make use of his anti-essentialism as a licence for a degree of imprecision which obscures important problems and conflicts. Political beliefs, according to Popper, are not certifiable by any form of intellectual intuition. To the extent that they are evaluative they are not verifiable propositions at all, but demands or proposals. To the extent that they assert or assume causal connections in the social domain, they are conjectural and are only rational in so far as they have been exposed to the social process of critical discussion. Most political convictions embody both evaluation and beliefs about social causation, the relation of means to ends in social action. In putting forward the thesis that certain types of absolute political principle are paradoxical, a further limitation is implied on, as it were, the logical form of such principles. To avoid paradox we must not say "X ought always to be done" but, much less categorically "in most circumstances X is probably the best thing to do."

The principles that Popper holds to be paradoxical are sovereignty, democracy, freedom, and tolerance. In fact they make up two closely related pairs. The principle of democracy is a special case of the principle of sovereignty; tolerance is logically connected with freedom, being abstention from interference with it in its intellectual and personal forms.

In what way are these principles paradoxical? A principle of sovereignty—for example, the democratic one: *the people at large should have absolute political power*—allows for the possibility that the people may exercise its power by assigning its sovereignty to a tyrant. This is not a point that is original with Popper. It lies behind the insistence of many traditional definitions of sovereignty on its inalienability. A practical recognition of this liability to mishap is made by systems of law which distinguish constitutional laws from laws of other kinds. The principle of sovereignty gives the central core of the constitution, and the law-making power which it assigns does not extend to

[9] *Ibid.*, I, 111.

the constitution itself. (Normally, of course, some provision is made for amendment of the constitution, but the distinction becomes otiose if the amending authority is not in some way different from the ordinary law-making sovereign.)

This has its merits as a practical device, although it is not indispensable. There is no such distinction in the legal and political arrangements of Britain. It is, however, intellectually unsatisfactory. Whatever reason there may be for assigning authority for making positive laws to a person or group will equally be a reason for giving them authority over the constitution. If the people at large are more qualified than anyone else to make laws in general, how can the founding fathers of a previous age be regarded as specially qualified to draw up just one particular set of laws?

Principles of sovereignty of an unrestricted sort are only paradoxical in a fairly weak sense. Consider a full-blooded logical paradox: "this statement is false," where the intended reference of the phrase "this statement" is to the very statement in which it occurs. If we suppose it to be true, it follows that it is false; if we suppose that it is false, it follows that it is true. An unrestricted principle of sovereignty does not even entail its own falsity. It entails only the potentially inconsistent conditional "if the sovereign says someone other than he should be sovereign, that someone, and not he, should be sovereign." It would be better to describe such principles not as simply paradoxical, but as potentially self-refuting.

The logical defects of the principles of unlimited freedom and tolerance are even less formal. Popper's point is that if everyone is left absolutely free of control by the government then the strong will be able to oppress and enslave the weak, and there will be less freedom all round. The solution to this puzzle is surely that since freedoms are competitive, since one man's freedom is another man's bondage, there can be no such thing as absolute freedom for all. In particular, freedom is not going to be maximised by leaving people free to diminish the freedom of others.

Popper concludes that tolerance should not be extended to the intolerant. But what is tolerance and who are the intolerant? There are very real problems about the application of this forthright-looking principle. Intolerance can take many forms.

At its mildest it is a matter of believing that certain things should not be allowed, should, perhaps, be forbidden by law; and giving reasoned expression to these beliefs. Next there is the stage at which people are incited to prevent the disliked activities by non-legal violence or the threat of it. Finally there is the situation in which the intolerant have, constitutionally or otherwise, acquired control of the state and make and enforce intolerant laws. Popper maintains that if the final possibility is realised it is reasonable to use violence so as to put state power back in tolerant hands. As for the second possibility, since it involves violence, the threat of it, or incitement thereto, it is not only non-legal but illegal. One does not have to adopt an essentialist view of Max Weber's definition of the state in terms of its monopoly of legitimate violence to suppose that any adequate legal system will prohibit all but the most marginal kinds of violence not positively authorized by the state—for example, for immediate self-defence against physical assault. Non-legal violence is forbidden because it is violence and not because of its object. Violent intolerance is on the same footing as violent theft.

But what of the first possibility, that of merely intellectual intolerance? Would Popper have thought the Weimar Republic justified in banning *Mein Kampf*? There is surely something to be said for letting the enemies of freedom come out into the open. It is even more important, for the sake of freedom, to put the onus of forbidding free expression very firmly on the intending suppressors and not to license intervention generally against anything about which a charge of intolerance can be contrived.

An interesting feature of *The Open Society* is the extent to which it reflects the political experience of Central Europe in the years between the wars. Popper concludes many of his chapters on Marx with illustrations from the melancholy history of that time and place. In this connection he discusses the problem of international security as it presented itself at that time and states his belief that the aggressive criminality of nations, taken as natural by Hobbes and exulted in by Hegel, could be controlled by an extension of the methods by which nation-states keep crime under a measure of control within their own borders.

To help justify this belief he argues against the idea that the nation is an especially real or natural community. Of Wilson's principle of national self-determination he says, "how anybody who had the slightest knowledge of European history, of the shifting and mixing of all kinds of tribes . . . could ever have put forward such an inapplicable principle is hard to understand." [10] He goes on: "even if anyone knew what he meant when he spoke of nationality, it would be not at all clear why nationality should be accepted as a fundamental political category, more important, for instance, than religion, or birth within a certain geographical region, or loyalty to a dynasty, or a political creed like democracy." [11]

It is natural that the concept of nationality should seem particularly indeterminate to a German-speaking Austrian, born under the Hapsburg Empire, and coming to maturity in the truncated Austrian republic created by the treaty of Versailles. But for all the difficulty of supplying a clear and explicit criterion for the concept (a fact which should not be all that discreditable to the anti-essentialist Popper), it remains a large and emotionally important feature of most people's notion of themselves. Whatever forms of international organisation men are led by political and economic prudence to develop, it seems certain that the bricks out of which the construction is built will be nation-states.

There is a great deal more to *The Open Society* than has been discussed here. The greater part of the book is devoted to the interpretation and criticism of Plato and Marx, carried out with the greatest scholarly thoroughness and, at least as far as Plato is concerned, with epoch-making originality. There are important developments of Popper's general theory about the nature and growth of scientific knowledge as applied to the social sciences and history. There are numerous parenthetical discussions of the greatest interest of philosophy, education, the relations of morality and religion, and of the tradition of irrationalism in post-Kantian German thought.

As a contribution to political theory the importance of the work seems to me to be twofold. In the first place, it carries fur-

[10] *Ibid.*, I, 50–51.
[11] *Ibid.*, I, 51.

ther the project of supplying empirical foundations for democratic liberalism, beyond the point to which Mill brought it, in much the same way as Mill advanced from the only abstract or formal empiricism of Bentham and his father. The instrument of this important revision is Popper's correction of Mill's theory of the nature of scientific knowledge. For any utilitarian, political justification is necessarily based on knowledge of the social consequences of human actions. Bentham acknowledged this principle, but relied in practice on nothing more than the psychological common sense of the Enlightenment. Mill saw that the social sciences would have to provide the required knowledge of consequences and recognized that that knowledge would take a much more complex and tentative form than the naive proverbial wisdom thought sufficient by his utilitarian forebears. Popper's aim is directly continuous with Mill's, and the measure of his superiority to Mill in this respect is that of the superiority of the *Logik der Forschung* to Mill's *System of Logic*. This would be enough to make *The Open Society* a really substantial addition to the liberal canon.

Second, although in the earlier part of this essay I have questioned the closeness of the connection between the historicism it is Popper's main object to refute, and the anti-liberal or totalitarian politics of this century, I should not deny that there is a connection between them. Ideologies typically ground social and political valuations in general theories about the universe, human nature, or society and its history. In our age social and historical foundations for ideologies have, through the influence of Hegel and Marx, come to prevail over cosmological or psychological ones. Large historicist theories have not, I think, been as positively productive of totalitarian ideologies as Popper suggests. But those that have, in the circumstances of our epoch, supplanted the law of inevitable progress of nineteenth-century liberal optimism, have created the presumption that the liberal experiment is doomed to fail. If blind faith in progress has turned out to be an error, Popper has shown that its opposite is no better founded.

Bertrand de Jouvenel:
Efficiency and Amenity

by CARL SLEVIN

Bertrand de Jouvenel's interest in political theory derives from his efforts to improve political and economic organisation rather than from academic contemplation. He was deeply concerned with the turmoil of American and European events in the wake of the First World War. As a foreign correspondent he journeyed through the United States in 1933 to report on the effects of the depression; in 1936 he interviewed both Hitler and Mussolini. It is not surprising, therefore, that his work bears little trace of the intellectual isolation characteristic of so much French thought since the late 1920s.[1]

Jouvenel's reputation as a political theorist rests mainly upon four books published since the end of the Second World War: *On Power, Sovereignty, The Pure Theory of Politics,* and *The Art of Conjecture.*[2] They belong to the great tradition of political philosophy from Plato to Marx after its supposed demise at the hands of the neopositivists. *Sovereignty,* in particular, was an important indication of the tradition's continued vitality in the mid-1950s and was received as such. Those who believed political philosophy to be a significant area praised the book, sometimes extravagantly; those who did not, simply ig-

---

[1] See H. Stuart Hughes, *The Obstructed Path* (New York, 1966), pp. 1–18.

[2] *Du pouvoir* (Geneva, 1945), published in English as *On Power,* trans. J. F. Huntingdon (London and New York, 1948); *De la souveraineté* (Paris, 1955), trans. J. F. Huntingdon as *Sovereignty* (Cambridge, 1957); *The Pure Theory of Politics* (Cambridge, 1963), written in English; and *L'art de la conjecture* (Monaco, 1964), trans. N. Lary as *The Art of Conjecture* (London, 1967). All page references are to the English editions.

nored it.[3] All four books tend to be unsystematic and exploratory in varying degrees, seeking to display every side of the questions examined rather than to reach final conclusions about closely defined topics. They were not written as parts of an integrated system; but together they present a sophisticated general analysis of politics and relate this view to the kinds of decisions which actually face contemporary societies.

The basis of Jouvenel's thought is a dual conception of human nature. Man has a capacity for changing himself and his environment, but this capacity tends to conflict with his need for physical and psychological stability. Jouvenel's political theory seeks to show how a satisfactory balance may be achieved, combining the maximum degree of improvement in human life with the minimum of disruption.

The difficulty involved in achieving this balance is most obvious in Jouvenel's work on economics, and he examined this aspect of the question in his first book, *L'économie dirigée*,[4] as early as 1928. Here he denounces the unregulated market economy because the mechanism by which it is supposed to ensure efficient production and low prices is self-destructive. Under this system, enterprises which do not compete successfully are eliminated or taken over by their more efficient rivals. Gradually, the number of firms in any sector is reduced until so few remain that they can fix an inflated level of profits by agreeing price and output policies amongst themselves and preventing the entry of new competition. Once dominant, such firms tend to discourage innovation. The system is plagued by periodic crises and mass unemployment. This rejection of a free market system did not lead Jouvenel to embrace central planning, for he thought it differed only marginally in results from its supposed opposite. To try and plan a whole economy is so complex a task that it cannot be done without immense waste and inefficiency. It removes the danger of unemployment only by abolishing the individual's freedom to choose his type and place of work. Although property is collectively owned, the relationship

---

[3] Possibly the most ecstatic review was published in the *Times Literary Supplement*, 18 October 1957, and refers to *Sovereignty* as "a great work of political philosophy which . . . must be firmly placed in the ranks of the masters."

[4] *L'économie dirigée* (Paris, 1928); originally published as articles in the monthly *Notre Temps* between October 1927 and June 1928.

between workers and managers does not differ significantly from that of the market economy. Thus, the theoretical advantages of both systems are far outweighed by their shortcomings in practice. Consumers suffer from the failure to encourage and utilise innovations which would secure maximum quantity and quality of output and from the fact that their preferences are not reflected in what is produced. Workers suffer complete subjection to machines and overseers and are always under the threat of unemployment or of arbitrarily imposed mobility. Most serious of all in the long run, neither system shows any concern for the future—wasting natural resources and destroying the environment, haphazardly but very effectively.

The way to avoid all these evils is to institute what Jouvenel calls the "guided economy." [5] According to this conception, the processes of production and distribution are to remain in (or be restored to) the hands of independent entrepreneurs, but within a framework provided by the state and enforced through its fiscal and monetary powers. The state would guarantee minimum wages and conditions by distributing government orders and allowing credit facilities to entrepreneurs who upheld or exceeded those levels and by withholding them from those who did not. Similarly, the state would undertake guidance of consumption patterns, encouraging some sectors of the economy to grow and others to decline, using criteria other than profit or crude maximization of output. Within each sector of production, support would be given to new entrants and to technical innovators against the attempts of established firms to stifle them. Overall demand, and consequently the level of employment, would be maintained at a high level by careful management of taxation and public expenditure. Altogether, Jouvenel wishes to create a system in which individual enterprise, stimulated by the desire to accumulate property, would ensure the most efficient and rapidly expanding production, under the guidance of a central authority concerned both with the good of society as a whole and of each member individually, as against the claims of organised interests. Extended from the economic sphere, the view expressed in *L'économie dirigée* summarises

---

[5] This is the nearest translation of *L'économie dirigée*, which is certainly not to be rendered as the "planned economy."

Jouvenel's notion of the proper function of the state in relation to individuals and groups although many important questions which he has since examined in detail are only hinted at or are altogether absent. The starting point for Jouvenel's mature political theory was the Second World War, which provided the theme of *On Power* and led to his stay in Switzerland, between 1943 and 1945, thus affording him the leisure to write his book. In *On Power* Jouvenel explains how and why central governments have continually tended to increase the extent and intensity of their control over the societies of Western Europe and the United States. The best index of this development is the growing scale of warfare, so that Jouvenel can use the Second World War, uppermost in the minds of his readers when the book was published, as a striking illustration of his argument. If conflict occurs between states, the degree of destruction will vary with the extent to which the governments can command the resources of society. The growth of centralized power, however beneficent its original purpose, is therefore extremely dangerous. Some commentators, concentrating on this polemic to the exclusion of all else, have seen Jouvenel as no more than an outdated liberal.[6]

In fact, although Jouvenel's approach to problems of politics and social freedom shows a certain kinship with the ideas of, for example, Benjamin Constant and Alexis de Tocqueville, his own work unmistakably deals with the contemporary situation. Even *On Power*, which gave rise to the misunderstanding, contains not only the attack on governmental expansion and centralization, but also a recognizable if incomplete statement of the political philosophy developed and refined in his three other major works. The four books differ widely as to content, but the underlying approach is the same throughout so that a detailed chronological analysis is unnecessary. While *The Art of Conjecture* develops a particular facet of Jouvenel's political philosophy, *Sovereignty* and *The Pure Theory of Politics* be-

[6] For example: Judith N. Shklar, *After Utopia* (Princeton, 1957), pp. 236, 248; Jean Touchard, *Histoire des idées politiques* (Paris, 1959), II, 825–26; J. P. Mayer, *Political Thought in France*, 3rd ed. (London, 1961), p. 142; David Kettler, "The Politics of Social Change," in *The Bias of Pluralism*, ed. William E. Connolly (New York, 1969), pp. 229–30.

tween them present the system as a whole, and attention will therefore be centred on them.

The best starting point is Jouvenel's view of the human condition, contained in his "axioms of man." [7] Human beings develop in the structured environment provided by the society into which they are born. Experience of this structure starts from the narrowest and most intimate links with parents or their substitutes and increases over time until the individual's capacity to relate to ever wider circles is exhausted. The individual's modes of thought and action, and his notions of right and wrong, result from the structure in which he grows up and the way in which he reacts to it. His reaction, however, is not determinate. He is free to choose between the alternatives with which he has become familiar, and his actions cannot be predicted with certainty. Given this freedom, he is open to the promptings of others seeking to influence his behaviour and can himself try to influence them. Finally, because he is free and because he can hope to influence the actions of others, he projects images of the future in the hope of being able to secure their realization.

The basic duality of human nature can therefore be characterised as, on the one hand, a will to power and on the other, a desire for social security.[8] Ability to control others is the means by which an individual can hope to bring about the changes he would like to see. Stability guarantees that what he enjoys in the existing situation will not be taken from him as a result of changes effected by others. All men partake of both characteristics to a certain extent though some are dominated by one and some by the other.

Not only individuals but also the patterns of group life which they form within societies can be analysed in terms of the dichotomy. Jouvenel distinguishes two models of groups at opposite extremes, one of which embodies man's conservative tendency and the other his potential for change.[9]

The most basic example of the first model is "the hearth" or domestic group—held together by ties of parenthood, mar-

---

[7] *Pure Theory*, pp. 46–47. The main references in Jouvenel's other major works are *Sovereignty*, pp. 33, 41–70, 220; *Conjecture*, pp. 3–11, 25–32.

[8] *Power*, p. 12.

[9] *Sovereignty*, pp. 56–59, 62–67.

riage, and adoption—in which children are brought up and (typically though not invariably) the aged are preserved. This kind of group is characterised by inequality and stability, for the very young and the very old are incapable of providing for themselves and depend upon the completely regular and dependable support of active adults. But the necessities of sustenance do not entirely explain the character of hearth groups. The child's originally enforced obedience gradually becomes the tendency to accept willingly the suggestions of others, which is the basis of all human cooperation whether aimed at conservation or change. Jouvenel's analysis is incomplete and somewhat confusing because he deals with this model solely in terms of the family example. In fact, the model is inadequate for Jouvenel's purposes if it does not include all groups which seek to maintain and exploit existing situations.

The second model, "the team of action," is dealt with in general terms and is not reduced to a particular example. It is the direct opposite of the first model, for its aim is not living and consuming together in stable conditions but deliberate modification of the *status quo* in a particular direction. It is held together by the conscious will of its founder and leader who, having conceived some project which he cannot realize unaided, draws together a number of his fellows to assist him in the task. All human progress is brought about by such active groups.

Jouvenel uses the dichotomy from a different point of view to classify various kinds of society. For this purpose, he considers the individual's "milieu of existence," the pattern of his relations with others.[10] At one extreme, in a primitive or closed society, the individual is known personally by all those with whom he has any contact and they all know each other. Such a society is necessarily small and isolated, for the capacity of individuals to know their fellows is limited and foreigners by definition stand outside the social structure. Because a primitive society is so closely knit in a physical sense, it forms an extremely coherent moral community where the actions of each are almost completely predictable in terms of norms accepted by all. The more closed or primitive a society is, the more it approximates

[10] *Ibid.*, pp. 1–2, 119–28, 136–38, 271–75; *Pure Theory*, pp. 59–61.

to the domestic group and the less it gives rise to teams of action. At the other extreme, is what Jouvenel calls an "open social network." Here, the individual is known by only a small proportion of his contacts and very few of them know each other. This kind of society tends to be large and outward looking. Its own heterogeneity means that foreigners do not appear to threaten its diffuse moral order, and the actions of its members are no longer predictable except where legal sanctions are applied to secure uniformity. Jouvenel sees Rousseau and Hobbes as the outstanding modern advocates of closed and open societies respectively. In his view, both of them base their theories on incomplete models of human nature: Rousseau omitting man's will to change; Hobbes, his desire for emotional (as opposed to legal) security. Jouvenel's own work seeks to combine the advantages of both, retaining the open society's potential for progress while salvaging as much of the moral coherence of the closed society as possible.[11]

What holds these various groups and societies together? In all cases, "authority," which Jouvenel defines as the ability of some men to rally the wills and direct the actions of others.[12] Authority can take either a natural or a juristic form and, in *Sovereignty*, Jouvenel refers to these as *de facto* and *de jure* authority respectively. In *The Pure Theory of Politics*, he abandons this usage and calls the two notions "authority" and "Authority," with only a capital letter to distinguish them. This is confusing and as there seems to be no good reason for it, the earlier terminology will be used here. Authority *de facto* is, as its name indicates, a matter of fact. If some obey another because they respect him and are willing to comply with a proposal because he is its author, they are accepting his authority in the *de facto* sense. If, on the other hand, they obey not simply through personal loyalty, but because they accept a pre-existing framework of rules which identifies the holder of authority and delimits his

---

[11] *Sovereignty*, pp. 123–28, 231–40. Jouvenel has written several pieces on Rousseau, the most important of which is a prefatory essay to his edition of *Du contrat social* (Geneva, 1947), and they have earned him the respect of leading Rousseau scholars. See, for example, C. W. Hendel, *Jean-Jacques Rousseau, Moralist*, 2nd ed. (New York, 1962), pp. ix–x; and Judith N. Shklar, *Men and Citizens* (Cambridge, 1969), p. 230.

[12] *Sovereignty*, pp. 29–31, 71–84; *Pure Theory*, pp. 99–101, 118–28.

sphere of competence, he may be said to exercise *de jure* authority. The state [13] is the only organization through which full *de jure* authority can be exercised; other groups give rise only to quasi *de jure* authority. The difference arises not because of the state's legal monopoly of the legitimate use of force, for that explains obedience in very few cases; [14] but rather because membership of it alone is involuntary. Acceptance of state authority forms part of an overall socialization process and does not normally involve deliberate choice. Recognition of the authority of other associations is normally a matter of choice, and disobedience is ultimately no more than withdrawal of that recognition.

Because *de jure* authority is defined beforehand by its framework of rules, it tends to be static in operation and conservative in effect. *De facto* authority, on the other hand, is essentially dynamic and progressive, setting its own bounds at the moment it is brought into play. Sometimes, however, either of the two kinds of authority may adopt the character of the other. To deal with this, Jouvenel distinguished the preserving from the innovating authority (*de facto* or *de jure*), calling the one *rex* and the other *dux*. The balance between them is the chief subject of political science in his view.[15]

There is no more than a vague connexion in terms of meaning between Jouvenel's concepts of preserving and innovating authorities and the Latin words he uses to designate them. *Rex*, usually translated as "king," was applied to the seven (absolute) kings of Rome before the Republic and later to subordinate kings within the Empire. *Dux* meant general or military leader with absolute power within the commission granted him by the king or the senate and people or the emperor. Jouvenel comes closest to these usages when he traces the origin of the separate preserving and innovating authorities to certain primitive tribal societies,[16] where the head priest may be identified as *rex* and the warrior chief as *dux*. The *rex* medi-

---

[13] "State" is used to translate Jouvenel's term "Pouvoir," by which he means: "l'ensemble des éléments gouvernementaux." *Power*, p. xiii.

[14] Jouvenel, "Authority: The Efficient Imperative," in *Authority*, ed. C. J. Friedrich (Cambridge, Mass., 1958), p. 161.

[15] *Sovereignty*, p. 298.

[16] *Power*, pp. 83–84; *Sovereignty*, pp. 98–99.

ates between society and its gods, acting as a lightning conductor against their possible displeasure by means of the appropriate rituals. In particular, he authorizes and sanctifies the *dux*, whose actions would otherwise call down divine wrath upon the people. In secular terms, the *rex* bestows *de jure* authority in a ceremonial procedure intended to instil into the *dux* his duty to act in the general interest. The ritual and its effect upon the manner in which the *dux* rules gives his *de facto* authority the legitimacy it previously lacked.

Only in primitive societies, where the *rex/dux* dichotomy is institutionalized, can the terms be used to classify, not different types of authority, but actual individuals wielding it. Nevertheless, Jouvenel sometimes seems to use them in this way for more complex societies where there is no such clear distinction.[17] St. Louis, giving judgement under the oak at Vincennes, is contrasted with Napoleon, leading his troops into action at the Bridge of Arcola, but this is not meant to classify one as pure *rex* and the other as pure *dux*.[18] It is a striking image of the contrast between the two functions and, as is often the case with Jouvenel's historical examples, must be seen as a forceful illustration rather than an addition of substance to the argument.

Not only may the same person carry out both *dux* and *rex* functions to some extent, but any society beyond the most primitive will contain many people exercising one or both of them. A few of these will do so in the name of the state—that is to say, with *de jure* authority. Although Jouvenel denies that there is a qualitative difference between state *duces* and *reges* and others, he pays special attention to the way in which the state carries out its share of the two functions. In *On Power*, indicating that his view at that time was provisional,[19] Jouvenel equates the functions with what he sees as the dual nature of the modern state: egoistic on the one hand as *dux;* concerned with the social good on the other as *rex*. As *duces*, governments seek to extend their power both for the fruits it will yield and for its own

---

[17] This usage was pointed out by Roy Pierce, *Contemporary French Political Thought* (London, 1966), pp. 196–97, who regards it as a substantive confusion on Jouvenel's part.

[18] *Sovereignty*, pp. 40–41.

[19] *Power*, p. 83.

sake. This is not merely a case of plundering subjects for material gain, although that could indeed be one of the aims. Rather, Jouvenel sees it as a reflection of the desire of every man to extend his personality by organising others in order to realise his visions of the future. Depending upon the visions, such egoism on the part of the state may benefit society, but the dangers are very great. The most extreme and typical form taken by governmental egoism is war, of which the benefits are always uncertain, but the costs, in both economic and human terms, inevitable. Although it may be possible to curb the dangers, there is no way of eliminating egoism without destroying the state, for "in the order of nature everything dies which is not sustained by an intense and brutal love of self." [20]

The state's concern for the social good is at first a direct consequence of its egoism. Exploitation is only possible, let alone worthwhile, if a society is at least collectively wealthy, and the satisfaction of command increases with the size of the operation. The state can thus be led by pure egoism to encourage the population it controls to grow and to prosper, but, in so doing, it tends to develop a genuine concern for its subjects apart from selfish considerations. When its actions are the result of such concern, the state is acting as *rex*, according to Jouvenel's definition in *On Power*. The difference between the two functions is therefore one of motivation rather than of actual tasks. Beyond this, Jouvenel says little, in *On Power*, about the state as *rex* and simply lists order, justice, security, and property as matters which should concern it.[21] His treatment of *dux* deals only with warfare and acquisition of the means to wage it. For a more complete—and considerably modified—treatment of the *dux/rex* dichotomy, we must turn to *Sovereignty* and *The Pure Theory of Politics*.

In these two later works, Jouvenel classified *dux* and *rex* in terms of the effect of the actions of authorities (*de facto* or *de jure*) upon society, divided between those which bring about change and those which maintain the existing order and integrate changes into it smoothly, avoiding overall disruption. As far as the state is concerned, the *rex* function of preservation

[20] *Ibid.*, p. 120.
[21] *Ibid.*, p. 109.

and adjustment is the more basic of the two,[22] for if it is not carried out effectively, society would quickly become chaotic. On the other hand, an excessively effective sovereign *rex* would, while it lasted, have a stultifying effect preventing all change.

Despite Jouvenel's explicit denial, a significant distinction between state and society does emerge from his treatment of the state's functioning as *rex*. It falls into three parts. First, the state adjudicates between disputants and attempts to restore situations which it decides have been unjustly disturbed. Second, it chooses between various changes advocated by social *duces* and encourages those which it regards as just and practicable, supporting them against groups trying to maintain the *status quo*. Third, it legitimizes those changes brought about *de facto* without its encouragement, if it comes to regard them as just after the event. This role as arbitrator between the *dux* and *rex* elements in society seems to put the state on a higher level: it appears to turn into a kind of super-*rex*, guiding social *reges* and *duces* so that they continue to balance each other, providing a stable but nevertheless progressive society. The *rex* function is thus extremely complex and raises the difficult and fundamental question: what is justice?[23] The state must know the answer so that it can choose between the conflicting claims of the various social *duces* and *reges*.

Jouvenel rejects the idea that justice is a static quality of particular social arrangements which somehow ensure that everything is shared out with perfect fairness. Such a view is quite unreliable because it takes no account of the dynamic nature of society. Instead he accepts the ancient and medieval notion of justice as an attribute of human will, a constant determination to render every man his due. This formulation provides clear directions in particular cases only in a stable situation where an established right has been infringed and it is simply a question of returning things to their previous state. Where substantial and frequent changes are taking place, however, innovators will seek to create new rights and to adjust those already established to fit in with new developments. In such a case, every man's

[22] *Sovereignty,* p. 53.
[23] *Ibid.,* pp. 139–65.

due must be discovered before it can be maintained or restored, and there is little likelihood of agreement unless those concerned feel closely united for the achievement of a common purpose. Such a feeling might well exist in a closed, morally homogeneous and static society; but it is not expected in a dynamic open social network except in extreme cases such as the prosecution of war.

The difficulty of deciding what is just in a rapidly changing environment would vanish if justice were no more than obedience to rules emanating from a legitimate source whatever their nature happened to be. Jouvenel rejects this solution and admits that there can be no certainty of complete agreement in any particular case, even among completely disinterested and well-meaning judges. In his view, however, such judges would share a common approach, seeing justice as the distribution of whatever is to be shared out in accordance with some relevant criterion. For example, if size of family rather than output is considered to be the relevant criterion in the allotment of wages, then someone whose family is twice as large as that of another should receive twice as much in wages even though he produces only half as much. A proper understanding of the situation and the criterion applicable should leave no room for dispute. Selection of a criterion, however, is not determinate. The requirement of relevance restricts quite narrowly what would otherwise be an infinite choice, although its boundaries are by no means fixed. Within the limits of relevance, selection depends upon the arbiter's own choice between the various alternatives. Returning to our example, colour of hair or expertise at poker would be quite irrelevant, except for rare occupations. On the other hand, size of family, product per worker, or hours worked would all seem relevant under normal conditions; and from different points of view, each would produce a just result.

One important distinction which can be made between different opinions about relevant criteria reflects Jouvenel's classification of groups into progressive and conservative types. Anything to be shared out may well become the object of competition between these two types of groups. The first type will see the resources involved as means to action; the second, as means for satisfying existing wants directly. Further, the way in which any group uses the resources it has obtained will vary in accordance with its type. A progressive group will distribute its resources so as to maximize the chances of producing the changes it desires: the problem of choosing the relevant criterion is automatically solved because members of the group support the common purpose. For a conservative group, on the other hand, a criterion is not automatically indicated and must still be chosen.

In fact, there are a number of different but equally "just" distributions in any situation, and there is no objective way of putting them in order from best to worst unless a decision is made beforehand about precisely what should be achieved. Selection of the relevant criterion allows a just distribution to be made, but this does not mean that it will satisfy everyone. The existence of claims for resources which simply cannot be met is the essence of politics for Jouvenel. There is no such thing as a "political problem," for the concepts indicated by the two words have nothing to do with one another. Problems can be solved perfectly, as in the case of determinate algebraic equations. Politics implies decisions to satisfy some people and, inevitably, to disappoint others.[24] Nevertheless, having regard to the social context, meaningful debate about the merits of different distributions can take place, and the decisions reached should be generally acceptable in a society where public discussion is free and influential.

Given that justice consists of choosing amongst various relevant criteria and applying the one (or the combination) chosen, the extent of the state's functioning as *rex* still has to be determined. Despite some changes of emphasis, Jouvenel's basic attitude has remained much the same since he produced his scheme for the guided economy in the late 1920s. He has always believed that the state cannot possibly regulate the distribution of everything in society with any hope of success because of the magnitude and complexity of the task. Most of the process of distribution is much better split into an infinity of small units, each handled by the groups directly concerned and best able to understand their particular part of it. The main function of the state is to settle disputes when groups come into conflict with each other or with the interests of society as a

---

[24] *Pure Theory*, pp. 204–12.

whole. This role requires the state to possess three qualities: it must desire justice; it must know how to discover it; and it must be able to impose its decisions upon those who dissent.[25]

The decisions of the state, however, will appear to be definitive only in an almost static society where justice is embodied in established usage. Elsewhere, the state must direct itself to the future, attempting to discern the direction in which the ideas of justice are evolving so that its decisions will retain their validity for as long as possible. Since he wrote *Sovereignty*, Jouvenel has become aware of a need to extend the area of state activity beyond its rectifying and stabilizing role as *rex*, towards the active leadership and creativity of *dux*. As a by-product of increased output, the use of technological developments tends to cause unplanned and often unforeseen changes, mostly detrimental, in the environments of advanced societies. In view of this, the state must not only control the groups concerned; it must choose the most desirable direction and level of changes and ensure they are realized.[26] Although Jouvenel's categories of authority do not really cover the possibility, the state may be seen as a super- *dux*, on analogy with its role as super- *rex*. There is a parallel between Jouvenel's wish to direct the unruly economic system which produced the depression of the 1930s, and his concern to control damage to the environment now.[27]

In one sense, society itself may be taken as a means of reducing uncertainty about the course of future events. This is especially clear where custom rules the actions of men from one generation to the next and ensures that their expectations will be fulfilled. People who live in dynamic societies have not somehow ceased to need a guarantee against disturbances, but

[25] Jouvenel's concern with these qualities reflects his view of political life in France between the first and second world wars. One of the main reasons why he rejected parliamentary democracy in the Third Republic after 1934 was that in his opinion successive governments lacked all three qualities to a significant degree.

[26] Interview with M. de Jouvenel, 26 August 1971.

[27] In between, circumstances caused Jouvenel to be less keen to allow such an active role to the state. In *On Power*, as we have seen, his distrust of the state was at its height because of the war. By the time he wrote *Sovereignty*, the spectres of unemployment and stagnation had retreated before generally high levels of economic activity, and environmental questions had not yet assumed major proportions in his view.

they can no longer find it in a fixed pattern of traditions. As the rate of change and the accompanying insecurity increase, men tend to look more and more to the state for stability, thereby adding to its natural tendency to expand. The state can best fulfil this function by encouraging forecasts of the various possible ways in which society might be developed, choosing between them after wide consultation and then guaranteeing that the chosen policies will be carried out.[28]

In rapidly changing societies, forecasting is at least potentially significant in a number of ways apart from acting as the counterpart of custom in static societies. Within a governmental system, it is a prerequisite for ensuring that present decisions actually produce the results intended. Consciousness of this leads naturally to consideration of the varying effects of different governmental structures in preventing or encouraging such forecasting.[29] One possibly dangerous aspect of forecasting is that it may help men to gain or keep positions of power within a system. Since practitioners have long since mastered the techniques involved, however, there is little danger in developing the theory; and it may have the benefit of suggesting ways of controlling the actions of those who seek power.[30] Jouvenel has also delineated the mental habits upon which forecasting is based in order to reveal its potentialities and limitations.[31] Jouvenel himself recognizes that his work on forecasting may be dismissed as mere journalism in traditional academic circles,[32] but it is an integral part of his political theory which cannot be ignored without completely distorting the whole.

Forecasting does not imply that there can be knowledge of the future in the same sense as we know the past. The future is not determinate and can be foreseen only within a greater or lesser margin of probability. Jouvenel rejects astrological and any other deterministic views of the future because they deny the possibility that deliberate human action can change the

---

[28] *Conjecture*, pp. 237–49.

[29] Both these aspects are dealt with in *Le rôle de la prévision dans les affaires publiques* (Paris, 1965–66).

[30] *Pure Theory, passim*, especially pp. 29–40.

[31] *Conjecture*, pp. viii, 127, *passim;* "Prévision et action," *Analyse et prévision*, 9, no. 3 (March 1970), 178–84.

[32] *Futuribles: Essai sur l'art de la conjecture* (written by Jouvenel for the second Futurible Symposium held in Paris, 6–8 July 1963), p. 119.

course of events. For any agent, future events will be divided between those which can be affected by the agent's own action and those which cannot—the masterable future and the dominating future, in Jouvenel's terminology. What is dominating for one agent—a recession foreseen by an individual entrepreneur for example—may be masterable for another—the government which controls the economy in which he operates. Their ability to influence future events imposes upon the agents concerned a duty to consider the effect upon others, both now and in the future, as well as upon themselves. It is not true, of course, that all action is consciously directed to the future in this way; and Jouvenel distinguishes the action which is, denoted by the Latin word *ut*, from mere reaction to present circumstances, which he calls action *quia*. To encourage action *ut* to the maximum, Jouvenel proposed a plurality of forecasts about the effects that different actions would have. He classifies primary forecasts as those which suggest what will happen in any situation if no steps are taken to alter it; secondary forecasts list the outcomes conditional upon various specific kinds of action; tertiary forecasts attempt to predict the action which will actually be taken by those concerned in the light of primary and secondary forecasts.

Systematic forecasting is an extremely ancient activity, but until very recently governments restricted their use of it almost entirely to diplomatic and military affairs. The two world wars and the great depression in between, along with the example of Soviet planning, gave Western governments a glimmering of the need to take a wider view; but only in the last twenty years or so have they even begun to take forecasting seriously as a necessary part of decision making. Jouvenel has sought to encourage this view and to replace the essential antagonism and secrecy of forecasts connected with international struggles by social forecasting aimed at furthering progress through cooperation. Extended in this way, forecasting can no longer be the state's exclusive preserve; indeed, a wide selection of forecasts and forecasters, openly competing, is an essential part of the process. If the forecasts on which decisions are based are kept secret, neither their accuracy nor the appropriateness of the decisions can be judged, and government becomes a magical procedure to be carried out only by officially accredited sorcerers. However skilled the forecasters and the governors, there would be no chance of the state fulfilling the role allotted to it by Jouvenel, that of choosing among the multitude of legitimate claims made by different social groups. Jouvenel's desire to see an expansion of forecasting activities had been to some extent realised. In France, the Centre International de'Etudes Prospectives, set up in 1957 by Gaston Berger, was the first organisation concerned entirely with forecasting as a means of allowing rational choice between the various possible alternative futures. Since 1955 Jouvenel had been director of SEDEIS,[33] an organisation that published a small information weekly specializing in economic affairs. In 1960, with the help of the Ford Foundation, he was able to extend the interests of this organisation and associate many leading intellectuals with his scheme for social forecasting in the Comité International Futuribles.[34]

One especially important part of Jouvenel's concern with forecasting is his stress on the conservation or improvement of both natural and social aspects of the environment. His involvement with this issue dates from the 1930s, long before the present wave of interest appeared, and was at first part of his reaction against the productivist ethic of Stalin's five-year plans and the capitalism symbolized by Henry Ford. Production should not be simply a matter of maximising quantity output, and consumption should not be considered purely in terms of income directly expended by individual or household units. Quality is as important as quantity, and increasing household consumption tends to require an increasing rate of public expenditure. Jouvenel, thinking of the ancient world, goes so far as to define quality civilization in terms of the excellence of public amenities. The working and living conditions imposed upon the mass of men by the economic system need to be considered in a new light for real improvement to result.[35] Espe-

---

[33] Société d'Etudes et de Documentation Economiques, Industrielles et Sociales.

[34] SEDEIS-Futuribles France publishes two monthly periodicals, *Analyse et prévision* and *Chroniques d'actualité*, and a series of separate volumes, the Futuribles Collection. Since the termination of the Ford grant in 1965, the organization has been self-supporting.

[35] The same kind of attitude is revealed in *Le réveil de l'Europe* (Paris, 1937), pp. 219–20 and *Conjecture*, pp. 154–57.

cially in the most industrialized countries work tends to be completely cut off from any satisfaction for the worker, who does it purely for the wages he receives. Urban life centred on the factory leaves much to be desired and requires a special planning effort to remedy its disadvantages.[36] Beyond these considerations, there looms what is, in the long run, the greatest difficulty facing humanity in the twentieth century—the rate at which raw materials are being used up and the environment polluted and destroyed. Taking this into account, much so-called economic progress is merely long-term and grand-scale self-destruction. The technique of National Accounting [37] tends to hide these dangers because it includes only goods and services which are or could be exchanged in the market. It leaves out services freely given, external diseconomies of production, and natural resources used up. If taken into account, such factors would make a great deal of difference to the picture and the policies derived from it. In the light of forecasting, a large part of the efforts of technologists should henceforth be devoted to undoing the harm already done and to discovering methods of production which will fit into natural "ecosystems" instead of destroying them irretrievably.

Through the development of Jouvenel's political theory we have in a sense come full circle from the guided economy to an extended version which might be called, in another of his phrases, the "guided civilization." Let us now turn to Jouvenel's conception of the nature of political theory. Unfortunately he has never produced a fully developed argument about this subject, but he has written enough to provide a reasonably clear picture of his views in spite of some residual ambiguities.

Jouvenel sees three basic aspects of political science: configuration, consequence, and recommendation. The first is description and explanation of political situations at a particular

---

[36] *Arcadie: essais sur le mieux vivre* (Paris, 1968), *passim*, especially pp. 120–21; "Prospective économique," in *Problemes économiques de notre temps*, Jouvenel *et al.* (Paris, 1966), pp. 26–28.

[37] "Proposition à la Commission des Comptes de la Nation, 6 mai 1966," *Arcadie*, pp. 266–71. Jouvenel was specifically referring to the French situation—he was a member of the Commission from the mid-1950s to 1969—but his point is generally valid.

moment. The second deals with the evolution of configurations over a period. The third involves trying to point out the "right" course which ought to be followed by political actors.

The first two areas start out, in some sense, from "the facts." Jouvenel points out that even after a manageable number of observations have been chosen for investigation, they have no meaning or significance until they have been arranged in various classes and relationships posited between the classes.[38] In other words, non- or extra-factual considerations help to determine both the scope (in delimiting its boundaries) and the substance (in classifying the data and positing relations between its parts) of any investigation. This process provides a model of the topic in question, and the set of relations which compose it can thereafter be refined or altered by applying them to further sets of data and observing whether or not the framework remains suitable—another non-factual judgement. Because of the limitations of human intellect, such models must at first be formulated in very simple terms and then increased in complexity in the light of the knowledge gained at each stage. Once started, the process is (or should be) self-perpetuating in a progressive sense.

But while this is indeed the case with the natural sciences and with economics, political philosophers have failed to produce a representative theory which could be perfected over time. Instead, they have elaborated a series of normative theories, each of which is separately based and is independent of the others.[39] Instead of being representatives of reality (albeit with a degree of non-factual input), these theories present their authors' visions of how politics ought to be organised with little reference to what actually happens. Any approximations to representative political theory which have taken notice of reality have been of a low-level configurative type rather than the more sophisticated consequential type, describing once-for-all situations rather than providing dynamic models with predictive capabilities. While Jouvenel insists on the validity of the prescriptive (third) function of political science, he feels not only that it has been stressed to the disadvantage of the other two, but that

---

[38] *Pure Theory*, pp. xi, 30; "Invitation à la théorie politique pure," *Révue Internationale d'Histoire Politique et Constitutionelle*, June 1957, pp. 86–91.
[39] *Pure Theory*, p. 30; *Sovereignty*, p. 229.

they are essential to provide a reliable basis for prescriptions.[40] His aim in *The Pure Theory of Politics* is to provide the elements of a consequential representative theory as a contribution towards fulfillment of the second function of political science.[41] His reflections on why previous political scientists (in the broad sense indicated by Jouvenel's enumeration of the three functions) have not produced such a theory lead to his view of the ethical third function.

Political scientists have always been inhibited by the belief that political activity is inherently dangerous. They have therefore concentrated upon guiding politicians along the path of righteousness, rather than run the risk of allowing evil to be perpetrated with greater efficiency by showing how politicians actually operate.[42] Economists have escaped this difficulty, not because they disregard the moral consequences of their science, but because they are optimistic about its outcome, in the long term. Short-term evils are unfortunate but can be ignored because the overall tendency of economic activity is assumed to be beneficial.[43] Jouvenel, however, feels justified in producing such a potentially dangerous political theory because, negatively, those active in politics have not in fact been inhibited from developing "the technology of politics" outside political science, and, positively, such a theory could be useful in suggesting ways of curbing undesirable political activity.[44]

Although Jouvenel bemoans the almost complete triumph of prescriptive over representative political science in the past, and despite formulations which clearly separate one from the other,[45] the two are closely interrelated in his work. There is some tension between Jouvenel's views about the nature of political theory (chiefly expressed in *The Pure Theory of Politics*)

[40] *Ibid.*, p. 30; *Sovereignty*, p. 229.

[41] *Pure Theory*, pp. x, xi, 3–13.

[42] *Ibid.*, pp. 31, 35–37, 106. Jouvenel does not see this fear as the whole explanation. Political science has also been retarded (as was, he thinks, medical science in the 2,000 years prior to Harvey's discoveries) by a tendency to regard every pathological state as a deviation from an assumed condition of 'health.' This has prevented close study of the various kinds of 'disease.' *Ibid.*, pp. 38–40.

[43] *Ibid.*, pp. 33–34.

[44] *Ibid.*, p. 38.

[45] *Ibid.*, p. xi.

and the way in which his own political theory (including that of *The Pure Theory of Politics*) is actually formulated. On the one hand, he suggests that it is possible to undertake the configurative and consequential aspects of political science quite separately from that of recommendation—that is, to admit values only in so far as they affect the behaviour of those under scrutiny. On the other, his own theory is an amalgam of fact and value which cannot be separated without considerable distortion. Equally, Jouvenel's practice suggests that he rejects the idea of attempting the third function without the first and second, for he attacks the validity of theories based on *a priori* assumptions about man instead of observation of actual men. Despite his claim that *The Pure Theory of Politics* is concerned only to describe, it is in fact just as much of a mixture of fact and value as is *Sovereignty*, of which the subtitle, *An Inquiry into the Political Good*, is enough to indicate the ethical intent. Political science, in Jouvenel's view, is concerned with social cooperation, and social cooperation is not a matter of measurement and calculation but of moral feelings.[46]

It is possible to relate Jouvenel's theories quite closely to the problems which have faced French society since 1918. At the end of the war, the French economy, still dominated by peasant agriculture and family businesses of all sorts, was somewhat backward compared with those of the United States, Great Britain, and Germany. As a result, economic difficulties in France during the inter-war period differed somewhat from those of the other three advanced countries and centred on the transition to mass production which continues even today. Jouvenel's idea of the guided economy, which sought to combine industrial efficiency with traditional small-scale ownership, was intended partially as an answer to these problems. One particular feature of French society which Jouvenel first noticed in the economic sphere was a preference for letting things take their course, however disastrous that might be in the long run, rather than trying to plan deliberate changes for the better. His concern with social forecasting is clearly related to his dislike of this aspect of French conservatism. From a political standpoint, victory in the First World War gave to the Third Republic an air

[46] *Sovereignty*, p. 303.

of legitimacy and permanence that it had previously lacked. This lasted a few years but then wore off. Failure to obtain the expected reparations from Germany, diplomatic isolation, economic disorder, and suspicions of governmental corruption led eventually to the disturbances of 6 February 1934 and left considerable sections of French society dissatisfied, not just with a particular party or government, but with the whole system. After the Second World War, the Fourth Republic presented an amazing panorama of rapidly changing governments, none of which was strong enough to govern effectively. Jouvenel's ideal of society as a plurality of groups competing within a system of rules enforced by a firm central authority can be seen as a reaction to this anarchic tendency of French political life.

Behind these reactions to particular problems, however, lies Jouvenel's commitment to a doctrine of natural law. Nowhere does he provide anything like a full statement of his view, but he certainly believes that if different people honestly consider a question of justice, they will tend to produce very similar answers. The convergence of those answers implies the existence of a universal order of justice which can be perceived by all human beings if they are willing to make the effort.[47] Jouvenel bases the argument on theology, which once led Leonard Woolf to condemn him for avoiding difficulties by producing God much as a conjurer produces a rabbit out of a hat.[48] This is hardly fair because any view of human nature which is adequate for the construction of an overall political theory must involve some non-factual and non-logical propositions as a starting point. Jouvenel is a Roman Catholic and his picture of man has its roots in the personalist wing of liberal Catholicism.[49] Such explicit reference to theology is not frequent amongst British and American writers but is by no means unusual in Continental Europe.

[47] Ibid., 276–94.

[48] Political Quarterly, 29 (1958), 187.

[49] Personalism stresses the importance of the individual human being seen in all his aspects as a combination of matter and spirit and as a member of various kinds of groups, particularly his family, profession, and locality. In France today it is mainly associated with the name of Emmanuel Mounier and the journal he founded, Esprit, but it was originally the common property of various groups of youthful intellectuals set up between 1927 and 1932 to oppose the désordre établi of French society.

This combination of theology with practical considerations in Jouvenel's political theory makes it difficult to identify the style of discourse in which he is engaged. His career provides no answer, for he has been neither a member of the French academic establishment (until very recently at any rate) nor a practising politician. Yet his work is far too substantial to be labelled "journalistic" in British or American use. In France, however, there is a well-established tradition by which academics may quite normally write articles for newspapers and journalists may write books of an academic nature. In a real sense, such academics and journalists both belong to a recognisable intelligentsia of a kind that hardly exists in the English-speaking world. This may help to explain why many British and American political scientists have taken less notice of Jouvenel than they might have done, or have tended to patronize him as a brilliant but unsystematic amateur.

Jouvenel nevertheless retains considerable importance in the development of the study of politics since the Second World War. Apart from the substance of his thought, *Sovereignty* remains a landmark in the continuation of traditional political theory, written in direct opposition to the brash and self-conscious claims of the advocates of a narrow, positivistic "science."

Raymond Aron:
A Modern Classicist

by GHITA IONESCU

It is somewhat surprising to see that so little has been written until now about the political work of Raymond Aron. His writings are not only known to most practitioners of the social sciences and to the general public, but permeate academic thinking more than may be generally realised. Still, for various reasons, contemporaries seem to find it difficult to consider his work in broad perspective.

One reason may be that Aron's work is still in the making. Aron is particularly productive, indeed prolific, and his unusually diversified work includes articles and chronicles in newspapers and reviews, lectures and courses at the Sorbonne and now at the Collège de France, and ranges from short polemical books to magisterial treatises. Not only does the political observer have the sense of hearing Aron constantly in the background, but one also expects to listen to him directly at certain points in the rapidly developing politics of our time. (He was, for instance, particularly impressive before and during the events of 1968 in Paris, when his stern reasonableness brought upon him the vindictive attacks of the extreme *groupuscules*.) [1]

His is a characteristically "open" *oeuvre*, especially compared with the "closed" methodological system of, say, David Easton or the "closed" ideological system of Herbert Marcuse. These men, too, are our contemporaries, but they are already judged and interpreted in endless commentaries by fervent disciples or by virulent critics. This openness might well seem to be an advantage for Aron, the creative springs of whose work

[1] See his *La révolution introuvable* (Paris, 1968).

have not yet been channelled and diverted into authorized interpretations. He seems to have escaped until now the danger of exegetes who might distort his work.

Another reason why Aron's significance has not yet been generally interpreted is that it is densely inter-disciplinary. (Indeed, the first part of this essay is a reflection on how difficult it is to separate political science in Aron from history, sociology, and the rest.) Real inter-disciplinarism is that which emanates from the creative work itself. In Aron's works, philosophy, history, international relations, economics, sociology, and politics are mingled in the very crucible of the creative labour. But each discipline is addressed in its own language and considered by means of its own approaches. The synthesis is effected in the unity of interpretation, and in the broad conclusions which his major works contain. And so perfectly is the work fused in its entirety that the student has great difficulty in trying to divide it synoptically.

One of the more widely accepted divisions is that between Aron's philosophical works, his works in international relations, and his sociological and political works.[2] But whereas the studies of international relations prove to be easier to separate from the rest of Aron's work, it is more difficult to distinguish between the other divisions, particularly the sociological and political writings.

The singularity of the works on international relations is perhaps caused in part by the fact that, for reasons of Aron's own creativity, these works—and above all, *Les guerres en chaîne* (*Century of Total War*) and *Paix et guerre entre les nations* (*Peace and War*) [3]—are the most finished. As used here the word "finished" must be taken in two senses. First, the works are the most finished because, in them, Aron blends together most effectively various fields of knowledge—history, strategy, economics, sociology, and politics—linking them boldly together in a general and pessimistic reflection upon the causes of war, its place in human nature, and its effects on the evolution of the industrial society. It should be noted that these

---

[2] Although Aron himself, if one is to judge on the basis of the division he proposes on the guard-page of his works, prefers a tripartite division: philosophy, politics, and sociology.

[3] Respectively, Paris, 1951; 1962.

reflections were produced comparatively early in Aron's career. Now, when we see new disciplines such as polemology on the one hand, or the science of peace on the other, becoming fashionable and indeed extremely popular with students of this generation, Aron's early approaches and interests seem, in retrospect, much more familiar. But these works are also finished because they are distinctively self-contained in their respective volumes and under their respective titles, unlike his sociological or political reflections, which defy the boundaries of individual volumes and articles and continue from one publication to the next in a sort of prolonged argument carried on by the author with himself.

When it comes to distinguishing between sociology and politics one is impressed by Aron's own hesitations and doubts. It is the theme which he belabours most and to which he returns again and again, either in articles or, significantly, in introductions to books which are inevitably on the border line between the two disciplines. So absorbed is he in this perennial argument that he seems to be impervious to the danger of being repetitious. At least five of his major works take up the theme at the very outset, and new variations are constantly added to it.

In principle Aron is a sociologist. From an academic point of view, he was professor of sociology at the Sorbonne. And it was on "the historical condition of the sociologist" that he chose to speak in his autobiographical inaugural lecture at the Collège de France when he joined that august body at the end of 1970.[4] In principle again, Aron considers politics to be a subsystem of the totality which is the society. Thus: "in the history of ideas sociology could almost be defined by the primacy of the concept of society over the concept of politics . . . ." "Society, at any epoch, forms a totality. Sociology is the science of that totality."[5] Or "within the western societies in which contemporary political science grew . . . the constitutional-pluralistic regime . . . contains a relatively clear differentiation of the 'po-

[4] "De la condition historique du sociologue" was the inaugural lecture at the Collège de France, December 7, 1970. Later published by Gallimard, NRF (Paris, 1971).

[5] These two texts come from the article "Les sociologues et les institutions représentatives," which represents a significant turning point in the substance of the argument. *Archives Européenes de Sociologie*, I (1960), 1; reproduced in *Etudes Politiques*, Paris, 1971.

litical sub-system.'" This sub-system, in turn, contains a differentiation of the organs and of the functions. It is this double differentiation of the political sub-system "in its relations with the social whole and within itself which is the immediately recognisable origin of the different trends of political science." [6]

In principle therefore, Aron does consider political science as a sub-system or a part of sociology. This view would be opposed to the view expressed, for instance, by Giovanni Sartori that "if the demarcation between sociology and political science is sought—as it should be—at the level of their respective conceptual frameworks, it soon appears that the formal theory of the social system leaves off where the formal theory of the political system begins." [7]

But, in reality, reaching conclusions almost identical with those of Sartori, Aron gradually elaborated a critique of classical sociology—that of Marx, Comte, and Durkheim (hence his distinct preference for Weber)—as being primarily concerned with the study of the deterministic evolution of the industrial society as a whole, and consequently ignoring the perennial reality of politics, both as the realm of organisation and as the factor of voluntarism. In these writers the idea of "politics as a sub-system" is contradicted by that of the global relations between the rulers and the ruled—although, in Aron's view, global relations reveal the essentially political aspect of all societies and, even more so, of the industrial society. For even if and when industrial society abolishes some of the causes of economic conflict, as for instance the private ownership of the means of production, it yet reproduces the conflicts of hierarchies of organisation through the perennial process of social stratification. "The originality of industrial societies does not reside in the permanence of a political sub-system, but in the differentiation of ruling hierarchies." [8] The proper "*political* conflicts between the ruling minorities and the masses" ought to be distinguished from the "*economic* conflicts between classes." [9] "The social

---

[6] "A propos de la théorie politique," in *Etudes Politiques*, pp. 158–59.

[7] Giovanni Sartori: "From the Sociology of Politics to Political Sociology," in *Government and Opposition*, 4, no. 2 (Spring 1969).

[8] *Progress and Disillusion: The Dialectics of Modern Society* (London, 1968), p. 27.

[9] *Ibid.*, p. 63.

sector, which in a restricted meaning is called political, is the sector in which those who rule and the proceedings by which they rule are chosen. It follows that this sector of social life reveals to us the human or the inhuman character of the whole community." [10]

The direct critique of sociology—or at least of classical sociology—on account of its short-sighted indifference towards politics is contained in "Les sociologues et les institutions représentatives." In this article Aron attacks both Marx and Comte with gusto for "substituting the global society for politics as a privileged subject of study. Agreeing on explaining the political regime through social and economic conditions, Auguste Comte and Karl Marx did not perceive either the crisis which they witnessed, or the solution of the future." From there Aron continues to criticise classical sociology as a whole for having asserted that "scientifically, the study of the social whole has conserved a primacy over the study of the political regime, the latter being seen as a reflexion or expression of the economic-social structure, rather than as an autonomous determining factor."

He asserts, in the same essay, that now "relations between societies and representative institutions are entirely different." All industrial societies show obvious similarities in their productive forces. But "the political regime has an autonomy, an efficacity of its own . . . . Once the specificity of the political order is asserted, the sociologists could no longer ignore the im-

[10] *Democracy and Totalitarianism* (London, 1968), p. 12. Aron elaborates on this theme in his important essay: "Pensée sociologique et droits de l'homme": "Do human rights still belong to the philosophy of our time? In the eighteenth century they were one with the rights of the citizen, the personal rights, the political rights. . . . In the twentieth century they were enlarged by economic and social rights. Was this a new stage?" In order to answer the question Aron discusses Maurice Cranston's distinction between the *practicability* and the *paramount importance* of rights. He considers that our epoch by broadening the concept of human rights has also weakened it. Aron ends: "What conclusions can we draw from these analyses? Should we rejoice at the extension of the traditional notion of human rights to the political and social domains? Or should we deplore the fact that these rights have been lost, or seem to have lost their unconditional and somewhat sacred character? Probably we should accept both conclusions at the same time; our time had the merit of having recreated the number of subjects and the sphere of the objects of the rights proclaimed universal, but this broadening did not go without a weakening of the substance." In *Etudes Politiques*, pp. 216–34.

portance, at least potential, of the rules characteristic of the regime." "Against both [Marx and Comte] we have learned that politics is a perennial category of human existence, a permanent sector of all societies." "The political regime conditions in great part, the style of the collectivity. In the age of industrial society it is the political regime which provides the specific difference between collectivities belonging to the same type." This conclusion is expressed even more sharply in Aron's essay on "Machiavelli and Marx." [11] Thus: "Marx is the prophet of a time in which the economy, the productive forces, take the shape of fate. Machiavelli, however, is much more our contemporary, not so much by what he teaches us, as by an interrogation which remains unanswered." This is where in substance Aron's conclusions coincide with those of Sartori: starting from opposite points on the journey between political science and sociology they meet halfway. In Aron's words, "all our *objective certainties* are increasingly exposed to, and conditioned by, *political uncertainty. . . .* The sociologist should catch up with the hazardous uncertainties of politics." [12]

But, be this as it may, what are Aron's principal, or indeed original, contributions to contemporary political science? One is his very profound examination of the different types of political regimes of the industrial societies. Indeed, let it be first said that the principal lesson that contemporary political science can draw from Aron's work is his concentration on the specific politics of the industrial society. Instead of searching for a comprehensive "model" or "system" or "paradigm" which would comprehend in its essentiality all the political societies, Aron chose from the beginning to concentrate on one historical type of society, or as he makes adamantly clear, of *societies:* the industrial type.

It is this type that he theorizes; and, by applying clear comparative indicators, he compares it with non-industrial societies, and individual industrial societies with each other. For this work Aron uses his different skills: as a political theorist, he relates the historical phenomenon of the industrial society to the perennial political processes of all communities in history,

[11] In *Etudes Politiques*, p. 74.
[12] *Ibid.*, p. 214.

and the specific theories of industrial politics to the main body of political theory—from Plato and Aristotle, to Machiavelli and Hobbes, to Montesquieu and Tocqueville. As a sociologist and historian of industrial societies, he ascertains the origins and delineates the general characteristics of such societies and, particularly relevant for their political characteristics, points out the elements of their social stratification and organisation. As a political scientist, he analyses the principal features of the politics of different regimes in industrial societies and finds out their similarities and differences. Thus his "model" is a historical one; his "system" is a real one; and his "comparative political analysis" is based on the direct observation of one general type of existing societies. It should also be noted that at the time when Aron was writing his first books on the subject, most American political science was still very abstract and "developmental," while most European political studies were still concentrating on describing the institutions of the respective individual states.

Aron's division of the two foremost political types of industrial societies is, I submit, much subtler and more precise than is generally realized, and will therefore increasingly prove its theoretical usefulness. It is a thousand pities that either he or his publishers chose to use in the title of one of his most thorough studies of the politics of the industrial societies the battered notions of democracy and totalitarianism. For in reality what Aron does in his study is to debunk both these notions and to propose replacing them by other, more adequate, terms. But this goes unnoticed and students at large continue to believe that Aron is still dealing with the opposition of the two cold war concepts.

To take first the worn-out notion of totalitarianism. Aron does not oppose the concept either in principle or for ideological reasons. He finds it useful, and he defines it with the help of five conceptual prerequisites which are not entirely dissimilar from the seven prerequisites framed by C. J. Friedrich and Z. K. Brzezinski in their more enthusiastic description of the totalitarian model.[13] But what Aron does is to restrict totalitarianism first to the age of industry; and then (like Hannah Arendt) to

[13] *Totalitarian Dictatorship and Autocracy* (Cambridge, Mass., 1956).

specific periods in the history of the USSR: 1934–38 and 1948–52, and also to the last years of the Third Reich. He warns explicitly against confusing the comparison between these periods with a comparison of other so-called totalitarian regimes in history, meaning by this all authoritarian and one-party regimes. Here again Aron preceded the reorientation in comparative political studies against the indiscriminate use of the concept of totalitarianism, which, as I have said elsewhere, like anything total, cannot be graded. But if totalitarianism is and should be restricted only to the "real thing," what is a more flexible concept which would fit most of the one-party states in industrial societies? Aron shares in the belief that contemporary political regimes can be characterised by the modality of the party struggle. He proposes therefore the notion of the "monopolistic party regime," with the focus on the monopoly of power assumed by one party alone. One might have reservations about the notion of monopoly itself (which Aron confesses to have borrowed from the semantics of economics), but one can see that in the absence of any other criterion, "monopolistic" is a more precise adjective than "totalitarian"; it is nearer to the reality of power in such states than "monolithic," and it is more relevant to the economic and social aspects of the industrial society than "autocratic," "despotic," "dictatorial," or "totalitarian."

But it was Aron's inspired description of the other, Western type of industrial society which, because of its felicitous simplicity, seemed to me bound to become popular with the students of "free" or "open" politics. He describes what everybody else still calls "Western democracies" or "liberal democracies" or "democratic states," as *constitutional-pluralistic states*. Now this description seemed to me at the time (and still does) to answer a longing which most students of politics—even those who were not prepared for all-round reconceptualisations—experienced after the Second World War. Especially during the cold war, students of politics wished that the basic descriptions of the non-totalitarian regimes could be refurbished. Terms such as "democratic" (a particularly ambiguous expression which should never have been detached from the limited, even if pejorative, meaning which Aristotle in his wisdom gave to it), "Western," or even more so "liberal" (another ambivalent term, in its economic and political equivocations), and especially any combination of these three favourites, were found radically normative, useful perhaps in an ideological confrontation, but increasingly valueless for academic work.

Aron's simple concept of constitutional-pluralistic states eliminated much confusion reigning at the time he advanced it. Through creation of a new term, the normative sting was taken out of other, more inflated notions—and a value-free notion easily appeared. If one looks more closely into how this had been effected, one realises the importance of the hyphen. It links the judicial or political value-free notion of "constitutional" (all states have constitutions) with the sociological value-free notion of "pluralistic" (all societies are implicitly and explicitly pluralistic). Even Soviet sociology, which was the last communist sociology to accept the concept of pluralism,[14] has now acknowledged it.

In the expression "constitutional-pluralistic," the hyphen enabled each of these two notions to reverberate conditionally on the other, so that—as in another political-constitutional hyphenated concept, the "king-in-parliament"—once associated in a new logical structure they could not be separated again; and only when united did they form a new, integrated, and integral, concept. For what the hyphen shows is that whereas all societies are pluralistic regardless of their political regimes, there are some in which the economic, social, and political pluralism of the society is guaranteed by the constitution; and, vice-versa, the continuous functioning of the pluralistic society will see to it that the constitution will be observed. Moreover, although Aron initially stressed the political pluralism (i.e., the constitutional guarantee extended to the competitive multi-party system and the legal functioning of opposition), he made it clear that in the particular case of the industrial society, pluralism means the pressure and bargaining of *all* forces in this particularly diversified, heterogeneous, and interdependent form of society.

This brings us to Aron's choice of representative institutions as the central principle of his political taxonomy of industrial societies. His interpretation of this principle contains two

[14] At the Evian World Congress of Sociology of 1966, the Soviet delegation still lagged behind the Czech or the Polish delegations, which acknowledged the pluralism of their societies and the fact that they contained conflicts.

qualifications. The first is historical. Together with Montesquieu, Aron considers modern representation "as the appearance of a new phenomenon," [15] which renders modern sovereignty conceptually different from its late-mediaeval predecessors. "Montesquieu understood the importance of representation; the formal holder of sovereignty was no longer identical with the real holder. From the time when the phenomenon of representation intervened, the theoretical holder of sovereignty no longer actually ruled." [16] This principle links up directly with Aron's principle that constitutional-pluralistic states are ultimately oligarchies, and it draws the barrier between Montesquieu's realistic appraisal of sovereignty and Rousseau's utopian "will of the people." But it should also be noted that the former principle, in the collective noun "representative institutions," includes not only parliament ("the seat of sovereignty"), but the representative government which derives from parliament, and the representative or competitive parties which form it. Thus: "By the same token, the phenomenon of parties *became* essential since the unity or the plurality determined the *modality* of representation." [17]

The second qualification derives to a certain extent from the first. Because they are historical phenomena, representative institutions will continue to be torn from within between the longing for the old, "Greek," form of democracy,[18] when *"the holder of sovereignty* was capable of *exercising power* effectively," and the less effective forms of exercise of power which representation offers, and which are contrasted with "direct action" or "self-government." Aron makes it clear, as was noted above, that classical sociology, as elaborated by Marx and Comte, felt a distinct lack of interest in representative institutions, and, what is more, in the phenomenon of politics itself, which is intrinsically linked with the mechanism, and with the philosophy of representation. "Sociology, as it was conceived by its founding fathers in the last century . . . considered the representative institutions only as a secondary aspect of the modern society, a legacy of the past, a survival of the transi-

[15] *Democracy and Totalitarianism*, p. 58.
[16] *Ibid.*
[17] *Ibid.*
[18] *Ibid.*

tional phase." [19] Both Comte and Marx see in the future the
need for an organic dictatorship: "the progressive dictatorship"
for Comte, "the dictatorship of the proletariat" for Marx—both
of them, however, ultimately conditioned by the inevitable
"withering away" of the state and of politics, which are to be
absorbed in the harmonies of the de-institutionalised society of
the future.

The trend is continued, according to Aron, in modern socialism (which he sees, in any case, as the normative twin of sociology).[20] This is clear not only in the Leninist theory of dictatorship of the proletariat, but in the fact that Karl Kautsky, who
wanted to combine socialism with parliamentarism and to remain faithful to the representative institutions "could not find
in the doctrine decisive arguments to answer the Bolshe-
viks." [21] Moreover, Aron finds Durkheim "more interested in
organising production than in saving or reforming the representative institutions." [22] He contrasts from this point of view, and
very sharply,[23] Durkheim's old-fashioned political views—almost identical with those of Saint-Simon and Comte—with
those of Weber who understands, in a modern sense, the importance of politics, and especially of politics in industrial societies.

For if industrial societies reproduce the processes of social
stratification, those of rationalization as well as the functional
hierarchies, the relations thus engendered between the rulers
and the ruled make politics a perennial activity. The problem of
politics—and above all the problem of representation—can no
longer be considered as a "thing of the past"; it becomes on the
contrary very much a concern of the present. The litmus-paper
test of this was to be found precisely in the evolution of the
USSR and of the other socialist states after industrialization.

[19] "Les sociologues," p. 275.

[20] "Sociology, the science of modern society, has as its central category
the social, differentiated from the traditional concepts of the political and of the
economic. Similarly socialism, as doctrine of action, strives to bridge the contra-
diction between political equality and the economic inequalities by a reform
bearing upon the constitution of the society itself." "De la condition historique
du sociologue," p. 15.

[21] "Les sociologues," p. 281.

[22] *Ibid.*, p. 280.

[23] Especially in *"De la condition."*

"The industrial society is now rather the present than the future. Also, in the USSR, in the countries of Eastern Europe since 1945, in China, a society has now developed which can be called industrial because it presents, as far as the organisation of production is concerned, multiple and obvious similarities with the Western societies. But then the similarity of productive forces does not exclude either the diversity of relations of production and of social stratification, or the radical opposition of ideologies and of political forces. . . ."[24]

Aron shows that the leaders of the USSR have preserved in their constitution elections with universal suffrage, and that in practice the competition for power from within the party is a distorted form of the political conflicts which the representative institutions try to regularise in the West.[25] Aron must therefore be given full credit for having sensed the reorientation towards politics of both sociology *and* the socialist states, previously meant to be on their way towards de-politization. The communist regimes are on the contrary in an agonizing need of some institutionalized form of real representation. But this, alas for them, cannot happen without some real accountability. It is, in other words, easier to allege representation than to arrive at accountability, which is the other side of the coin of representation. To whom are the representatives and their representative governments accountable, in the Soviet type of states? The realistic answer is: to the party. But this distorts the very logic of representation, which is based on the principle that the elected are accountable to the electors, who hold the final sanction. The political crisis of the socialist states can be defined as the need to find a coherent and effective system of public accountability.

Aron's analysis of this trend towards politics reflects an aspect which, while still pivoting around the problem of representation, differs not from his view but from the arguments he uses to back it. Two authors—one only too often used by Aron as a sparring partner, Durkheim, and the other not quoted by him, Samuel H. Beer—are relevant for the development of this aspect (as well as Theodore Lowi, Robert Dahl, and Stein Rok-

---

[24] "Les sociologues," p. 281.
[25] *Ibid.*, p. 282.

kan), which pushes Aron's trend of thought into situations not explicitly considered by him. For the two concentrated on the problems of the corporate forces in the industrial society: Durkheim, on the effect of their action on politics; Beer, on the interweaving of political and of corporate representations.

Although there is no room here for a serious discussion of Aron's antipathy towards Durkheim, a word must be said about Durkheim's actual thinking on society and socialism. In "De la condition" Aron reduces Durkheim's definition of socialism to the "statist control of economic power." In fact Durkheim made an explicit distinction between two forms of socialism: state-socialism and workers' socialism (which he described sometimes as "anarchism"). But it was workers' socialism which Durkheim described as the true and unique socialism, since he took it to be synonymous with the de-centralised, uncontrolled self-management of the producers organised in corporations. He explicitly revived the expression "corporations," distinguishing it from its old mediaeval meaning and showing that corporations were new forms, as required by the functional society of the industrial age, rather than anachronistic revivals. This was no Rousseauian longing for unanimities of will, whether in canton, polis, or modern state. Durkheim had in view the vast and harsh structures of the pluralist industrial society which would break the power of the centre of decision-making of the nation-state and transform it, from within, into the administration of corporations and, from without, into larger international forms of co-operation. Be it said in passing that Aron's constant lack of intellectual sympathy for Durkheim remains one of those very odd family quarrels in which the onlooker has somehow no business to mix. Even intellectual families have their quarrels.

Samuel H. Beer's *Modern British Politics* [26] is concerned above all with the interweaving of political representation and corporate representation in British politics, especially since the advent of the Labour party. Beer was particularly interested in the corporatism of the post-industrial societies and poses the question whether corporate representation will not increasingly replace the older forms of political representation. By now,

[26] London, 1956.

when the problem of corporate pluralism is so much with us, one might carry the question further and ask whether what is really happening in the politics of post-industrial society is not a massive challenge to the representative institutions by the corporate producers (corporations as companies, corporations as trade-unions, and corporations as local and regional administration). Corporate producers attempt to replace the very process of political representation through direct action and decentralised self-government. They have the power now not only to prevent the national government from governing, but to impose upon it their own, direct, decision-making. This would, in very abstract terms, bring about a change from Aron's "representative oligarchies" to what could be described as "functional oligopolies." Here, then, is one line of development which is related to Aron's lucid way of locating the modern political problem at the intersection between representative institutions and the industrial society.

If, in sum, one were asked to define in a single phrase Aron's distinctive mark as a political scientist, perhaps the most comprehensive answer would be to describe him as a modern classicist. Obviously he is a modern: his work has the quality of modernity built into it insofar as it addresses itself, with initial directness and with life-long tenacity, to the modern political subject *par excellence,* the transformation of the political processes and institutions under the impact of the industrial and post-industrial revolutions. If one looks in retrospect at the *Weltanschauung* of the "new" post-Second World War political science, one will have to recognise that its long excursion into, and fixation upon, the underdeveloped societies, not only as a preferred subject, but as a preferred paradigm for modern comparative politics, was a sterile diversion. In the meantime economists alone were addressing themselves to the formidable problems of the industrial society—its national and international structural aspects, which have transcended the problems of the nation-state and are exploding the frail limits of its institutions. The admirable and valid techniques of reconceptualisation and of comparative politics elaborated during the post-war period were and will remain of great import to political science. But the model was wrong; and the extrapolating projection from the elementary to the advanced, from the simple to the complex, and from the primitive to the historical was formalistic.

The revolt of the generation of the 1960s against the formal-
ism of the new political science was to a certain extent a reaction against its ultimate escapism. The popular success of John
Kenneth Galbraith and, for that matter, Herbert Marcuse was in
great part due to their critiques of the industrial society, sensed
as the "real thing." But then how much more relevant in its
modernity is Aron's focus, which never lost sight of the "real
thing," and which brought to bear upon it, in order to scrutinise
it, all the methodological tools available! And how characteristic
that he should be led from youth to this interest by his very
modern form of *Angst*. In the intellectual autobiography which
he offers in "De la condition historique du sociologue," he
stresses in a remarkable passage the initial element of anxiety
in his work, which transformed itself into his "active pessimism." "Since 1930," he says, "as a lecturer at the University
of Bonn or as a fellow of the Academic House of Berlin, I
sensed, almost physically, the coming of the storms of history.
History is again on the move, to use Arnold Toynbee's expression. I was marked forever by this experience, which inclined
me towards an active pessimism. Once and forever, I ceased to
believe that history follows by itself the imperative of reason or
the wishes of the men of goodwill. I lost faith but kept, not
without some difficulty, hope." [27]

With regard to Aron's classicism, the predisposition towards pessimism (i.e., the particular pessimism inspired by the
behaviour of men, as individuals or as collectivities) is characteristic of the founding fathers of political science, Machiavelli,
Hobbes, Suárez, and Bodin; whereas the founding fathers of sociology, Saint-Simon, Comte, the young Marx, and Durkheim,
were inspired, or claimed to be inspired, by a natural, romantic
optimism based on the trust they put in reason and science, and
on their faith in the almost teleological progress, or determinism, of the evolution of technology and culture. This, Aron
himself defines as the great incompatibility between his own attitudes "and the attitudes, at the same time resigned and confident, still related to Auguste Comte's positivism: acceptance of
social determinism, comparable to a natural determinism, and
unshakeable optimism concerning the long-term prospects." [28]

[27] "De la condition," p. 20.
[28] *Ibid.*

Aron, then, is a classicist in his method. He believes that in order to study his subject one should not throw away the tools of observation and of conceptualisation, which had served this science from Aristotle to Tocqueville, and replace them exclusively with new mechanistic gadgets. Here is how he describes modern political analysis (in the context of the constitutional-pluralistic states):

> 1. The political system must be considered in the light of a particular social system, from the elections up to the decisions taken by the government touching upon the structure of the parties, the function of the assembly and the selection of ministers.
> 2. The political system is related to what can be called the social infrastructure. The exercise of power or decision-making depends on social groups, on their interests, their rivalry, their ambitions, their possible agreement and their permanent competition.
> 3. Our analysis must comprise the administration or the bureaucracy.
> 4. Then we must study what I shall call for want of a better expression, the historical environment of the political system. Every political system is in fact influenced, if not determined by an accumulation of tradition, values, ways of thought and of action peculiar to each country.[29]

The classicism of the method is obvious in the three fundamental conditions of the study of politics which these recommendations entail: equal concentration on political institutions and on political processes, or as it were on the anatomy and the physiology of the body politic; full use of the new methods of investigation on the principal elements of the politics of the industrial society, groups and bureaucracy; and the inseparability of the study of politics from, on the one hand, the historical environment of the respective unit of study and, on the other, the accumulated wisdom and "relevance" of political theory from antiquity to the fourteenth century.

This balanced, integrated, and yet multi-dimensional approach differs from the unifying drive by which it was expected that the study of politics would become a science. The *élan* of that drive looks, in retrospect and by direct contrast with what

---

[29] *Democracy and Totalitarianism*, p. 68.

has been described here as classic, somehow romantic. It was romantic to proclaim that, given the profound transformation of the political world, all its meanings should be "reconceptualized" around a perspective—essentially political concepts like state, sovereignty, or citizen having become overnight, presumably, irrelevant. The same *élan* made many people think that infallible methods of quantification would render the fallible human philosophical vision and political acumen redundant. And a new generation, strangely predisposed for intellectual parricide, hurried to bury for good the works of the "founding fathers" of politics.

In an epoch in which, exalted by the technical advance and the economic progress of powers with more recent historical origins than Europe, a great part of the apprentices in the social sciences of today are inclined to believe that "relevance" starts only with Marx or Weber or Sorel, Aron's stand is exemplary. For the posture in which he obviously prefers above all to be seen is that of the humble continuator of the old masters: Aristotle, Saint Augustine, Machiavelli, Hobbes, Montesquieu, Tocqueville. He professes that their wisdom will be valid for as long as men are wise. Their "conceptual framework," to use an expression generally associated with the reconceptualizing schools of thought, will serve for *all* human situations, provided the situations are seen in their real perspectives, that is, within the perennial—tragic, in Unamuno's sense—limitations of human freedom. Aron's great discourse on liberty—*Essai sur les libertés*—[30] is characteristically classic in the way it transcends the stoicism of the reasoning with dedication to the cause of human dignity.

Finally, like all classics of politics, Aron's work is *hard*. It deals with hard facts and its approaches are direct. It avoids the ultimate escapism of systemic extrapolations. Modern political science, which had been asked [31] to look beyond the countries of Western Europe to the new nations of Asia, Africa, and Latin America, is brought back by Aron from these picturesque peripheries to the hard centre of industrial power, ugly as it might be. From this centre, then, he adjusts his comparative sights.

[30] Paris, 1970.
[31] Sidney Verba: "Some Dilemmas in Comparative Research," *World Politics*, XX, I (1967–68), p. 111.

The global view thus obtained contains of course the third world, but not at the price of leaving out the United States, the Soviet Union, and Western Europe, or of interpreting these highly developed societies from within "frameworks" devised for the more elementary ones.

It is this blending of an acute sense of the uniqueness of the situations of the post-industrial world with a profound sense of the continuity of history and culture that Aron achieves. And it is this achievement which gives him the distinctive greatness in the realm of political science which this essay has tried to isolate from the other realms of which Aron is also a master.

Jean-Paul Sartre:
Solitary Man in a Hostile
Universe

by MAURICE CRANSTON

In his autobiography, *Les Mots*, Sartre tells us that he grew up in a world of words. The only child of a widowed mother, he lived in the house of his grandfather, a language teacher with a well-stocked library. Reading was Sartre's solace for his loneliness as a child, and it was the main source of his knowledge of the world. But, as Sartre himself points out, the world we learn about from books is ordered, coherent, systematic, and purposeful. Reading, as a child, led him to expect the universe to be the kind of rational whole that is depicted in the metaphysics of a Leibniz or a Newton or a Descartes. When the universe of experience turned out to be very different from this—to be contingent, confused, and "messy"—Sartre was repelled by it. He was one of those people for whom a rational and purposeful universe was an emotional necessity. In his autobiography, he adds that he remained possessed by this metaphysical hunger until he was converted to Marxism during the Second World War.

However, the reader of Sartre's writings is bound to wonder: was Sartre really "converted," has he ever lost his metaphysical hunger, and is the political philosophy to which he has subscribed since the Second World War rightly to be considered Marxism? His writings, both as a political philosopher and as a political pamphleteer since the early 1940s, have been voluminous. For a time there did not appear to be any clear connection between Sartre's politics and his philosophy. His philosophy was existentialist, and existentialism as such seems to have no specific political implication. Some existentialists, such as Heidegger, have been fascists; others, like Gabriel Marcel, were *conservateurs;* yet others, like Camus, were liberal-socialists. Sartre was far to the left. Soon after the Liberation he tried to found a new movement of like-minded leftists, but when that failed he became for nearly twenty years a somewhat unreliable fellow traveller of the French Communist party. This is to say, he approved in the main of the politics of the French Communist party, but he detested its philosophy. When he disagreed with it in political matters, it was because he favoured a more extreme, militant, and revolutionary policy. During the lifetime of Stalin, he occasionally criticised communism and the Soviet Union, but he would always spring to the defence of it when others (such as Camus) attacked it. After Stalin's death, when official communist policy became more directed towards co-existence than towards revolution, and the hard line seemed to "thaw," Sartre began to lose patience with the communists. At the time of the *évènements* of May 1968, when the French Communist party seemed chiefly concerned to exploit the panic of the bourgeoisie to extract higher wages for the workers, Sartre exploded with anger against the party: the communists, he said, had sabotaged the chance of revolution in France, and he could have no more respect for them. After 1968 he felt more at home in Maoist company, and even acted for a time as editor of an extreme revolutionary newspaper, when the young editors were accused of inciting public disorder and imprisoned.

It was in these political circumstances that Sartre worked out his own political theory, a fusion of existentialism and Marxism. This theory is set out in its greatest detail in Sartre's *Critique de la raison dialectique,* published in Paris as long ago as 1960, but not as yet translated into English.[1] Two further books of his, both ostensibly works of literary criticism, *Saint Genet*

---

[1] The first section of the prefatory essay *Question de méthode* has, however, been translated by Hazel Barnes as *Search for a Method* (New York, 1963) and *The Problem of Method* (London, 1964). Excerpts may be found in R. D. Cumming, *The Philosophy of Jean-Paul Sartre* (New York, 1965; London, 1966). *Reason and Violence* by R. D. Laing and D. Cooper (London, 1964; New York, 1965) contains a summary in English of the argument of Sartre's *Critique* and his *Saint Genêt.*

(1952) [2] and *Flaubert* (1971) [3] may be read as extended and discursive footnotes to the argument of the *Critique*. The title *Critique de la raison dialectique* is an ambitious one, if only because of the obvious reference to Kant's *Critique of Pure Reason*. And indeed Sartre sees himself as doing something analogous to Kant; whereas Kant, as Sartre supposes, was making a synthesis of empiricism and rationalism, Sartre is attempting to make a synthesis of existentialism and Marxism. In a prefatory essay, *Question de méthode*, Sartre explains that he has set out to revitalize and modernize Marxism by giving it a new method. In the main body of the *Critique* he shows how this modernized, or existentialized, Marxism unfolds itself in a new *anthropologie* (in Kant's sense of that word)—that is to say, in a philosophical theory of man and society.

Sartre's approach to the subject is not, as he explains, purely academic. His *Question de méthode* appeared originally in a Polish journal in 1957, when "destalinization" first became the order of the day; and the theory is consciously put forward as a destalinized philosophy for bewildered communist intellectuals, and as a basis for reunion between such intellectuals and those of the left who remained outside the party: in other words, as something to fill minds left painfully empty by Moscow's repudiation of Stalin's teaching, and as a theoretical foundation for a new united front against the bourgeoisie. This polemical purpose in no way detracts from the academic interest of the *Critique*. Many of the best political theorists have had some such further motive; the philosopher and the pamphleteer are often the same man.

Sartre begins the *Critique* by paying the most lavish tributes to Marxism and making the most modest claims for existentialism. Indeed he says that whereas Marxism is one of the main philosophies of the modern world, existentialism is not even a genuine philosophy at all. Existentialism is merely an "ideology." It should be noted that Sartre does not use the word "ideology" in Marx's sense. He provides his own Sartrian definition both of that word and of the word "philosophy." Philoso-

---

[2] *Saint Genêt, comédien et martyr* (Paris, 1952). Translated by Bernard Frechtman as *Saint Genet* (New York, 1963; London, 1964).

[3] *Flaubert*, 2 vols. (Paris, 1971).

phies, he says, are the great creative systems of thought which dominate certain "moments" or periods of history, systems which cannot be got beyond (dépassé) until history itself has moved on to another stage. Thus in the seventeenth century, the philosophical "moment" was that of Descartes and Locke; at the end of the eighteenth century and the beginning of the nineteenth century, it was the "moment" of Kant and Hegel; our own age is that of Marx. No philosophy could go beyond Descartes and Locke in their time, or Kant and Hegel in theirs; and no philosophy can go beyond Marx today. We are compelled, Sartre says, to think in Marxist terms.

Not content with thus exalting Marxism, Sartre is at pains to diminish existentialism, the mere ideology. Ideologies, in this Sartrian sense, are little systems of thought which live on the edge of the great systems, and which "exploit the domain" of the genuine philosophers. Since the present century falls within the Marxist epoch, existentialism "exploits the domain of Marxism." Existentialism, then, is "a parasitic system which lives on the margin of a knowledge to which it was at first opposed, but into which it seeks now to integrate itself." [4]

This is a decidedly original perspective. There is also something audacious about the proposal that existentialism should "integrate itself" into Marxism, for no two systems of thought could be more dissimilar. Two things, at least, would seem to offer insuperable obstacles to any fusion. First, existentialists believe in free will, libertarianism, indeterminism; and Sartre in particular has always put great emphasis on this. No theme is more marked and recurrent in all his work than that man is "condemned to be free." Marx, on the other hand, belongs to that tradition of philosophy which would banish the free will problem altogether. Freedom, for Marx, is, in Hegel's words, "recognition of necessity." Marx holds first that all history is shaped and determined by the relations of production, which follow certain laws, and secondly, that men can master their destiny insofar as they understand those laws and consciously direct their action in accordance with them. Thus Marx thinks he is entitled to believe equally in both freedom and determinism. For Sartre, on the other hand, determinism is not

[4] *Critique de la raison dialectique*, p. 18.

only false, it is a form of *mauvaise foi,* or culpable self-deception, by means of which certain people evade their moral responsibility.

Next, there is the matter of individualism. Existentialists lay great stress on the isolation, the solitude, the "abandonment" of the individual; and no existentialist writer has stressed this more than Sartre, from his first novel *La Nausée* to his play *Les Séquestrés d'Altona.* But Marxism regards individualism as a "delusion of theory" and holds that man's true nature is social.

Sartre does not shirk these contradictions. He believes they can be resolved. He suggests that the trouble lies in the fact that Marxism—orthodox Marxism—has become out-of-date, hidebound, dogmatic; it has lost touch with humanity. This is where existentialism can help to renovate it—by "humanizing" Marxism. Sartre goes on to make this curious prediction:

> From the day that Marxist research takes on a human dimension (that is to say, the existential project), as the basis of its sociological knowledge, existentialism will no longer have a reason for being—absorbed, transcended and conserved by the totalizing movement of philosophy, it will cease to be one particular enquiry, and become the basis of all enquiry.[5]

Sartre insists that his quarrel is with the Marxists and not with Marx; indeed he gives an interpretation of Marx's essay on the "Eighteenth Brumaire" which suggests that Marx himself, in his most inspired moments, was an existentialist without realising it. Sartre's complaint about the Marxists is that they are lazy. Sometimes they are too metaphysical and sometimes too positivistic. Their thinking is old-fashioned, and often it is not thinking at all, but blind assent to authority.

Many of Sartre's criticisms of the orthodox Marxist hit the nail on the head. He shows, for example, how shallow is the judgment of those Marxist literary critics who dismiss Valéry as a "petit bourgeois intellectual." Sartre agrees: Valéry *is* a petit bourgeois intellectual, but the important point is that "not every petit bourgeois intellectual is a Valéry." Sartre also demonstrates the absurdity of the Marxist critical habit of bundling

[5] *Ibid.,* p. 111.

together such diverse writers as Proust, Joyce, Bergson, and Gide as "subjective"; he shows that this category of the subjective is not empirically viable; it is not drawn from experience; it is not based on the study of real men.

"Lazy Marxists," Sartre says, reveal their laziness not only in their unreflective use of categories but in their tendency to constitute the real a priori. Just as Communist party politicians use these methods to prove that what has happened had to happen, so Marxist intellectuals use them to prove that everything is what it was bound to be. And this, Sartre shrewdly observes, is merely a method of "exposition" from which one learns nothing. It is tautologous; it cannot teach us anything because it knows in advance what it is going to find out. Hence the need for giving Marxism a new method.

Sartre describes this method which existentialism offers Marxism as "heuristic"—that is, it is a method serving to discover truth; it is also "dialectic." Sartre claims that whereas the lazy Marxist when confronted with any problem immediately refers to abstract principles, his own new method works by means of cross reference (va-et-vient) within the flux and movement of the real world. For example, Sartre's method would seek to explain the biography of individuals like Flaubert or Robespierre by an equally deep study of the epoch which shapes the individual and of the individual who shapes the epoch. He calls it the "progressive-regressive" method. It is progressive because it seeks part of the explanation in the aims of conscious beings; and it is regressive because it looks at the conditions in which each conscious being pursues his objectives. People have to be understood both in terms of their own aims and in the light of the circumstances in which they formulate and seek to realize their aims.

Sartre gives an interesting example of what he has in mind in discussing the case of Flaubert. Sartre is as quick as any lazy Marxist to classify and castigate Flaubert as a petit bourgeois. But this is only the beginning. The important thing about Flaubert, for Sartre, is not that he belonged to the petit bourgeois class, but what he did to rise above that condition. Flaubert, in Sartre's words, "threw himself across the several fields of possibility toward the alienated objectivation of himself, creating himself ineluctably and indissolubly as the author of *Madame*

Bovary and as the petit bourgeois that he refused to be." [6]

Flaubert's career is thus seen as an instance of "the project" (*le projet*). This is a characteristically existentialist concept and one of which Sartre has often made use. It figures prominently in the most substantial work of his earlier years, *L'Etre et le Néant* (1943), where the project is defined as the way in which a person chooses his mode of life and creates himself in action. The design according to which we make ourselves is our project. Of Flaubert's project, creating himself as an objective being in the shape of an author, or more precisely as *the* author of *Madame Bovary* and other novels, Sartre writes:

> This project has a *meaning*. It is not a simple negativity, the flight [from the petit bourgeois predicament]; but rather through it, the man aims at the production of himself in the world as a certain objective totality. It is not the pure and simple abstract choice to write that makes the nature of Flaubert, but the choice to write in a certain fashion so as to manifest himself in the world in a certain way—in a word, it is the particular meaning that he gives [in the framework of contemporary ideology] to literature as the negation of his original condition, and as the objective resolution of his contradictions. [7]

A man "defines himself" by his project. We make ourselves what we are by what we do. Sartre has had something to say about this in several of his earlier books. For example, in his play, *Huis-clos* (1943), the male protagonist, Garcin, tries to maintain that he has a noble and courageous nature in spite of the fact that he has done cowardly deeds, and the *farouche,* plain-speaking Lesbian, Inès, tells Garcin that a man has no nature apart from his actions—his actions define him—so that a man whose behaviour is cowardly *is* a coward. We *are* what we *do*. Sartre is equally emphatic in saying that what we do is what we choose to do. We are totally responsible for our actions; since as beings "condemned to be free" we could, if we had chosen differently, have acted differently. Garcin, in *Huis-clos,* could have done better deeds and died a hero. Flaubert, in the real world, could have made a worse choice and lived in idleness as a *rentier*, but then he would not have been *the* Flaubert, the author of *Madame Bovary.*

[6] *Ibid.*, p. 93.
[7] *Ibid.*

In *L'Etre et le Néant,* the notion of the project is bound up with existence and in the *Critique,* Sartre speaks of the project as a kind of "uprooting of oneself toward existence"; and by existence, he adds, "we do not understand a stable substance, which abides in itself, but a perpetual disequilibrium, an uprooting of the whole body. And this drive toward objectivation takes different forms in different individuals as each projects himself forward through a field of possibilities—of which one realizes some to the exclusion of others. We existentialists call this Choice, or Liberty." [8]

I think it is clear from this quotation, and from what I have so far summarized, that Sartre has retained the free will doctrine of existentialism and by no means assimilated the Marxist theory of necessity. So in spite of all that Sartre said at the beginning of the *Critique* about Marxism being the true philosophy and existentialism being a mere ideology, it is obvious that an essential part of the so-called integration between the two will have to be the surrender by the Marxist, and not by the existentialist, of one fundamental belief. To modify the shock of this demand, Sartre invokes the aid of the Marxist concept of *Praxis.* This word is often used by Marx and his followers, though not always in the same sense. At different places in Marxist writings, *Praxis* appears to mean (1) the common sense that stands opposed to speculation; (2) the process of acting, as opposed to meditation, by which understanding is acquired; (3) empirical, scientific, or industrial work. Now Sartre, with some adroitness, has taken this ambiguous and rather rough-and-ready Marxist notion and made it more or less identical with the existentialist notion of the project; in other words, he uses the idea of *Praxis* as a means of injecting into Marxism his own notion of project, which entails freedom of the will. If the notion of *Praxis* could be interpreted as meaning what project means, and the Marxist admits to believing in *Praxis,* then the Marxist might be shown to believe in free will without knowing it.

Sartre, however, can hardly expect to have this ploy pass unchallenged. The project is by definition something that can be undertaken only by men who have free will, whereas *Praxis,* however loosely the word may be used in Marxist writings, is

[8] *Ibid.,* p. 95.

always represented there as something undertaken in full consciousness of the laws of necessity. Hence, as already indicated, if the concepts of project and *Praxis* are to be united, it is the Marxist, and not the existentialist, who is going to have to make a radical revision of his categories.

Let us next consider the other subject on which existentialism and Marxism are notoriously at variance: individualism. Existentialism as it is commonly understood, and certainly as it is expounded by Sartre, entails an extreme form of individualism, whereas Marxism has no more conspicuous feature than its rejection of individualism—its belief that man must be seen in terms of the social whole or common humanity. Sartre attempts to resolve this antithesis by putting forward in his *Critique* a theory of society which he claims to be both Marxist and existentialist. How far can he be said to have succeeded?

Once again Sartre makes free use of the kind of technical language which is favoured by Marxists. First, he invokes the notion of alienation. But Sartre, as we shall see, has a different theory of alienation from that of Marx. Whereas Marx saw alienation as the result of the exploitation of one man by another, Sartre sees alienation as a universal feature of the human predicament. Indeed Sartre's notion of alienation cannot be understood in purely Marxist terms. The words Sartre shares with Marx are words they have both rifled from Hegel. Sartre's theory of alienation is an existentialized Hegelian concept, not an existentialized Marxist concept. His alienation, already explained in *L'Etre et le Néant*, is *metaphysical*. Nevertheless he does not forget that his subject here is *l'anthropologie* as opposed to *l'ontologie;* and that a fresh and, so to speak, specifically sociological reason has to be given for what he has always regarded as the fundamental characteristic of human relations—mutual antagonism.

The principle Sartre introduces at this point is that of shortage, or *scarcity*. He says that all human history—at any rate, all human history hitherto—has been a history of shortage and of a bitter struggle against shortage. There is not enough in this world to go around, and there never has been. And it is this *scarcity*, according to the *Critique*, which makes human relationships intelligible. Scarcity is the key to understanding the attitude of men to one another and to understanding the social structures men have built up during their lives on earth. Scarcity, says Sartre, both unites and divides us. It unites us because it is only by united efforts that we are able to struggle at all successfully against scarcity; it divides us because each one of us knows that it is only the existence of others which prevents there being abundance for oneself.

Scarcity then is "the motor of history." Men cannot eliminate scarcity altogether. In this sense, they are powerless or impotent. The best they can do is to try to overcome scarcity by collaboration with others. But such collaboration is itself paradoxical, for each of the collaborators knows that it is only the existence of the world of others that makes scarcity. I am a rival to you, and you are a rival to me. When I work together with others to struggle against scarcity, I am working with those whose existence makes that work necessary; and by my work I nourish my competitors and rivals. Scarcity, then, not only shapes our attitude to the natural world but shapes our attitude to our neighbours. Scarcity makes us all rivals, yet compels us to collaborate with our rivals; being impotent alone, we can struggle effectively against scarcity only by the division of labour and other such joint endeavours.

Nature, however, is "inert" and indifferent to human welfare. The world we inhabit is in part the world of nature and in part the world that has been made by our forebears in the course of their long struggle against scarcity. Sartre calls it the world of the "Practico-Inert." The world is the world of *Praxis* insofar as it is a world shaped by the work and projects of its past and present inhabitants. This is the world to the extent that it is man-made. But the world is also the passive, or inert, world of nature on which man has had to work. Ironically, many of the things that men have done with the aim of making the world more bearable, with the aim of diminishing scarcity, have had the effect not of improving but of worsening the world. Sartre gives the example of Chinese peasants cutting down wood to make fires and to build houses, and doing this on so large a scale that they effectively deforest their land, and so expose themselves to the hazards and disasters of constant floods. Men are tormented by their own inventions in the world of the Practico-Inert.

Thus, in a hostile universe, defined by scarcity, man becomes the enemy of man. In a typically Sartrian phrase, man becomes anti-man, *le contrehomme*. And in a paragraph which is dramatic enough to be a speech in one of his plays, Sartre writes:

> Nothing indeed—neither wild beasts nor microbes—could be more terrible for man than this intelligent, flesh-eating, cruel species, which knows how to follow and outwit the human intelligence and of which the aim is precisely the destruction of man. This species is manifestly our own, as each of us sees it, in the Other, in the context of scarcity.[9]

The conflicts—or relationships of antagonism—between man and man are thus given an *economic* explanation in the *Critique*. We come next to a piece of "dialectic." Antagonism is negative reciprocity; but that negation is itself negated in the collaboration between neighbours which is necessary to overcome scarcity. This is Sartre's "dialectical" theory of the origin of society.

He distinguishes two forms of social structure: one, in the language of the early nineteenth-century French sociologists, he calls the "series"; the other, the "group." The two are significantly different. A series is a collection of people who are united only by external proximity. It does not exist as a whole "inside" any of its members. The example Sartre gives of a series is a queue or line at a bus stop. This is a collection or gathering of people that can be observed. You can look at it, count the number of people in it. Everyone is there for the "same" purpose; but they do not have a *common* or collective purpose. No one is interested in the other. Indeed, each member of the queue is a rival of the others. Because of the scarcity of seats in the bus, each wishes the others were not there. Each is superfluous; each is one too many. But because everyone *knows* that he also is one too many to the others, just as each of the others is one too many to him, all agree to take it in turn to get on the bus when the bus comes. They form an orderly series to avoid a fight or war on the platform of the bus. The forming of an orderly series like a queue waiting for a bus is thus a negative reciprocal relationship which is the negation of antagonism; it is the negation of itself.

[9] *Ibid.*, p. 208.

The people in the queue form a plurality of solitudes. And Sartre maintains that the whole social life of mankind is permeated by series of this kind. A city is a series of series. The bourgeoisie is a series of series, each member respecting the solitude of the others. But in human society, there is another kind of collection or gathering which Sartre recognizes; and this is what he calls the "group." A group is a collection of people who, unlike those in a series, *do* have a common objective or end. A football team is the example Sartre gives. The difference between a group and a series is inward. From the outside you cannot tell the difference. What makes a group is the fact that each member has committed himself to act as a member of that group. The group is held together, and therefore constituted, by commitment. Each member, as Sartre puts it, has converted his own individual *Praxis* to a common or social *Praxis*. The working class becomes a group when its members commit themselves to socialism. A group can get things done, whereas a series is impotent, since each member pursues only his own *Praxis*. And indeed it is precisely *because* the series is impotent that the group is constituted in the first place. The origin of the group, Sartre suggests, can be summed up in the discovery that "we must either live by working together, or die by fighting each other."

Scarcity again is the driving force, since it is scarcity, and scarcity alone, which makes men work together for a common end. Scarcity is thus seen as the origin of human societies, as groups rather than mere series. And in developing this thought, Sartre introduces three colourful notions: the pledge (*le serment*), violence, and Terror. Sartre explains that the group comes into being when each individual gives his pledge to become a member of the group and not to defect from or betray the group. Society as a group is *pledged* group. But the pledge must be enforced, and the members must be assured that it will be enforced. This is where violence and Terror come in. It is fear which drives men to form groups in the first place, and it is fear that must keep them in these groups. The fear which keeps men in their groups is Terror. Indeed the pledge itself, says Sartre, is a demand for violence to be used against oneself if one break one's own word; and the existence of Terror is an assurance that violence will be used against any other member of the group who tries to break his pledge.

All groups, says Sartre, are in constant danger of dissolving into seriality. Everyone is conscious of the threat of dispersion in himself and in others. Hence Sartre can say that "Terror is the statutory guarantee, freely called for, that none shall fall back into seriality." Terror is more than this: it is "mortal solicitude," for it is thanks to Terror that man becomes a social being, created such by himself and by others. Terror is the violence that negates violence. Terror indeed is fraternity. For Terror is the guarantee that my neighbour will stay my brother; it binds my neighbour to me by the threat of the violence it will use against him if he dares to be "unbrotherly."

The most important example of a group which Sartre gives is the state. The state, he says, "is a group which reconstitutes itself incessantly, and modifies its composition by a partial renewal—discontinuous or continuous—of its members." [10] Sartre argues that the group in fusion throws up leaders; later the group perpetuates itself by founding institutions. This is the basis of sovereignty. Authority is connected with Terror in the sense that the sovereign is the man who is authorized to exercise Terror. In a serial society, I obey because I have to obey. But in a state I obey myself because it is I, by my pledge, who have merged myself in the group and authorized the sovereign to command. Sartre does not, of course, fancy that every member of a state has actually given his pledge personally—he has been pledged *by proxy*—but the pledge is no less a pledge.

Nor is this all. Sartre claims that Terror is not only fraternity, it is also liberty. For I freely merge my individual project in the common project when I pledge myself (or am pledged by proxy) to the state; and when the sovereign, fortified by Terror, commands me on behalf of the state, he is giving me back my freedom.

Such, in summary terms, is Sartre's theory of social structures. How far can it be considered a Marxist theory? There is not much doubt that it is a thoroughly *Sartrian* theory, one which harmonizes completely with the theory of human relationships put forward in *L'Etre et le Néant*, and summed up by a character in his play *Huis-clos* with the remark "hell is other

[10] *Ibid.*, p. 610.

people." This theory is, briefly, the following: If I speak, I objectify myself in words. Those words, once uttered and heard by other people, become *things* in the external world. Other people can hear them, think about them, talk about them. My words are part of the furniture of *their* world. Once I have spoken them they are no longer, strictly speaking, mine. I can no longer control them. This is what leads Sartre to say that in communicating with other people, or indeed even in being seen and heard by other people, I lose part of my self to other People. I cease to be a Self to myself and become an Other to another. At the same time, you become an Other to me. It is the Other Person, the Witness, who makes each of us an object in the universe—and to that extent robs each of us of our complete freedom. The word Sartre uses for this otherness is "alterity" (*alterité*).

This theory of alterity (which owes much to Hegel) Sartre developed in his earlier exposition of existentialism, *L'Etre et le Néant*, where he argued that relations between people are inevitably subject to mutual tensions because each individual, acting toward others as an objectifying Other, robs others of their liberty. This is what leads Sartre in *L'Etre et le Néant* to say that all relations between men are forms of metaphysical conflict, each individual trying to outdo the other, each robbing the other of the other's freedom by objectifying him as a *thing* in the world, and each trying to defend his own freedom from being thus objectified. Sartre's conclusion in *L'Etre et le Néant* is that the only possible relations between people are those which tend toward the sadistic and those which tend toward the masochistic. Togetherness, harmony, love, the *Mitsein* is impossible; all relationships between men are relationships of conflict.

In the *Critique*, Sartre gives a new reason for this conflict, but the conclusion is the same. He still maintains that each individual is at war with all the others; and though social groups are formed, these groups are held together only by the pledge and Terror—they are in constant danger of relapsing into the individualistic condition of the series. Just as love, togetherness, friendship is rejected in *L'Etre et le Néant*, so in the *Critique* is any Aristotelian notion of man being social by nature.

Now, precisely because this social and political theory of

Sartre is so close to his own earlier teaching, it is all the further removed from Marxism. For Marx, though ambiguous in many ways, was unambiguous in his rejection of the picture of mankind as divided into individualistic and competing atoms. Marx believed in community or human togetherness as the natural condition of man. All Sartre's talk about pledges and political societies being held together by Terror is the antithesis of Marxism. Moreover, Sartre's theory of scarcity has nothing in common with Marxist economics, which is, indeed, directly opposed to the scarcity theory as put forward by Malthus and other economists of the classical school, whom Marx regarded as bourgeois *idéologues*. Marx says that men lived originally together in a state of primitive communism; then with the invention of things like iron tools and machinery, some men learned to exploit others. Expropriation reduced the dispossessed to a condition of penurious slavery; the exploiters stole from the slaves the difference between what they produced and what was needed to keep the slaves alive. And this, as Marx said, is a theory of *surplus*, not a theory of scarcity. The scarcity is the result of exploitation, not a characteristic of nature.

So Sartre's aim of producing a modernized Marxism can hardly be said to have been achieved. Indeed one has the impression that Sartre himself forgets his original modest intention. His early talk about Marxism being the great philosophy and existentialism being the mere ideology gives way to increasingly bold assertions about the metaphysical status of his own system. Already by page 153 of his *Critique* Sartre says he is going "to establish a priori (and not as the Marxists think of doing, a posteriori) the heuristic value of the dialectic method." He goes on to explain that starting with the discovery of the existential validity of the dialectical reason, he proposes to show that "the dialectical method will be efficacious as a method insofar as it will become permanently *necessary* as a law of intelligibility and as the rational structure of being." [11]

Sartre is thus making for his theory higher claims than Marx makes for his; Sartre is determined, as he puts it, "to establish an order of certitudes." And this is something more than Sartre allowed in his preliminary essay, *Question de méthode*,

[11] *Ibid.*, p. 158.

to Descartes, Locke, Kant, Hegel, *or* Marx; all these "great philosophies" had validity only within the context of their historical periods and as expressions of the aspirations of the rising class of the time. Sartre's own system, however, is going to be *necessarily* true, a law of the rational structure of *being*. So much for existentialism as "mere ideology."

Sartre's "restatement" of Marxism is certainly more sophisticated than the original, but how far can it be considered a "modernization"? One striking feature of Sartre's theory is that it moves from nineteenth-century philosophy back to that of the eighteenth and even seventeenth centuries, not forward to that of the twentieth. This is not only a question of language, although Sartre's talk of "Liberty" as "Terror" and "Terror" as "Fraternity" might come straight from a speech by Robespierre. It is the basic elements of the theory which belong to pre-Hegelian thought. For Sartre is putting forward a doctrine of social covenant which is virtually identical with that of the seventeenth-century English philosopher Thomas Hobbes. Sartre then adds to Hobbes's doctrine something which comes directly from one of Hobbes's critics—that is, the theory of scarcity put forward by the eighteenth-century Scotsman David Hume.

Hobbes's word is not "Violence," it is "War"; he does not speak of a "Pledge," but a "Covenant"; he does not speak of "Terror," but of a sovereign who keeps peace between men by "holding them all in *awe*." The words are slightly different, but the theory is uncannily the same. Neither Hobbes nor Sartre offers what is, strictly speaking, a social contract theory of the kind one finds in Locke or Rousseau, but both Hobbes and Sartre hold promise-and-force theories. And although Sartre's theory of sovereignty is a little more elaborate, perhaps, than Hobbes's, Sartre says exactly what Hobbes says about fear being the basis of political society and about the sovereign being *authorized* by the people to do whatever he decides to do, and so giving them back their freedom when he commands them to act as he wills. And just as Hobbes is haunted by fear of political society relapsing into the intolerable condition of the state of nature where no man is safe, Sartre goes on and on about the danger of the group's relapsing into an intolerable condition of seriality. Sartre writes:

The group is not a metaphysical reality, but a certain practical relationship between men toward a shared objective and among themselves. If certain circumstances of the struggle lead to a disbanding, and if this is not followed by a regroupment, the group is dead, the contagious panic reestablishes the dominion of the Practico-Inert—*voilà tout*.[12]

Voilà everything indeed—and how extraordinarily Hobbesian everything looks. And what does not look Hobbesian looks Humeian. The theory that scarcity lies at the origin of society (though anticipated in some of the unpublished works of Locke) was first elaborated by Hume in the third book of his *Treatise of Human Nature*, in this memorable passage:

Of all the animals with which this globe is peopled, there is none towards whom nature seems, at first sight, to have exercised more cruelty than towards man, in the numberless wants and necessities with which she has loaded him, and in the slender means which she affords to the relieving of these necessities. . . . It is by society alone he is able to supply his defects, and raise himself up to an equality with his fellow-creatures and even acquire a superiority above them. . . . When every individual labours apart and only for himself, his force is too small to execute any considerable work; his labour being employed in supplying all his different necessities, he never attains a perfection in any particular art; and as his force and success are not at all times equal, the least failure in either of these particulars must be attended with inevitable ruin and misery. Society provides a remedy for these *three* inconveniences.[13]

Although Hume argues that society, which comes into being because of scarcity, requires what he calls a "convention" being entered into by all its members, he denies that this convention is "of the nature of a promise": society arises only "from a general sense of the common interest." Hume was attacking, among other sorts of promise, the Hobbesian notion of the "covenant"; but Sartre, though taking the Humeian notion of scarcity, has to restore the Hobbesian notion of promise because, like Hobbes, Sartre puts great emphasis on the idea of

[12] *Ibid.*, p. 427n.
[13] David Hume, *Treatise*, bk. III, pt. II, sec. 2.

war between men as part of their natural condition. In the world of the Practico-Inert, as in Hobbes's state of nature, there is no "general sense of the common interest," for all men are enemies and rivals.

Are we to conclude that there are no elements of Marxism in Sartre's theory? That, I think, would be an unjustified conclusion. If he has not produced an "existentialized Marxism," he can fairly be said to have produced a "Marxified existentialism." He has kept the central teachings of *L'Etre et le Néant* and his other earlier writings, but he has given them a socialistic formulation. Conflict, still the central feature of human relationships, is presented in his later writings as the effect of an economic cause. The possibility of human collectives is now admitted, even if only by going against nature. And the old doctrine of conversion or personal salvation which was put forward in *La Nausée* is restated as a gospel of revolution. Sartre has taken from Marx a good deal of his theory of classes, and Marx's vision of a classless society has obviously inspired Sartre's belief in the possibility of the transformation of human society from bourgeois seriality into the socialistic group.

Logically, since he believes that historical man is anti-man, Sartre puts more stress than does Marx on the need for violence to bring about the revolution. One of the first plays Sartre wrote after his "conversion" to revolutionary politics in the war years was called *Les mains sales* (*Dirty Hands*). Its theme, which was also that of several later works, was that socialism could not be introduced with clean hands. Blood would have to be spilled. Sartre is far from being a pacifist, and if he shares Hobbes's view of the origin of civil society, he has none of Hobbes's horror of war. Indeed, in 1966, Sartre went so far as to urge the Russians to send their forces into Vietnam against the Americans, even at the risk of a Third World War. In the preface he wrote in 1960 to Franz Fanon's celebrated book *Les damnés de la terre* (*The Wretched of the Earth*) he endorsed Fanon's suggestion that revolutionary violence was a "cleansing force"; and added: "The native cures himself of colonial neurosis by thrusting out the settlers by force of arms." Sartre sometimes gives the impression of hungering for violence: not at all of accepting reluctantly the necessity of force, as Marx did. And this again fits perfectly with the theory of *L'Etre et le Néant*, according to which we have to choose either to be masochistic or to be sadistic.

There is no lack of logic or coherence in Sartre: his philosophy is a completely integrated system; all the parts stand or fall together. Again, he offers us a characteristically "existentialist choice": either to accept his theory as a whole or to reject it.

Hannah Arendt:
Hellenic Nostalgia and
Industrial Society

by NOEL O'SULLIVAN

If the first victim of a sceptical age is always religion, the second is invariably politics. It is therefore no surprise to find one contemporary political philosopher writing that

> Politics, we know, is a second-rate form of human activity, neither an art nor a science, at once corrupting to the soul and fatiguing to the mind, the activity either of those who cannot live without the illusion of affairs or those so fearful of being ruled by others that they will pay away their lives to prevent it; [1]

nor is it surprising, again, to find another, no less eminent philosopher remarking that politicians show no understanding of their place in society, no awareness of the significance of their activity, no apprehension of any but the most trivial details of life, and concluding that they are "with few exceptions, entirely blind." [2] If instead we were told by a philosopher that politics provides the only guarantee of our sanity, that political activity alone confers meaning upon life, and that in it the highest form of happiness is to be found, then curiosity would immediately be inspired; and if the philosopher who proffered this doctrine had supported it with such an extensive body of systematic argument as Hannah Arendt has, it would naturally also command respect and demand careful consideration.

It need hardly be said that admiration for the ancient

---

[1] Michael Oakeshott, in his introduction to Thomas Hobbes, *Leviathan*, Blackwell, ed. (Oxford, 1960), p. xiv.

[2] G. Santayana, *Dominations and Powers* (London, 1951), p. 196.

world has waned somewhat since the days of Machiavelli and Renaissance political thought. What principally distinguishes Arendt from other contemporary political philosophers is the fact that her enthusiasm for that world goes considerably beyond even Machiavelli's. It is indeed not so much Livy (although Rome stands high in her estimation) as the life of the Greek polis (as theorized by Aristotle), which constitutes the focal point of all her thought. Hellenism determines even her definition of politics; thus she can write, for example, that "we understand the political in the sense of the polis." [3] The influence of the polis is transmitted from this definition to the remainder of her system by way of two related sets of concepts; they are those of labour, work, and action on the one hand, and of a private and public realm of activity on the other. Taken together they constitute the structure of her most ambitious work, *The Human Condition*.

Labour, work, and action are not merely different forms of activity but comprise a scale in which each marks the achievement of a progressively higher level of consciousness. At the bottom of the scale is labour, an activity in which man enjoys a solipsistic, herdlike level of consciousness. In labouring he shares with the rest of creation bondage to necessity, being concerned simply with the maintenance of life as such. "The mark of all labouring," Arendt writes, is that "it leaves nothing behind, that the result of its effort is almost as quickly consumed as the effort is spent." [4] If labour produces objects, it produces them only incidentally, as a means to its own reproduction; strictly speaking, its only product is life itself.[5] Work, on the other hand, produces durable objects, and has the production of such objects as its primary aim. In work, man emerges for the first time to self-consciousness, since he becomes aware of his difference, as subject, from the object upon which his efforts are directed. But because the world in which he moves, *qua* worker, is a world of things, and not a world of men, he does not reach the highest level of human development. In so far as he does encounter his fellow men, it is only in their limited capacity as producers; he meets them only within the confined

[3] *The Human Condition* (New York, 1958), p. 76.
[4] *Ibid.*, p. 76.
[5] *Ibid.*, p. 77.

context of a market relationship, and never in their full stature as human beings. Both labour and work are therefore relegated to what Arendt terms the "private realm" of existence.

In adopting this scale of activity she is deliberately rejecting the modern hierarchy and reverting to the ancient position as expressed, for example, by Aristotle, who considered that neither labour nor work possessed sufficient dignity to be termed a way of life (a *bios*) at all, since they were not "autonomous and authentically human" [6] activities. In the modern world, by contrast, labour has acquired a dignity which has placed it above all other activities and lifted it out of the oblivion of the private realm to which the Greeks consigned it. The modern development culminated in the thought of Adam Smith and Karl Marx (although both these thinkers, Arendt considers, confused labour with work).[7]

The highest level of development is attained only in action, which is "the only activity that goes on directly between men without the intermediary of things or matter." [8] More will be said about action, which belongs to the "public realm," in due course; at present it is essential to make clear why Arendt considers that only action is authentically human, and hence superior to labour and work. This follows from a view of human essence which lies behind her categories but has not yet been brought into focus. The nature of this essence is indicated in a passage in which she uses an interpretation of Greek thought as the vehicle for a presentation of her own position:

> The task and potential greatness of mortals lie in their ability to produce things—works and deeds and words—which would deserve to be and, at least to a degree are, at home in everlastingness, so that through them mortals could find their place in a cosmos where everything is immortal except themselves. By their capacity for the immortal deed, by their ability to leave nonperishable traces behind, men, their individual mortality notwithstanding, attain an immortality of their own and prove themselves to be of a "divine" nature.[9]

The essential nature of man, then, is to seek immortality, and the attainment of immortality is only possible when man

[6] *Ibid.*, p. 14.
[7] *Ibid.*, pp. 76–77.
[8] *Ibid.*, p. 9.
[9] *Ibid.*, p. 19.

enters the public realm and moves amongst his peers, for only his equals are able to judge his actions, and only through their presence as witnesses will the memory of his deeds survive and assure his immortality. And this is what politics is about; it is the art which "teaches men how to bring forth what is great and radiant," [10] and only a man who abandons labour and work in order to engage in politics can properly be described as human, truly free, and completely happy.

This view of action obviously possesses marked affinities with existentialist philosophy. Like the existentialists, Arendt believes that the source of value and the meaning of existence are to be found only within action itself, and that it is only in acting that a man defines himself, by making his essence into a tangible reality in the form of deeds. Interwoven with her existentialism, however, is a deeply romantic strand of thought which harks back to Nietzsche. Admiration for the hero or superman takes the form, in her case, of an unqualified admiration for Achilles as the embodiment of political virtue [11] and a corresponding contempt for the meaningless everyday life of the mass in which there is no place for great deeds exhibiting the creative will.[12] Her romanticism reaches its greatest height when it leads her to insist that one who would win the favour of the gods by his political exploits must die young, a view which is arrived at in the following way. Since the essence of who somebody is "can come into being only when life departs, leaving behind nothing but a story," it follows that whoever consciously aims at leaving behind a story and an identity which will win immortal fame "must not only risk his life but expressly choose, as Achilles did, a short life and premature death. Only a man who does not survive his one supreme act remains the indisputable master of his identity and possible greatness, because he withdraws into death from the possible consequences and continuation of what he began." [13]

It must be added immediately, however, that Arendt rejects in principle the idea of abandoning politics completely to the superman: the creative will she admires is not identical

[10] *Ibid.*, p. 184.
[11] *Ibid.*, p. 73. She writes that Achilles's story has "paradigmatic significance."
[12] *Ibid.*, p. 39.
[13] *Ibid.*, p. 173.

with the will to power, which "as the modern age from Hobbes to Nietzsche understood it in glorification or denunciation, far from being a characteristic of the strong, is, like envy and greed, among the views of the weak, and possibly even their most dangerous one." [14] Whether this distinction amounts to much in practice is another matter; in so far as it does, it would seem to require an emphasis upon constitutional safeguards for individual liberty, but it will become clear in a moment that they are noticeably absent.

We are confronted, then, with three assumptions about the human condition. The first is that man is distinguished from the rest of creation by virtue of his desire for immortality; the second is that this desire can only be satisfied through action, or *praxis;* and the third is that action must take place before a peer group of spectators who can transmit the memory of it, much as Homer did for Achilles. The highest form of action, that is to say, is politics; and politics, for Arendt, means what the ancient Greeks (or some of them, anyway) took it to mean.

When looked at from this position, the Western tradition of political thought naturally appears somewhat disappointing, since it has not paid much attention to the ideal of a society in which men can emulate Achilles. Arendt's criticism of that tradition is as follows. Ever since Plato there has been a tendency to confuse rule with authority, with results fatal, not only to liberty, but to the very existence of political activity. Rule implies a division of the community into rulers and ruled, into those who command and those who obey. It originates in man's need to escape from the realm of necessity, and is therefore a pre-political relationship. Because our tradition of political thought has primarily stressed the idea of rule, Arendt regards it as no more than a series of attempts to escape from politics. To the idea of rule she opposes the idea of authority. Authority, unlike rule, is essentially a relationship between equals, each of whom initiates action and then seeks supporters to help him carry it through. Some indication of what she means by authority may perhaps be found in the fact that she credits the Romans with having grasped that it is (in Mommsen's words) "more than advice and less than a command, an advice which one may

[14] *Ibid.*, p. 182.

not safely ignore"; [15] but at the bottom her view of authority would seem to be much closer to that of Rousseau. He too began with a rejection of the notion of rule (as developed, for example, by Hobbes), and of the consequent division of the community into those who command and those who obey. He went on to dismiss representative government as incompatible with human freedom and demanded its replacement by a form of social organisation which would provide the benefits of government whilst leaving men as free as they were before they created it. Arendt follows in his footsteps.

She does not deny that representative institutions have provided a considerable measure of freedom of speech and thought, but argues that the sort of freedom they have made possible is worthless, since it "no longer opens the channels for action, for the meaningful exercise of freedom." [16] Such freedom constitutes no more than a series of purely negative safeguards, necessary "to protect the lives of labourers and to shield them against the encroachment of government." [17] In other words, it leaves men in the private realm, with all the futility that entails. Through parties and pressure groups the voter can indeed exercise influence over his representatives, but only with regard to his interest or welfare; and since "interest" is an essentially private matter, no genuine common good can emerge. What the representative system fails above all to provide for is the expression of opinion. True opinion can be formed only in a process of open discussion, and this requires a society in which men possess a public realm where genuine equality prevails. There is instead a universal emphasis on a false form of equality, false because based on "the conformism inherent in society and possible only because behaviour has replaced action as the foremost mode of human relationship." [18] True equality, by contrast, is based on "a fiercely agonal spirit," which leads each to distinguish himself from all others, instead of conforming with them.[19]

Arendt is close to Rousseau, again, in the stress she lays

[15] Quoted in *Between Past and Future* (London, 1961), p. 123.
[16] *New York Review of Books*, 12, no. 4. (27 February 1969), 31.
[17] *On Revolution* (London, 1963), p. 63.
[18] *Human Condition*, p. 38.
[19] *Ibid.*

upon an ever-renewed consent as the basis of authority. In her case, however, the stress is generated not so much by a desire to preserve an egalitarian order in which each can lead an existence which is undisturbed by the need for social conformity as by a desire to preserve opportunities for initiating new enterprises; for it is in beginning, initiating, and founding political enterprises and institutions that the creative will finds its supreme expression. She is therefore naturally reluctant to accept the maintenance of settled institutional forms as an appropriate style of politics; no matter how satisfactory they may be found by the bulk of the community, acquiescence in the routine and undramatic conduct they require becomes identified with conformism. It would seem, then, that only permanent revolution would prevent human spontaneity from being enchained by the external consequences of its earlier manifestations. Although Arendt does not explicitly draw this conclusion, the inference derives support from the fact that the political arrangements she favours (considered below) are ones which have arisen under revolutionary conditions, and have ceased to exist when those circumstances disappeared.

Only consent or promise involves no external restraints upon action: it is to be regarded as a control mechanism built into the faculty of action itself, arising directly out of "the will to live together in the modes of acting and speaking." Far from creating sovereignty, promises merely produce "an equal purpose for which alone the promises are valid and binding." [20] Since there is obviously danger that anarchy will result if promises are not kept, or if disputes arise about the kind of things which people commit themselves to by their promises, the question arises of how she avoids the introduction of force and its concomitant, rule. One part of her answer (like that given by Rousseau) amounts to no more than a tacit assumption that the ideal society will be sufficiently harmonious for occasions of conflict to be very rare. This harmony will be guaranteed by the fact that its members will no longer be motivated by the selfish and competitive interests which men at present pursue, but will be guided instead by principle, and above all by what she calls "the principle of solidarity," [21] which leads them to will what

[20] *Human Condition*, p. 220.
[21] *On Revolution*, p. 87.

is, in effect, a general will. If conflict nonetheless occurs, it would seem that it must almost inevitably be regarded as originating in selfishness, or in putting one's "actual" will above one's "real" will.

The second part of her solution also resembles Rousseau's thinking: it introduces the idea of a supra-political saviour who, standing above private interests and party, points out the direction in which the general will is to be sought. For Rousseau this figure is, of course, the legislator; for Arendt, he is the intellectual. He alone enters the political arena in a neutral role, his sole aim being, not to act, but to report the truth.[22] On entering the public realm, however, he is likely to be confronted by the most malevolent of all political figures, the deliberate liar. The liar, unlike the non-partisan intellectual, is a man of action, dedicated to re-shaping the world in line with his perverted vision. What is even worse, the intellectual who has the task of reporting truth is likely to encounter lying in an organised, institutional form, supported by the mass media and reinforced by professional manipulation of the propaganda image. When organized lying comes to dominate the life of a society, the danger is that there will emerge at any moment the totalitarian state.

The interpretation of totalitarianism as a lie so monstrous that it leads to the creation of an entirely fictitious world will be examined later; the thing to be noticed at present is that there is an almost Manichean naivety in the way in which Arendt reduces the political world to black and white terms by dividing it up into liars and truth-tellers. Such a division naturally presupposes that there is one right answer on all major moral and political issues, and this belief scarcely contributes to an atmosphere in which discussion and argument are appropriate. The dogmatic character which her thought sometimes assumes as a result of this conviction is revealed when she asserts that the true intellectual is the guardian of a body of factual truth which lies at the bottom of every healthy body politic, and adds that factual truth "like all other truths, peremptorily claims to be acknowledged and precludes debate." [23] She refers on a number of occasions to the omission of Trotsky's name from the Stalinist

[22] "Truth and Politics," in *Political Theory and Social Change*, ed. D. Spitz (New York, 1967), p. 23.

[23] *Ibid.*, pp. 22–23.

version of Soviet history, as an example of the denial of factual truth. The idea of factual truth seems, however, to be a red herring. The real difficulty lies not so much in determining what factual truths are, as in deciding what implications they have for policy. Thus even if Stalin's history had been better, he might still have insisted without any inconsistency on the necessity for pursuing identical policies, on the ground that Trotsky had (for example) misunderstood the nature of revolution, or of the Russian revolution, or of the role of the party, and so on.

The third part of her answer is unusual; it consists of emphasizing the political significance of the idea of forgiveness. The ideal society has, at least politically, nothing to support itself except "the good will to counter the enormous risks of action by readiness to forgive, and to be forgiven, to make promises and to keep them." [24] The power of forgiving enables each man to release his fellows from the consequences of their actions and to make a new start. She attributes the discovery of the importance of forgiveness to Christ,[25] which is puzzling in view of the fact that his interest in it was as a means of releasing men from the burden of sin, rather than as a way of facilitating the pursuit of personal and temporal immortality through mighty actions. The alternative to accepting sovereignty and rule, then, appears to be complete dependence upon the indulgent forgiveness of each of one's fellow citizens. Not everyone would find the prospect as attractive as Arendt does.

Her criticisms of the liberal conception of freedom derive only in part from the radical incompatibility of true liberty with rule. They stem also from the further incompatibility of liberty with modern notions of happiness. There has been a growing tendency to identify happiness with material comfort. Happiness, so understood, satisfies only the "private" side of man's nature and further intensifies alienation by creating relationships of inequality, such as that between employer and employee. When politics itself becomes a vehicle for pursuing material happiness, the alienation of man from his true public existence is complete. Arendt is therefore opposed to the welfare programme which has dominated domestic politics in the

[24] *Human Condition*, p. 221.
[25] *Ibid.*, pp. 214–16.

present century and writes that "nothing could be more foolish and more dangerous than to attempt to liberate mankind from poverty by political means." [26] Paradoxically, her desire to restore men to enjoyment of the freedom and happiness provided by participation in public life serves only to intensify the very inequality which she castigates in previous political thought, since it leads her to recommend that the mass of mankind who lack any inclination to pursue such a life should be deprived of the suffrage.[27] When she insists that this would not be a real deprivation at all, but would amount to no more than a formal recognition of the fact that to prefer a private or social existence to a public one is automatically to consign oneself to oblivion, it would seem that we are back once more in the realm of discourse Rousseau introduced when he spoke of forcing men to be free.

Happiness in the modern sense, then, has meant the invasion of politics by economics; and this has resulted in the creation of a new sphere of life, totally unknown in the ancient and medieval world, which Arendt terms "the social realm." This realm "takes nothing into account but the life process of mankind," and within its frame of reference all things become objects of consumption.[28] Her attitude towards this development is ambivalent. She recognises that the existence of the social realm is desirable in so far as it permits individuals to develop differences of character and taste, and readily grants that its appearance has brought an enormous enrichment of private life.[29] Yet at other times she emphasizes, not the contribution it has made to individual liberty, but the harm it has done by destroying the public realm. Because the social realm allows activities which by their nature are private to assume public significance, it has in a relatively short time "transformed all modern communities into societies of labourers and jobholders." [30] It is this view which predominates in her writings.

The idea of the social realm completes the intellectual schema which Arendt wishes to substitute for the inadequate

[26] *On Revolution*, p. 110.
[27] *Ibid.*, p. 78.
[28] *Human Condition*, p. 38.
[29] *Ibid.*, p. 35.
[30] *Ibid.*, p. 42.

categories of traditional political thought; in conjunction with the concepts of the private and the public realms it provides her with an exhaustive classification of human activity. Some of the difficulties presented by the schema can be brought out by considering the one serious attempt Arendt has made to apply the classification to the analysis of an actual issue in contemporary political life. In a highly controversial article entitled "Reflections on Little Rock," published in the journal *Dissent* in 1959, she used the schema to criticize the administration's endeavour to end racial discrimination in the southern states. Two of her criticisms are of especial interest in the present connection. The first is of a general nature and applies to the civil rights programme as a whole. The principle of the public realm, she writes, is equality, and government can therefore only act legitimately in the name of this principle. The principle of equality, however, is inapplicable in the face of ineliminable natural, physical characteristics, amongst which she includes racial differences. Government, accordingly, should not try to interfere with what she refers to as the "visibility" of blacks in the public realm; on the contrary, the more that government respects the principle of equality, the more strongly are ineliminable physical characteristics thrown into relief. This, then, is the basis of her objection to the policy of social, economic, and educational equality for blacks pursued by the Supreme Court and federal government. Whilst she does not go so far as to conclude that the civil rights programme should be abandoned, she does insist that intervention should be restricted "to the few instances in which the law of the land and the principle of the Republic (viz. political equality) are at stake." [31] Arendt's second criticism applies more especially to the federal government's attempts to desegregate schools, with which she is primarily concerned in the article. Education, she argues, falls not in the public realm but in the social realm; and whilst the principle of the political realm is equality, the principle of the social realm is discrimination. What matters in the social realm is not personal distinction (which is only to be found in the public realm), but "the differences by which people belong to certain groups whose very identifiability demands that they discrimi-

[31] *Dissent* (Winter, 1959), p. 48.

nate against other groups in the same domain." [32]

There are points in the article which would command wide agreement, as when Arendt criticises government policy on the ground that the methods used for desegregating schools have shifted responsibility for implementing a political ideal from the shoulders of adults onto those of children.[33] What is problematic about her position, however, is the underlying assumption that every activity can be neatly classified as private, social, or public in nature, and that education in particular may be regarded as purely social. One is immediately reminded of John Stuart Mill's similar belief that all activities could be classified as either self- or other-regarding, and the objection in both cases is the same. No activity is exclusively private, social, or public, but will in fact display all three aspects. Arendt qualifies her position somewhat when she allows that the state is entitled to regulate the content of education, but insists nonetheless that it must refrain from interfering with "the context of association and social life which invariably develops out of . . . attendance at school." In practice, however, it is no more possible to make a rigid distinction between the content and context of education than it is to draw a sharp line between the social and political realms as a whole; it is hardly necessary to point out that both content and context may on occasion have serious political implications.

Whilst the concept of private, public, and social realms may be of doubtful value in determining the legitimate sphere of government action, the first two of these categories have provided notable results when applied by Arendt to the analysis of the most novel feature of twentieth-century political life, namely, the emergence of totalitarianism.

It has already been observed that for Arendt, lying is the greatest political evil; and the connection between lying and the emergence of totalitarianism has been briefly touched upon. In order to understand her interpretation of totalitarianism as a monstrous lie which has resulted in the creation of a totally fictitious world, it is necessary to notice three things: firstly, the connection that she postulates between political action and our

[32] *Ibid.*, p. 51.
[33] *Ibid.*, p. 55.

knowledge of reality, a knowledge which has been greatly affected by the disappearance of the public realm in the modern world; secondly, the general character of modern intellectual life, which reinforces the historical factors which have facilitated the destruction of an autonomous public sphere by encouraging a radically subjectivist attitude towards the world, culminating in what Arendt terms "world alienation"; and thirdly, the general movement in modern history from "classes" to "masses." As the last idea is a familiar one in contemporary literature, attention will be confined to the first two.

In the ordinary way, we do not think of political action as closely connected with the comprehension of reality; we tend to assume, rather, that such knowledge is independent of political action. Arendt rejects this view out of hand. For her, it is only "the presence of others who see what we see and hear what we hear" which "assures us of the reality of the world and ourselves." Thus, whilst the decline of the public realm in the modern world may well have been accompanied by an intensification and enrichment of the whole scale of subjective emotions and private feelings, the important thing is that "this intensification will always come to pass at the expense of the assurance of the reality of the world and man." In short, "our feeling for reality depends ultimately upon appearance and therefore upon the existence of a public realm into which things can appear out of the darkness of sheltered existence," so that "even the twilight which illuminates our private and intimate lives is ultimately derived from the much harsher light of the public realm." [34] The decline of the public realm, then, constitutes the necessary condition for the rise of totalitarianism, since the existence of that realm is the main bulwark against lying.

The loss of contact with reality which has followed upon the decline of the public realm has been accentuated by the nature of modern intellectual life, which is characterized by an "exclusive concern with the self" to such an extent that it tends to reduce all experiences, with the world as well as with other human beings, to experiences between man and himself. Arendt credits the discovery of this feature of modern life to

[34] *Human Condition*, pp. 46–47.

Max Weber: the greatness of his discovery about the origins of capitalism "lay precisely in his demonstration that an enormous, strictly modern activity is possible without any care for or enjoyment of the world whatever, an activity whose deepest motivation, on the contrary, is worry and care about the self." Hence, "world alienation, and not self-alienation as Marx thought, has been the hallmark of the modern age." [35] The consequence of world alienation, in conjunction with the factors which have destroyed the last vestiges of a common public world, has been the rise of the lonely mass man and "the worldless mentality of modern ideological mass movements." [36] It is this theme which is explored at length in her essay on *The Origins of Totalitarianism*. [37]

Totalitarianism as a system of government which is only possible in a world in which men no longer find reality itself bearable, owing to the destruction of the public world which gave their lives meaning and significance. What it offers is an escape from their loneliness into a world which offers certainty and intelligibility, but at the cost of sacrificing reality in favour of fiction. It can only offer this escape because of the disappearance from the world of the bedrock of "common sense" which once united men and stabilized their existence. Arendt uses the term "common sense" in an untechnical way, to refer to what our eyes and ears and personal experience generally tell us. It is what provides "a measured insight into the interdependence of the arbitrary and the planned, the accidental and the necessary." [38]

Now the principal characteristic of modern masses is precisely that "they do not believe in anything visible, in the reality of their own experience; they do not trust their eyes and ears but only their imaginations, which may be caught by anything that is at once universal and consistent in itself." [39] What modern man wants, in short, is system and coherence, and for this he is prepared to trade away whatever elements of common sense still survive, and push reality altogether to one side. Real-

[35] *Ibid.*, pp. 230–31.
[36] *Ibid.*, p. 233.
[37] London, 1958 (first published in Cleveland, Ohio, in 1951).
[38] *Origins*, p. 352.
[39] *Ibid.*, p. 351.

ity itself is pervaded by fortuitousness and accident; to systematize it is therefore inevitably to simplify it, and hence to distort
it, since these elements of contingency are then passed over.
Yet it is the fact that their very simplicity enables them to eliminate fortuitousness and accident—the things which make reality
so unbearable—which gives modern ideologies their appeal.
Totalitarian ideologies in particular have been able to satisfy
the demands of homeless men for an intelligible world because
they have realized that what convinces masses is "not facts, and
not even inverted facts, but only the consistency of the system
of which they are presumably part." [40] Instead of facts, with all
the contingency that surrounds them, the masses prefer to have
everything presented to them in the form of laws, elaborated
into an intellectual framework which "eliminates coincidences
by inventing an all-embracing omnipotence which is supposed
to be at the root of every accident. Totalitarian propaganda
thrives on the escape from reality into fiction, from coincidence
into consistency." [41]

This interpretation has the great advantage of enabling
Arendt to explain the element of irrationality in the conduct of
supporters of totalitarian regimes: the fact, that is, that their
behaviour often displays a complete disregard for the concept of
"self-interest" which has dominated Western ethical thought for
the past few centuries. In particular, it enables her to account
for the most irrational of all totalitarian phenomena—the
terror—which continues in existence even when a population is
completely subdued. This is because no matter how far totalitarian regimes succeed in conjuring up "a lying world of consistency which is more adequate to the needs of the human mind
than reality itself," the reality they seek to exclude still continues to exert pressure upon them, thereby creating "sore
spots." [42] Only terror can maintain the iron curtain of illusion
around the mass by preventing real experience from making itself felt; terror is thus the means by which the escape from reality into fiction is achieved, and the condition of untruth—the totalitarian lie—sustained. It is in fact "the very essence of its
form of government." [43]

[40] Ibid.
[41] Ibid., p. 352.
[42] Ibid., p. 353.
[43] Ibid., p. 344.

The most imaginative element in Arendt's interpretation of totalitarianism is undoubtedly her description of the organizational structure which gives institutional form to the escape from reality upon which totalitarianism rests. The totalitarian regime has, typically, an onion structure: that is, it consists of a number of different layers, at the centre of which stands the leader. The outermost layer consists of the less fanatical mass of supporters, with increasing degrees of fanaticism discernible as one moves inwards.

What makes this structure uniquely appropriate for the preservation of a fictitious world is the fact that members of each layer will find on their outside another, less fanatical layer, whose presence will serve to assure them of their own sanity, whilst at the same time reinforcing their feeling of superiority. On their inside, members of the layer will find a more fanatical grouping whose enthusiasm will inspire them to greater efforts, thereby preventing complacency or back-sliding. In this way the whole structure maintains its insulation from reality, whilst preserving the illusion that the fictitious world it occupies is a sane one. The leader, however, might appear to be in a more vulnerable position, since there is no layer beyond him to provide him with insulation; but Arendt argues that contact with reality never occurs even at this point, owing to the peculiar nature of "the leader principle." The leader represents the movement in a way totally different from all ordinary party leaders, in that he claims personal responsibility for every action, deed, or misdeed committed by any member or functionary in his official capacity; and because the leader alone is in the end responsible for all the activity of the movement through this total identification with it, "nobody ever experiences a situation in which he has to be responsible for his own actions or can explain the reasons for them." [44] The leader never encounters the external world in a simple, straightforward way, since the whole nature of the totalitarian movement is such as to create in him, in the highest degree, a conviction shared by all those within it—that politics is a form of cheating. Instead of emerging from this fictitious world when he encounters the international order, he merely transfers this attitude onto the scene of world politics.

[44] *Ibid.*, p. 374-75.

This brief outline does scant justice to the subtlety and scholarship which have gone into the presentation of one of the most interesting works of political science to appear since the war.[45] Certain difficulties, however, are presented by *The Origins of Totalitarianism*. The first attaches to the central idea of totalitarianism as a lie, or the creation of a purely fictitious world. The main disadvantage of this view is that it precludes any recognition of those similarities between (for example) the USSR and other countries, which have been highlighted by subsequent developmental and industrial society models of totalitarian regimes. For instance, the use of a "mature-industrial-society model" for analyzing the view of society prevalent amongst the large managerial class in the Soviet Union has suggested that there are "a large number of elements in the life and situations of these men and in their response to it which are indistinguishable from the situations and response of industrial managers in many other parts of the world." [46]

Whereas Arendt's model achieves its unity by presenting totalitarianism as a system created by the pursuit of pure power, later models have abandoned her almost exclusively political emphasis in order to stress the divergent socio-economic policies of Germany and the USSR and to exhibit points of resemblance between Soviet and non-communist economic goals. More generally, it would seem that her inability to account for important similarities between totalitarian and non-totalitarian regimes may ultimately be traced to her insistence on the absolute uniqueness of the totalitarian experience, arising from the conviction that it originates in forces which are completely alien to the Western political tradition and "can no longer be

---

[45] It is now generally regarded (together with *Totalitarian Dictatorship and Autocracy* [Cambridge, Mass., 1956], by C. J. Friedrich and Z. K. Brzezinski) as the classical theory. Subsequent work has tended either to revise and refine these early models, or else to abandon the concept of totalitarianism altogether. R. Burrowes sums up the current position when he writes that "The present view within the discipline . . . seems to be that the term "totalitarianism" suffers from the fact that it was developed in isolation and outside the mainstream of a rapidly changing field of comparative politics." See "Totalitarianism: The Revised Standard Version," in *World Politics*, 21 (January 1969), 272–94.

[46] A. Inkeles, "Models in the Analysis of Soviet Society," in *Survey*, no. 60 (July 1966). p. 10.

deduced from humanly comprehensible motives."[47] Her attempt to find in the onion structure of the regimes an institutional reflection of their uniqueness only accentuates the parochial element in her model, since something like this structure is to be found in any modern regime which confronts the problem of winning electoral support. The need to gain this support will inevitably generate a multi-layer structure extending from the broad, relatively unenthusiastic mass of supporters, through the more fanatical party workers, to the inner elite of power-holders or office-seekers.

When it comes to the tight centralized control based upon the leader principle, Arendt might appear to be on much firmer ground, since this would seem to be a characteristic peculiar to totalitarian governments. She has been criticized, however, for representing the leader as merely a function of the machine within which he is located, thereby minimizing the personal impact of Hitler and Stalin on their regimes.[48] It is also obvious that the bureaucratization of totalitarian society which Arendt stresses may very well dilute the impact of the leader in some quarters, rather than enhancing his personal control.

In 1967 a revised edition of *The Origins of Totalitarianism* appeared. The only important change was a new introduction in which Arendt tried to take account of developments which followed upon Stalin's death in 1951. She had originally argued, it will be remembered, that terror was the essential basis of the totalitarian system. The difficulty was that in the meantime new machinery of social control appeared to have emerged, capable of checking deviant behaviour "by more particular and indirect means" than terror.[49] In short, it seemed that there could be totalitarianism without terror. Arendt's solution was to circumscribe more narrowly the temporal duration of the totalitarian experience, arguing that Stalin's death had been followed by "an enthusiastic, though never unequivocal, process of detotalitarization."[50] By the 1960s it was clear that the Soviet

[47] *Origins*, p. lx.

[48] R. C. Tucker, "The Dictator and Totalitarianism," in *World Politics*, 17, no. 4 (July 1965).

[49] A. Kassof, "Totalitarianism Without Terror," in *World Politics*, vol, XVII, no. 4 (July, 1965), 573.

[50] *Origins* (New York, 1967), p. ix.

Union "had emerged from the nightmare of totalitarian rule to the manifold hardships, dangers and injustices of one-party dictatorship," although there remains the possibility that the country "can relapse into totalitarianism between one day and another without major upheavals." [51]

From a purely methodological standpoint, the least satisfactory aspects of Arendt's inquiry concern the historical method she adopts. Although she does not try to press Italian fascism into the model, on the ground that there the "movement was only a means of bringing the party to power and not an all-consuming end in itself," [52] the fact remains that the unity of her conception postulates a degree of similarity between German and Russian experience which is not to be found.[53] The laxity of her historical method is most evident, however, in her handling of the general "origins" of totalitarianism. The quest for them has an odd consequence: the net is cast so widely that totalitarianism itself ceases to be an inexplicable phenomenon, and what requires explanation is, instead, the existence of anything except totalitarianism. Burke, for example, becomes a precursor of the racialist element in totalitarian ideology on the ground that he described the rights of Englishmen as an "entailed inheritance" and concluded that such rights were preferable to the abstract ones claimed by other nations. In Arendt's eyes, this amounts to racialism merely because he regarded the English as "a kind of nobility among nations." [54]

Again, it is true that totalitarian ideology emphasizes the need for self-sacrifice in the name of abstract historical forces; but it is odd to conclude from the fact that T. E. Lawrence felt he incarnated the historical destiny of the Arab national movement and was obliged to sacrifice himself to it, that Lawrence was therefore in any significant sense a precursor of totalitarianism—yet Arendt does suggest this.[55] A last example is at least as unsatisfactory. It is true that totalitarianism favours secret societies and conspiracy theories; it is also true that

[51] *Ibid.*, p. xxi.
[52] *Origins*, 1958 ed., p. 259.
[53] See, for example, A. J. Groth, "The 'Isms' in Totalitarianism," in *American Political Science Review*, 58, no. 4 (1964).
[54] *Ibid.*, pp. 175–76.
[55] *Ibid.*, p. 219.

Disraeli liked secret societies and had a fondness for attributing political conspiracies to the Jews; but to conclude that he therefore foreshadows the rise of Hitler and Stalin is to adopt a methodology so loose that one can range over the whole of history, picking out precursors here and anticipators there according to taste.[56] Disraeli is indeed formally absolved from any direct responsibility for the rise of totalitarianism, but what was to be gained by introducing him in the first place is not made clear.

It was said earlier that totalitarianism is only an extreme response to a malaise that has afflicted the modern world as a whole, namely, the loss of contact with reality produced by the decline of the public realm. It must now be asked what steps Arendt considers appropriate for restoring the public realm; and secondly, what institutional form it would take, should it ever be restored. The answer to both questions is to be found in her theory of revolution.

Her pessimism about the contemporary world leads her to contemplate a radical solution; she believes that a taste for the kind of freedom she prefers can only be reacquired, and the conditions for it re-established, in and through revolutionary action. The thesis of her book *On Revolution* is that revolution is a modern phenomenon, involving the use of violence to bring about a complete change in the social order, and aiming at the foundation of a republic. Even if we ignore the curious implications of this definition—that revolutions which have aimed at creating a socialist society are not really true revolutions at all—it is impossible to escape the difficulties presented once again by Arendt's view of history, revealed this time in her account of the origins of the modern revolutionary spirit. This spirit has been inspired, she believes, by the desire to recapture "the Roman passion for foundation." [57] The evidence she produces in support of this belief derives from what one critic has acidly termed "a pedantic kind of lexicography, based on the quaint belief that a study of the roots of a political word used, for example, by the Americans in the eighteenth century can tell us what those Americans were really up to." [58]

[56] *Ibid.*, pp. 68–79.
[57] *On Revolution*, p. 49.
[58] Maurice Cranston, in a review in *The Listener*, 19 March 1964, pp. 485–86.

The most significant feature of her study of revolution, however, lies in her belief that revolutionary experience has provided the clue to the structure of the ideal society. This is to be found in the people's societies and councils which sprang up during the French Revolution, during the siege of Paris by the Prussian army in 1870, during the Russian strike of 1905, again during the February Revolution of 1917, and most recently during the Hungarian Revolution of 1956.[59] It is in fact in councils modelled on these revolutionary phenomena and linked together in a federal system which will provide opportunity for political action under conditions of perfect equality and community, that she finds "the best instruments . . . for breaking up the modern mass society." [60]

It cannot be said, however, that Arendt explores the difficulties presented by trying to convert institutions which have merged only under the exigencies of untypical situations, into ones suitable for more usual conditions of life. She contents herself instead with quoting an optimistic sentence from Jefferson to the effect that once they have been established they will soon reveal their merits.[61] Even if the council system is allowed to have the more general political relevance she attributes to it, it is difficult to share her opinion when she converts it into a device for understanding and sympathizing with the student movement, on the ground that this "derives from the best in the revolutionary tradition—the council system, the always defeated but only authentic outgrowth of every revolution since the eighteenth century." [62] The line of historical derivation is at least as vague here as it was in the case of the origins of totalitarianism.

Arendt's attitude towards the use of violence is hard to pin down, but there is strong evidence of a basic moderation and sanity in her views, even though she has occasionally entertained a sufficiently romantic view of it to be able to write that "it is as though Life itself, the immortal life of the species, nourished as it were by the sempiternal dying of its individual

[59] On Revolution, pp. 265–66.
[60] On Revolution, p. 283.
[61] Ibid.
[62] On Violence (London, 1970), p. 22.

members . . . is actualized in the practice of violence." [63] Her more conservative inclinations showed themselves at the time of Little Rock, to such an extent indeed that she suffered severe rebukes from radicals.[64] They are revealed also in the fact that she finds her ideal model of revolution in the American Revolution, which even Burke did not object to.[65] She has, again, explicitly rejected Fanon's belief that violence can regenerate human nature and create a new community.[66] Her main conclusion seems to be that "The practice of violence . . . changes the world, but the most probable change is to a more violent world." [67] The furthest she appears prepared to go is to countenance violence which pursues short-term goals and stands some chance of success, or else serves to "dramatize grievances." The implications of this principle remain ambiguous, but her tone is moderate.

What, then, is Hannah Arendt's contribution to contemporary political thought? If our own age has provided a further instance of the persistent tendency of Western political thought to assimilate the political relationship to some other relationship, by identifying it with the pursuit of greater productivity and a higher level of consumption, then she may be said to have provided a timely reminder of the autonomy of politics. On the other hand, exclusive emphasis on politics as the pursuit of personal immortality limits the significance of this achievement by making it difficult to extract the central concepts of the private and public realms from the confines of the small city-states of the ancient world out of which they arise; and those political units, of course, presupposed a slave economy. Her own solution is utopian: members of a community who have no desire to spend their lives in political activity should be disfranchised in order to leave the public realm open to political devotees. No institutional provisions are made to compel enthusiastic members of the council-state to pay the slightest regard to their interests thereafter. Since slavery is not to be contemplated as a

---

[63] *Ibid.*, p. 29.
[64] For example, by Melvin Tuman in *Dissent* (Winter 1959), pp. 65–71.
[65] *On Revolution*, p. 49.
[66] *New York Review of Books*, 12, no. 4(27 February 1969), 29.
[67] *Ibid.*, p. 30.

means of facilitating an escape from the private realm, it would seem that her political theory requires a large section of the community to undertake this voluntary withdrawal and presupposes their willingness to subsidize the heroic activities of the doers of mighty deeds; for how else can the latter escape completely from the futility of the realm of necessity? If these inferences are to be avoided, it can only be by abandoning the diametrical opposition which Arendt postulates between politics and rule on the one hand, and politics and private happiness on the other. Her view of politics, in other words, would have to be modified to include more mundane things than the pursuit of immortality, as well as safeguards for men who do not consider, as she does, that "to live an entirely private life means to be deprived of things essential to a truly human life." [68]

It is not only the concepts of private and public which are tied to the structure of the ancient city; the same is true of Arendt's categories of labour, work, and action. In the time of Aristotle it was easy enough to distinguish between the non-productive labour of a slave and the productive activity of the artisan—between, that is to say, labour and work. In the modern world, however, the abolition of slavery and the complexity of modern economies make such a distinction impossible, beyond the limits of a very loose and imprecise conventional usage. Even if these categories were readily applicable a serious problem would still remain, which is that of explaining how men accustomed to labour have come to develop political consciousness. In other words, since there is nothing in Arendt's classification of activity which would account for movement out of the solipsistic, herd-like life of the labourer, it would seem that her categories presuppose a static social order. So far as the concept of action itself is concerned, this is conceived of in such individualistic and theatrical terms as to leave some doubt about its political relevance. Politics does indeed contain a theatrical element, imposing an artificial persona on the actors; but the analogy breaks down when it is assumed that the political actor can rely on his audience to remain passive spectators, concerned only to judge his acts and either immortalize them or consign them to oblivion. In politics the audience is not passive;

---

[68] *Human Condition*, p. 253.

the actor therefore cannot confine himself to doing whatever he considers will define his unique essence most effectively, but must accommodate his course of action at every point to the interests and inclinations of his fellow participants.

In the last resort, the issue pressed upon us by Arendt is that of determining how much weight is to be given to her critique of existing liberal-democratic institutions on the one hand, and to her arguments in favour of a republican council-state on the other. As regards the former, the critique ultimately depends on an assumption which is crucial for the whole of her political philosophy. This is the identification she makes between the essentially public character of the human world and political action. It is of course true that human existence is public, in the sense that human consciousness rises above the solipsistic condition of animals. It does not follow from this, however, that the only completely satisfactory (or fully human) mode of publicity is that which occurs in political participation. Arendt may one day provide the philosophical basis required to justify her identification of the broad notion "the public" with the narrower notion of "the political," but until that time it cannot be said that her rejection of the liberal-democratic tradition is founded on convincing theoretical considerations. So far as her republican idealism is concerned, one can scarcely avoid reflecting that the ideal of a republic of virtuous men, *committed to willing the common good untainted* by any regard for private interest, is not after all a novel one. The first attempts to realise it go back to Robespierre, and all the evidence indicates that they lead inexorably to the autocratic system of government which Arendt abhors. Nothing, of course, could be further from her own intentions; but the record of history suggests that the best intentions in the world have in practice been powerless to prevent the connection.

C. B. Macpherson:
The Roots of Democracy and
Liberalism

by MICHAEL A. WEINSTEIN

The chief concern of C. B. Macpherson has been with the problems of democracy in the contemporary world. He has consistently held that the task of the political theorist is to determine the relevance of traditions of social thought to elucidating and directing social change. His aim has been to further a "humanistic political science," which would aid in the reconstruction of the moral foundations of political systems, rather than merely analyze ideas for their own sakes. In a criticism of the approach to political theory advocated by Leo Strauss, Macpherson wrote: "To reject any searching into the relations between ideas and social change is to say that the problem of political theory, or at least of the historian of political theory, is the investigation of ideas for their own sake only and not the investigation of society or social change."[1] He added that following Strauss's path "would lead to the eclipse of humanistic political science."[2] An idea of what Macpherson meant by a humanistic political science is contained in his comment: ". . . the purpose of scholarly reappraisals of political theories is to help us to see the limits and possibilities of a great tradition as applied to our own day. . . ."[3] In his studies of the moral foundations of democracy, Macpherson has attempted to achieve this purpose

---

[1] "A Disturbing Tendency in Political Science," *The Canadian Journal of Economics and Political Science*, 16, no. 1 (February 1950), 106.

[2] *Ibid.*

[3] "Halévy's Century Revisited," *Science and Society*, 31, no. 1 (Winter 1967), 37.

with respect to the liberal tradition.

Macpherson has opened several paths of inquiry in his efforts to clarify the limits and possibilities of liberal democracy and liberal democratic thought. He has developed a characteristic method of doing political theory based on trying to identify those social assumptions made by past political thinkers which are not automatically shared by contemporary readers. This kind of analysis has led Macpherson to develop a broad theory of democracy, of which liberal democracy is merely a special case. He has related this general theory of democratic politics to a vision of the contemporary human condition and has suggested some ways of moving from the present competitive social order to a future society marked by the enhancement of creative freedom. Thus, Macpherson is a theorist in the grand style. Following the central theme of clarifying contemporary democracy, he moves from a concern with methods of inquiry to recommendations for social change.

It is not surprising that in undertaking such a broad and difficult project, Macpherson has appeared to be inconsistent in certain places. In his discussion of the method he used to study the thought of such liberal writers as Hobbes and Locke, he offers us a way of dealing with his own apparent inconsistencies: "The presence of apparently clear inconsistency is to be treated as a clue to inadequately stated assumptions. The hypothesis that a thinker was consistent within the limits of his vision is useful less as a way of resolving inconsistencies than as a pointer to the direction and limits of his vision, which may then be established by other evidence." [4]

This essay has the dual purpose of summarizing the important points in Macpherson's political thought and criticizing his democratic theory in terms of his own method of theoretical inquiry. In order to accomplish this dual purpose it will be necessary to construct Macpherson's theory by looking behind his various critical writings to determine significant continuities of theme, and then to integrate the themes into a relatively coherent whole. Only after this constructive exposition is done will it be possible to make explicit what may be seen as the tacit assumption accounting for Macpherson's apparent inconsisten-

[4] *The Political Theory of Possessive Individualism* (Oxford, 1962), p. 8.

cies. Given these aims, there will be no discussion of the adequacy of Macpherson's treatment of specific political thinkers. Neither will there be criticism of Macpherson's basic moral and intellectual commitments to the enhancement of creative freedom and to socialist humanism. Such limitations will disappoint those who view Macpherson merely as a participant in debates about interpretations of the history of political thought, or who oppose his fundamental commitments. The assumption of this essay is that Macpherson is a serious and constructive political philosopher, whose works contain a distinctive and often compelling vision of the contemporary human condition.

All of the phases of Macpherson's political thought are mutually reinforcing. This is to be expected from someone working in a tradition stressing the close relations between thought and other aspects of experience. However, it means that there is no best place to begin the exposition. The discussion of method has been chosen as a starting point here, because it is a good way of placing Macpherson's work in the context of twentieth-century political thought. His distinctive method places him outside of both behavioral and traditional approaches, and provides some clues about the nature and aims of a humanistic political science.

Macpherson has not aligned himself with any of the more recent tendencies in Western political science. In a survey for UNESCO, "World Trends in Political Science," he remarks that despite the proclaimed goal of a natural science of politics, political science in the United States has been marked by the underlying policy aim of reaching "generalizations which would help improve the quality of American democracy." [5] Macpherson notes that attempts to be scientific and to reform political structures had not met with great success because sufficient research had not been devoted to exploring the moral implications of changes in basic social relations: ". . . the new matter which the accepted political theory cannot accommodate is not simply new factual phenomena, but new moral problems which have been brought into existence by changed social relations. When this is so, the requirement for valid political science re-

[5] "World Trends in Political Science Research," *American Political Science Review*, 48, no. 2 (June 1954), 434.

search is both fresh empirical inquiry and fresh philosophical thinking." [6]

This judgment led Macpherson to the conclusion that the goal of contemporary political science should not be a systematic empirical, or "positive," theory, or even the accumulation of studies to ground such a theory, but that research should be judged according to "whether either systematic theory or particular inquiries are being pursued with the requisite consciousness of the need to rethink a political philosophy adequate to the new moral problems posed by changes in society." [7] Thus, Macpherson's thought is essentially practical, in that its ultimate aim is the resolution of moral problems which emerge as societies change, and not the discovery of either moral or scientific laws.

In "Market Concepts in Political Theory," Macpherson argues that the aversion of current political scientists to examining fundamental social assumptions is no better shown than in the interest in formal economic models of political behavior. These models, which interpret democratic politics as a market are associated with moral justifications of liberal democracy which ignore basic social conflicts:

> The trouble with the equilibrium theory of democracy, we may conclude, is that, like the economists' marginal utility theory, it leaves out of account the historical determinants of effective demand. It treats class interests in advanced countries, and national aspirations in advancing countries, as just one among many kinds of political pressure. In doing so it averts its thoughts from the most serious problems of democracy. [8]

From this discussion, it is clear that Macpherson has placed the function of basic social criticism ahead of the other tasks of political scientists. Empirical studies, and whatever positive theories may appear, should grow up within the context of criticism. In his masterwork, *The Political Theory of Possessive Individualism*, Macpherson develops a method for

[6] *Ibid.*, p. 448.

[7] *Ibid.*, pp. 448–49.

[8] "Market Concepts in Political Theory," *The Canadian Journal of Economics and Political Science*, 27, no. 4 (November 1961), 496. Macpherson's ease in identifying "the most serious problems" is perhaps a result of an element of dogmatism in his socialist perspective.

doing political theory consistent with his broad approach to political science. He does not claim that it is the only method appropriate for a humanistic political science, but argues only that it is suitable for the task of considering the diagnosis that the weaknesses of liberalism can be repaired and that liberalism does not have to be abandoned as a progressive theory. This diagnosis is based on the notion that "the repair that was needed was one that would bring back a sense of the moral value of community, which had been present in some measure in the Puritan and Lockean theory," [9] and had made this theory progressive. Macpherson argues that the diagnosis is mistaken because the difficulties of liberalism lie in the assumption, latent in the liberal tradition, of possessive individualism—the idea "of the individual as essentially the proprietor of his own person or capacities, owing nothing to society for them." [10] He attempts to show that this assumption was at the root of seventeenth-century political theory and continues to influence twentieth-century accounts of liberal democracy.

Macpherson notes that the assumption of possessive individualism has not generally been clearly identified by commentators, has been beneath and beyond the notice of philosophical and historical critics because it appears in "uncertain mixtures of assumptions about fact and assumptions about right," and was not made explicit in the theories themselves. These considerations posed the problem for Macpherson of justifying his claim that seventeenth-century theorists were using some assumptions beyond those they explicitly formulated. He notes that his claims cannot be established with certainty and cannot be satisfactorily supported merely by showing that unstated assumptions are required to produce the conclusions of a theory. The presumption that unstated assumptions were used, however, could be supported if the assumptions were such that the author could take it for granted that his readers would share them, that they were used by the writer in other contexts than the one being examined, and that they filled gaps in the argument. Of course, an author might not even have been aware of some of his assumptions. In this case, if the assumptions are

---

[9] *The Political Theory*, p. 2.
[10] *Ibid.*, p. 3.

such that they "might readily have arisen from that thinker's experience of his own society" and are "repeatedly implied in various of his incidental arguments, the probability that he was using such assumptions is sufficient to entitle us to admit them." [11] Further, assumptions might have been concealed or disguised "either from fear of offending the readers whom he wanted to convert to his conclusion, or from fear of persecution."

Given the importance Macpherson attaches to unstated assumptions, his method depends on identifying "some real or supposed inconsistency in a theoretical structure." While he is guided by the hypothesis that the seventeenth-century thinkers tended to be consistent, he does not hypothesize that each of the theories they produced was consistent. Although sometimes the disclosure of an implicit assumption resolves an apparent inconsistency, more often the result shows that the theory was "in some respects strictly inconsistent, even (or especially) when its implicit assumptions have been given full weight." [12] Thus, the method achieves an explanation of how a theorist could have been unaware of key assumptions, but not a resolution of logical inconsistencies in his work. The aim of Macpherson's method is to reveal the directions and limits of a thinker's vision of the human condition.

Macpherson's discussion of method is not complete. One may ask how the investigator arrives at one particular set of possible unstated assumptions. Macpherson admits that more than one set of assumptions might be appropriate to produce a given conclusion, but in his analysis of the seventeenth-century thinkers he does not test any assumptions but those of possessive individualism. This leads to the possibility that the use of possessive individualism as a means for interpreting seventeenth-century thought did not arise out of a critical examination of early liberal writings, but was derived from the conceptual scheme of socialist humanism, particularly its critique of capitalism. While this possibility does not challenge Macpherson's method, it does challenge the independence of that method from prior substantive philosophical commitments.

[11] *Ibid.*, p. 6.
[12] *Ibid.*, p. 8.

Thus, Macpherson's method is chiefly a means of verifying hypotheses generated in a wider scheme of social criticism. This only strengthens the judgment that Macpherson's political thought forms a unity.

For Macpherson, method is subordinate to problem. He believes that the historian of political thought ought to clarify the limits and possibilities of a tradition as applied to the present. The tradition that Macpherson has attempted to understand is liberalism. His basic argument is that liberal-democracy is based on the assumption of possessive individualism and that the persistence of this assumption is in some measure "responsible for the difficulties of liberal-democratic theory in our own time." [13]

In "Market Concepts in Political Theory" he defines this assumption as an image of human nature:

> Man is the proprietor of his own person. He is what he owns. The human essence is freedom to do what one wills with one's own, a freedom properly limited only by such rules as are needed to secure the same freedom for others. On these assumptions, the best society (indeed the only possible good society) is one in which all social relations between individuals are transformed into market relations in which men are related to each other as possessors of their own capacities (and of what they have acquired by the exercise of their capacities.) [14]

Possessive individualism is the image of human nature generated by competitive capitalist market society. In "Elegant Tombstones," his critique of Milton Friedman's defense of capitalism, Macpherson distinguishes a capitalist economy from a simple exchange economy. In a simple exchange economy a number of independent producers, each one owning his own means of production, compete to make the most advantageous exchange possible. Since they have direct access to the means of labor, they have the option of leaving the system of exchange altogether and producing their own subsistence. The simple exchange economy does not fully concretize the image of possessive individualism because it assumes that labor is not a detachable resource capable of being sold on the market. In capi-

---

[13] Ibid., p. 4.
[14] "Market Concepts," p. 496.

talism, however, labor is something that can be bought and sold because it is viewed simply as a possession of the individual: "What distinguishes the capitalist economy from the simple exchange economy is the separation of labor and capital, that is, the existence of a labor force without its own sufficient capital and therefore without a choice as to whether to put its labor in the market or not." [15]

The separation of labor from capital is the key to capitalism as an exploitative system of property relations because the owners of capital levy a toll for access to the means of production. In a reply to Ronald W. Crowley's defense of Friedman, Macpherson observes: "The most freely competitive capitalist economy, quite apart from its inherent momentum towards monopoly or oligopoly, does entail the amassing of capital in the hands of a fraction of the members of the society, which gives that fraction economic power over the rest." [16] Thus, in a capitalist market society, even if it is fully competitive, incomes cannot be proportional to people's expenditure of energy and skill because the market must "reward ownership as well as exertion." [17] However, the deepest moral failing of capitalism goes beyond the appropriation of surplus value by owners and concerns the inadequacies of the assumption of possessive individualism itself. The detachment of labor from the person means that the majority of people are prevented from using strength and skill creatively: "The power of a horse or machine may be defined as the amount of work it can do whether it is set to work or not. But a human being, to be human, must be able to use his strength and skill for purposes he has consciously formed." [18]

While possessive individualism is the moral foundation for the alienation of labor, it is not sufficient to account for the dynamics of capitalist market society. In addition to possessive individualism, the assumption of a desire for unlimited appro-

---

[15] "Elegant Tombstones," *Canadian Journal of Political Science*, 1, no. 1 (March 1968), 98.
[16] "Interpretation vs. Criticism," *Canadian Journal of Political Science*, 2, no. 3 (September 1969), 357.
[17] *The Real World of Democracy* (Oxford, 1966), p. 58.
[18] *Ibid.*, p. 43. Presumably, this does not mean that purposes must be original if a human being is to be "human."

priation underlies the capitalist market model, although Macpherson does not appear to recognize it consistently. Nevertheless, he does take account of this assumption in his essay "Post-Liberal-Democracy," in which he shows how the principle of diminishing marginal utility is inconsistent with a fully capitalist system. He argues that the principle of diminishing marginal utility implies that some wants are more important than others. Thus, acceptance of this principle makes it difficult to justify severe inequalities of wealth or income on utilitarian grounds. The difficulty is avoided in recent capitalist thought by postulating ". . . that all men inherently desire to emulate others, or innately desire ever more." [19]

However, the assumption of a desire for unlimited appropriation is not logically derivable from possessive individualism, which is merely the notion that the essence of human beings is freedom to do what one wills with one's own. It is perhaps the assumption of a desire for unlimited appropriation rather than the notion of possessive individualism that is more important in contemporary capitalist societies. Macpherson sometimes realizes this: "The implacable force in the drama of liberal society was scarcity in relation to unlimited desire." [20] It has been this "implacable force," coupled with the idea that labor could be appropriated for private use, that has provided the dynamics of capitalist society. It is perhaps this same force, coupled with the idea that labor can be appropriated for use by the state or governing party, that provides the dynamics of communist and underdeveloped societies. Given that the "myth of maximization" is added to the assumption of possessive individualism, Macpherson's treatment of liberal society is intelligible. The next step is to follow Macpherson's argument that the liberal society is marked by a liberal state, which has become a liberal-democratic state.

The roots of the liberal state are in the exploitative aspects of liberal society, as well as in the need to coordinate activities of people freed from the authoritative allocations of traditional economy. With respect to the breakdown of tradition, Macpherson has written: ". . . in a market society in which everybody is

[19] "Post-Liberal-Democracy," *The Canadian Journal of Economics and Political Science*, 30, no. 4 (November 1964), 492–93.
[20] *The Real World*, p. 61.

put on his own, freed from the ties and protections of a non-market society, the only possible guarantor of individual freedom is a state strong enough to prevent the disintegrative forces of the market from breaking up the society." [21] However, far more important than the coordinative aspect of the state is its exploitative aspect. Macpherson declares: ". . . the market economy, in principle as well as in history, cannot prevail in any society until labor has been reduced to a commodity, which can only be done in the measure that the laborer is separated from the means and objects of labor, and this, as the classical economists recognized, requires continuous state coercion." [22]

According to Macpherson the liberal state arose to protect the interests of those who controlled the means to labor. At first it was not a democratic state, and only became so through the growth of pressures from below. The essence of the liberal state was "the system of alternate or multiple parties whereby governments could be held responsible to different sections of the class or classes that had a political voice." [23] The two functions of this state were to adjust conflicting interests held by different sections of the dominant class and to provide a check on arbitrary uses of state power. As the liberal state was democratized, democracy was liberalized: "By admitting the mass of the people into the competitive party system, the liberal state did not abandon its fundamental nature; it simply opened the competitive political system to all the individuals who had been created by the competitive market society." [24]

This account of liberal democracy presents a problem. It is reasonable to assume that as a capitalist society matures, and the means to labor are progressively concentrated in the hands of a small class, the liberal state will come to play more and more of an exploitative rather than a coordinative role. Macpherson admits this when he remarks that the dilemma of modern liberal-democratic theory is that "it must continue to use the assumptions of possessive individualism, at a time when the structure of market society no longer provides the necessary

<hr/>

[21] "Halévy's Century Revisited," p. 43.
[22] "A Disturbing Tendency," p. 101. A market economy is, of course, defined as one in which labor has been reduced to a commodity.
[23] *The Real World*, p. 4.
[24] *Ibid.*, p. 11.

conditions for deducing a valid theory of political obligation from those assumptions." [25] While the liberal state was once supported by the fact that "those who might have had doubts about its rightness were confronted with its inevitability," [26] today "bourgeois individualism is in retreat, pressed by socialist and other humanisms." [27]

Why, then, do the liberal democracies continue to exist, when the masses, who have the vote, are being exploited in a capitalist economy? Macpherson rejects the answer that the transfer payments of the welfare state and the growth of a managed capitalist economy have fundamentally changed capitalism. The exploitative labor market remains and the exploitation of taste has been added to it: ". . . the change to the welfare state and the managed market cannot be counted on to provide an improvement of the quality of life as judged by the liberal-democratic criterion. We can only count on the manufacture and control of tastes." [28]

What accounts for the persistence of the liberal-state in the twentieth century when it is morally flawed and when there are presumably more attractive possibilities attainable? In the *Real World of Democracy*, Macpherson remarks that the West has had "the peculiar good fortune" of not having to face the problem of regenerating people debased by an inhuman society, because it has "been able to coast on the liberal revolutions of the seventeenth and eighteenth centuries." [29] In order to make sense of this apparently inconsistent remark, it is necessary to consider Macpherson's argument that liberal-democracy is a special case of democracy rather than the essence of democracy.

As early as 1949, in "The Political Theory of Social Credit," Macpherson questioned the notion that the liberal variant of democracy was the fullest moral expression of democracy:

> Just as orthodox economic theory before Keynes was, without realizing it, dealing with a special case of economic equilibrium,

[25] *The Political Theory*, p. 275.
[26] "Market Concepts," p. 497.
[27] "Progress of the Locke Industry," *Canadian Journal of Political Science*, 3, no. 2 (June 1970), 326.
[28] "Post-Liberal-Democracy," p. 497.
[29] *The Real World*, p. 20.

. . . so, perhaps, orthodox political theory, which explains the alternate-party system as an essential mechanism of modern democracy, may be, without realizing it, dealing with a special case of democracy rather than with the general case.[30]

In the orthodox theory, the essence of democratic society is the multitude of group interests, and the essential function of the democratic state is to adjust these interests. However, Macpherson argues that the wide variety of interests, and the political function of adjusting them, only appears in conditions of expanding prosperity:

> The adjustment of multitudinous group interests is the *primary* task of democratic political institutions only in a peaceful and expanding society the economic and political power relations of which are generally acceptable, so that there is no strong or urgent pressure to establish, or having established, to consolidate a new structure of economic class relationships. It is for such a society that the need of the alternate-party system can be shown by the orthodox arguments.[31]

This means that there is a broader idea of democracy than that of liberal-democracy, and that, presumably, conditions of expanding prosperity in the West have been responsible for the maintenance of liberal-democracy despite the exploitative features of the underlying capitalist society.

In various of his writings, Macpherson defines the broader idea of democracy and sets up typologies of democratic systems. In *The Real World of Democracy* he remarks that while contemporary ideas of democracy differ on questions of means, they all prescribe the same ultimate goal: "to provide the conditions for the full and free development of the essential human capacities of all the members of the society." [32] In "The Political Theory of Social Credit," Macpherson used this criterion to show that a society with one-class rule, and with a one-party or no-party system, may be democratic. Such a system would promote democracy if it released "the productive force of society from previous obstacles" and if it developed "wide participation in adminis-

---

[30] "The Political Theory of Social Credit," *The Canadian Journal of Economics and Political Science*, 15, no. 3 (August 1949), 389.

[31] *Ibid.*, pp. 389-90.

[32] *The Real World*, p. 36.

tration." [33] It would be possible to think of a general will sustaining democracy without alternative parties in a society without class division and with popular franchise because "the people would regard that state's purposes as their own." [34] However, Macpherson added that even in such an ideal condition, "historical evidence" suggests that no-party or one-party democracy can only be sustained where there is wide popular participation in the administration and formulation of policy.

In his early works on the types of democratic systems, Macpherson opposed an ideal type of democracy in a classless society, to a more empirical type of liberal-democracy. In his later work, particularly in *The Real World of Democracy*, he has compared the same conception of liberal-democracy to other empirical types. He has essentially adapted his classless model to the ideas of democracy expressed in the underdeveloped countries. Macpherson argues that the theorists of emerging nations view their societies as classless and postulate a general will for national unity and economic development. Thus, while theories of liberal-democracy treat government as a consumer's good, theories of the general will treat it as a producer's good, or capital investment. Like all capital investments, government in the underdeveloped countries "cannot be controlled directly, but at most only indirectly and at one long remove, by consumer choices." [35] Yet even though a competitive party system is neither practicable in nor desired by these countries, their doctrines have in common with liberal-democracy a belief in "the ultimate worth of the dignity and freedom of the human being." [36] The determination of whether or not such a general will is present in many, or even some of, the emerging nations is beyond the scope of this essay. It is sufficient to remark that in the process of adapting his original model, Macpherson appears to have altered the conditions for success from releasing the productive force of society from previous obstacles and developing wide participation in administration, to the existence of a general will for national unity and economic development.

Macpherson also discusses a third empirical type of de-

---

[33] "The Political Theory of Social Credit," p. 390.
[34] *Ibid.*, p. 391.
[35] *The Real World*, p. 34.
[36] *Ibid.*, p. 29.

mocracy in *The Real World of Democracy*, the people's democracy of the communist world. He notes that communist regimes are revolutionary and are, therefore, faced with the problem of transforming a society which debases human beings through the efforts of those who have been debased by it. The heart of this problem is that "people who have been debased by their society cannot be morally regenerated except by the society being reformed, and this requires political power." [37] Yet despite their use of power in the service of moral reform, these regimes are democratic in their pursuit of "an equality [that] could only be fully realized in a society where no class was able to dominate or live at the expense of others." [38] Macpherson does admit that the people's democracies are not democratic in a narrower sense, but suggests that they could become so under the conditions of full intraparty democracy, open party membership, and a price of membership in the party that involved no greater degree of activity "than the average person can reasonably be expected to contribute." [39] Again, it is beyond the scope of this essay to evaluate the accuracy of Macpherson's analysis of people's democracy. It is sufficient to note at present that this type has no analogue in his earlier work and that its absence there is probably accounted for by the fact that Macpherson had not yet made the problem of moral regeneration one of his central concerns.

In his discussion of a broader idea of democracy, based on the moral end of promoting "the moral, intellectual, and active worth of all individuals," Macpherson answered the question of why liberal-democracy has persisted despite an underlying exploitative capitalist society, by arguing that the conditions for maintaining liberal-democracy are a peaceful, expanding, and prosperous economy. Further, he noted that under the condition of national revolution and economic development a regime based on a theory of the general will is viable, while under the condition of communist revolution a regime based on a theory of people's democracy is viable. From these conclusions, Mac-

[37] *Ibid.*, p. 19. "Moral regeneration" means at the minimum being purged of possessive individualism and at the maximum being oriented towards development of moral potentialities.

[38] *Ibid.*, p. 22.

[39] *Ibid.*, p. 21.

pherson develops an image of the contemporary human condition as it affects the West.

Macpherson holds that the contemporary world is characterized by multiple crises. The overriding crisis is perhaps the fact that "technical change in the methods of war, that has made war an impossible source of internal cohesion, has created a new quality of insecurity among individuals, not merely within one nation but everywhere." [40] Within this general crisis is the particular problem of liberal-democracy, summed up in the statement: "Liberal-democratic nations can no longer expect to run the world, nor can they expect that the world will run to them." [41] The climate of uncertainty and the challenge to liberal-democracy by other democratic systems raises the question of "whether we are likely to lose our unique system by our own doing, or on what terms can we keep it?" [42]

Macpherson reasons that if military technology has ruled out the use of force in settling major political conflicts, "the relative power and influence of different nations and sections of the world is going to have to depend on the degree to which their economic and political systems satisfy the desires of all their people." [43] At present the communist nations have a moral advantage in this competition because they do not levy a toll on access to the means to labor, but are at a moral disadvantage because they do not provide the same measure of political freedoms and civil liberties as the liberal-democracies do. However, Macpherson predicts that the people's democracies are likely to retain their moral advantage in the future, while the liberal-democracies are likely progressively to lose their advantage as the police states in the East loosen up. This means that "we in the West will decline in power unless we can discard our possessive market morality": "Power-oriented as we are, this argument should surely be decisive." [44]

What are the prospects for the "revolution in democratic consciousness" proposed by Macpherson? He summarizes the problem in "Market Concepts in Political Theory": "The jus-

[40] *The Political Theory*, p. 276.
[41] *The Real World*, p. 3.
[42] *Ibid.*
[43] *Ibid.*, p. 65.
[44] *Ibid.*, p. 66.

tification of liberal-democracy still rests, and must rest, on the ultimate value of the free self-developing individual. But in so far as freedom is still seen as possession, as freedom from any but market relations with others, it can scarcely serve as the ultimate value of modern democracy." [45] It appears that the key to resolving this problem is found in Macpherson's critique of contemporary economic theory. It was noted above in the discussion of liberalism that Macpherson argued that the principle of diminishing marginal utility was destructive of capitalism because it did not make all desires equal and, therefore, did not justify severe inequalities of wealth or income. In the same essay in which this analysis appeared, Macpherson endorsed Mill's rejection of the maximization of indifferent utilities as the criterion of social good and his replacement of it with "the maximum *development* and use of human capacities—moral, intellectual, aesthetic, as well as material productive capacities." [46]

In "Halévy's Century Revisited," Macpherson makes the same point even more strongly:

> . . . whatever one may say about J. S. Mill's elitism, he did have a more humanistic and democratic idea of the essence of man than any of his Utilitarian predecessors, and it was his attempt to square this with their purely bourgeois view of man as a maximizer of utilities that led him to confront the central problem of modern theory.[47]

Thus, it would appear that in order for liberal-democracies to persist in the contemporary world, they must lose their character as liberal-democracies, because it is only in a prosperous and expanding capitalist society that the liberal-democratic model is appropriate.[48] This paradox, or inconsistency, has been present throughout the discussion of Macpherson's thought. It is now time to analyze the inconsistency with a view to revealing Macpherson's own veiled assumptions.

According to Macpherson, investigation of a body of thought should be guided by the hypothesis that the thinker was consistent within the limits of his vision, and one should

[45] P. 407.
[46] "Post-Liberal-Democracy," p. 489.
[47] P. 38.
[48] "Market Concepts," p. 494.

therefore use apparent inconsistencies to clarify the limits and direction of the vision. In the following critique, these standards will be applied to Macpherson's thought.

Macpherson remarked in his discussion of method that "when we find inconsistent positions being taken in a single sentence we are entitled to ask whether any assumptions the writer may then have had in mind can account for such statements." [49] Such inconsistent positions appear in Macpherson's own writings. For example, in his argument about the problem of justifying liberal-democracy, Macpherson states that the justification of liberal-democracy rests on the ultimate value of the free self-developing individual and also states that liberal-democracy cannot be justified through the notion of freedom as a possession. Yet according to Macpherson, liberal-democracy has always rested on liberal society, which has in turn exemplified the assumption of possessive individualism. He states that the moral failing of liberal-democracies is that they are based on a possessive market morality rather than on a morality of creative freedom. Given the compulsory transfers involved in liberal society and backed up by the liberal state, whether or not it is democratic, it is difficult to see how creative freedom could supplant freedom from any but market relations in liberal-democracies.

A related inconsistency appears in Macpherson's discussion of the social conditions necessary for the persistence of liberal-democracy. Macpherson argues that liberal-democracy is supported by an expanding capitalist economy which promises enough affluence to mute class conflict. It would be reasonable to assume on these grounds that fundamental changes in liberal-democracy would arise from the disturbance of these conditions, such as an economic crisis that would intensify class conflict and lead ultimately to the dissolution of the capitalist system. Yet Macpherson does not mention such models of social change, but argues, instead, that a "revaluation of democratic consciousness" is needed in the liberal-democracies. He expects this moral regeneration to take place because it will aid the Western nations in the race for power. As an "operative" recommendation he does not call for transformation of a capital-

[49] *The Political Theory,* p. 8.

ist system that he has branded immoral, but urges the Western nations to give "massive aid" to the poor nations so that economic development will be speeded and "the moral stature and power" of the liberal-democracies preserved.

Still another related inconsistency appears in Macpherson's discussion of the people's democracies. He argues that the West has been able to avoid the problem of imposing moral regeneration on human beings debased by their society because it has been coasting along on the waves of the liberal revolutions. Yet, according to Macpherson, liberal society cannot be morally justified because it frustrates the development of human capacities through the alienation of labor and fosters "a money-grubbing, maximizing behaviour." In contemporary capitalist societies we can "only count on the manufacture and control of tastes." Are not those people whose tastes have been manipulated debased? If so, has the West really been so fortunate that it has been able to coast along?

Thus, there are three major inconsistencies in Macpherson's thought. First, he holds that liberal-democracy is justified by a commitment to human development and that liberal society frustrates human development. Second, he holds that liberal-democracy is maintained by economic factors, but should be reformed by changes in consciousness. Third, he holds that liberal-democracies need not face the problem of imposing moral regeneration and that liberal society debases human beings. These inconsistencies are closely related to one another and can be made sense of, though not resolved, by three assumptions.

It is best to begin with the third paradox because the assumption which explains it is explicit in Macpherson's thought and provides the key to the other assumptions. Why does Macpherson not claim that a large number of people living in Western democracies have been debased by their society? It is obvious that if tastes are manipulated and labor is alienated, the kind of moral, intellectual, and creative development prescribed by Mill is being thwarted. The solution to this problem seems to lie in Macpherson's assumption that "people who have been debased by their society cannot be morally regenerated except by the society being reformed, and this requires political power." It is reasonable to surmise that Macpherson has been unwilling to face up to the consequences of his own assumption when it is applied to the Western liberal-democracies. He does not, in short, want to believe that large segments of Western populations must be forced to be free, if freedom means human development in Mill's sense. Since he is unwilling to face the consequences, he covers over the problem by stating that the liberal-democracies have already undergone their revolutions.

The preceding analysis leads into the explanation of the second paradox. What can explain Macpherson's advocacy of ideological changes when he accounts for the stability of liberal-democracies in terms of economic factors? The assumption in this case is that people who are being exploited by the capitalist system will not complain so long as there is general prosperity. This assumption is consistent with the principle that moral regeneration must be imposed. For Macpherson, the masses living under capitalism are less concerned with intellectual, moral, and active development than with security and prosperity. They will revolt only in an economic crisis, and following Macpherson's line of argument it is reasonable to assume that in the event of a successful revolution moral regeneration would still have to be imposed by a vanguard. Since Macpherson is unwilling to face this consequence he is led to advocate peaceful change through transformation of consciousness and appeals to the enlightened self-interest of power-hungry men.

The final paradox can be explained by extending the preceding discussion. Macpherson proclaims the ultimate morality of liberal-democracy and denounces the immorality of liberal society because, given his failure to will the means to overcoming human debasement, he must attempt to rescue whatever human values are present in liberal-democracy and hope that they will eventually leaven the mass. The assumption here is contained in the fundamental question he poses about the contemporary human condition: ". . . whether we are likely to lose our unique system by our own doing, or on what terms can we keep it?" Thus, the final assumption, is that, given an aversion to imposing moral regeneration on significant numbers of debased people, the rescue of liberal-democracy is the best hope for the West. This assumption does not resolve the inconsistency, but does show clearly enough the limitations and directions of Macpherson's vision. His vision is that of an intellectual who cannot condone the use of force to impose moral transformation, but who believes that force is necessary to lead the unregenerate masses towards moral fulfillment. This fundamental dilemma leads a humanistic political scientist with socialist leanings to launch a rescue operation to save liberal-democracy and its accompaniment, the power-seeking nation-state. Yet the operation is doomed to failure from the beginning because Macpherson cannot avoid attacking liberal society at its very roots and showing how it is integrally related to liberal-democracy.

It is up to contemporary humanistic political scientists to leave Macpherson's inconsistencies behind and to resolve his dilemma. The first step toward resolving it is to repudiate the assumption that moral regeneration must be imposed by force. Abandoning this assumption may give rise to attempts at innovating new ways of actively encouraging self-examination among large numbers of people. In various liberation movements such self-examination is well under way and new methods of "consciousness-raising" are being discovered. These efforts do not merely aim at a change in attitude, but involve activity directed to recasting roles. It is up to humanists to participate in this activity with an eye to making sure that it is principled by the kinds of values Mill prescribed. It is up to social scientists to diffuse such methods as participant observation and the "sociological imagination," and such theoretical tools as the sociology of knowledge, as widely as possible. It is through such efforts that political theory will go beyond the latent pessimism in Macpherson's thought and the thought of those like him. The question will no longer be how to rescue liberal-democracy but will be, instead, how to attain human development most effectively.

John Rawls:
A Theory of Justice

by SAMUEL GOROVITZ

For nearly two decades in the 1950s and 1960s professional philosophers followed with increasing interest the developing work of John Rawls and eagerly discussed such examples of his writing as they could acquire. Occasionally, an essay would appear in a philosophical journal. Invariably, it would be well received, would prompt discussion and criticism, and would heighten curiosity about an oft-rumored but elusive major book. Rawls was little known outside academia—indeed, outside the ranks of the philosophically *au courant*. Then, in 1971, *A Theory of Justice* [1] appeared. Mammoth, complex, and ambitious, it sent the practitioners of moral and political philosophy into a reflective sequestration, as they sought to come to grips with the intricate argumentation of the book. In 1972, when reviews began to appear in prominent places, *A Theory of Justice*—and John Rawls with it—soared blazingly into prominence throughout the intellectual world. For what reviews they were! Scholars known for their high standards of critical judgment—Stuart Hampshire, G. J. Warnock, and Marshall Cohen—described the book as "magisterial," "a peerless contribution to political theory," and "a permanent refutation of the reproach that analytical philosophy cannot contribute to substantial moral and political thought." And they likened it in various ways to works by Plato, John Stuart Mill, and Immanuel Kant. No fit fare for the layman, this demanding treatise was nonetheless designated by the *New York Times Book Review* as one of five

[1] Cambridge, Mass., 1971.

significant books of 1972—in part on the grounds that "its political implications may change our lives."

In discussing the work of John Rawls, I shall focus exclusively on his remarkable book. My aim will be to provide a sense of the historical context in which it appears; to explicate its objectives, methods, and consequences; and to identify some of its most provocative points. But overall assessment is premature, for the book may not be adequately understood for years, and may well become the sort of classic over which disputes rage for generations. Indeed, although I shall highlight the fundamental features of *A Theory of Justice,* I cannot address even superficially the full spectrum of issues that fall within its scope. For the work consists of eighty-seven sections, many the length of small essays, covering not only the theory which Rawls develops, but many of its ramifications, under such diverse headings as "Toleration of the Intolerant," "The Concept of Justice in Political Economy," "The Problem of Justice Between Generations," "The Duty to Comply with an Unjust Law," "Self-Respect, Excellence and Shame," "The Concept of a Well-Ordered Society," "The Principles of Moral Psychology," and "The Idea of Social Union."

The basic objective of *A Theory of Justice* is to provide a coherent theoretical foundation for a conception of justice that can be offered in opposition to the utilitarian point of view that has been dominant since Jeremy Bentham. In order to appreciate the impact of this book, we should therefore review briefly the utilitarian tradition to which it is opposed.

Although there are elements of utilitarianism in the writings of David Hume, and sustained and detailed development of it constitutes a major component of the works of Bentham, the most prominent advocacy of utilitarianism as a moral theory is found in Mill's *Utilitarianism.* In *A System of Logic,* Mill had written that

> There must be some standard by which to determine the goodness or badness, absolute and comparative, of ends or objects of desire. And whatever that standard is, there can be but one . . . .

He then declared:

> That the general principle to which all rules of practice ought to conform, and the test by which they should be tried, is that of conduciveness to the happiness of mankind . . . .[2]

In *Utilitarianism,* Mill attempts to explain and support this point of view, and that attempt has provided the dominant influence in moral philosophy ever since. The principle of utilitarianism has enormous appeal, calling as it does for each agent to perform that action which will do more good for more people than any other. It seems hard to imagine how an action satisfying such a condition could fail to be the right thing to do. Many objections have been raised against utilitarianism, but the basic attractiveness of a theory that selects as right the action that maximizes human happiness has led moral philosophers for the most part to try to answer the objections in an essentially utilitarian way, rather than to abandon utilitarianism in light of the objections. However, while the debate about the adequacy of utilitarianism as a moral theory has continued, the influence of utilitarianism on legislative policy has been profound. Indeed, Bentham's doctrine of utilitarianism was developed largely in order to provide a justificatory framework for legislation, and Mill, both as a private citizen and as a Member of Parliament, maintained a deep and active concern with matters of governmental and legislative interest. Their heritage has been a profoundly influential one, and the liberal tradition in Anglo-American law has reflected ever since the basic view that the maximization of social welfare is the proper object of legislative activity.

The objections against utilitarianism have covered a variety of points. The consistency of the utilitarian principle has been challenged, on the grounds that what maximizes the total amount of happiness may differ from what maximizes the number of people whose happiness is advanced, and that the utilitarian principle thus is in reality an amalgam of two different, sometimes conflicting, principles. Questions have been raised about the clarity of the notion of utility, about the plausibility of a principle that requires quantitative evaluations of pleasure or happiness, about the intelligibility of comparative evaluations of utility, and about whose utility counts as the in-

[2] Bk. VI, Ch. 12, Sect. 7.

terests of actual people are weighed against one another and against those of future generations or of other sentient creatures. But the most serious challenge to utilitarianism is the charge that it sanctions violations of the principles of justice.

Mill had argued that such principles not only were consonant with the utilitarian principle, but that they followed from it. "To have a right," Mill claimed, is

> . . . to have something which society ought to defend one in the possession of. If the objector goes on to ask why it ought, I can give him no other reason than general utility.

And against the notion of justice as an independent standard, he continued:

> If the preceding analysis, or something resembling it, be not the correct account of the notion of justice—if justice be totally independent of utility, and be a standard *per se*, which the mind can recognize by a simple introspection of itself—it is hard to understand why that internal oracle is so ambiguous, and why so many things appear either just or unjust, according to the light in which they are regarded.[3]

But Mill's argument has not been entirely convincing. Those who have opposed utilitarianism because of considerations of justice have not responded to Mill's challenge that an intuitive sense of justice provides no coherent opposition to the principle of utilitarianism. Rather, they have argued that utilitarianism is untenable on the grounds that it sanctions, or could sanction, acts of a sort we know to be unjust. For example, one might imagine a state of affairs in which a maximum amount of happiness would be produced, and its distribution to a maximum number of people achieved by the enslavement of a minority. That such action may not in fact be the utilitarian thing to do is beside the point, so the argument goes. For it conceivably could be, and hence utilitarianism, in principle, is compatible with unjust institutions such as slavery. While the critics of utilitarianism have searched for more and more examples of morally culpable actions which they believe utilitarianism to permit—e.g., broken promises, punishment of the innocent, or denial of minority rights—the defenders of utilitarianism have

[3] *Utilitarianism*, Ch. 5.

reformulated their theory in an effort to show that such actions are not, in fact, sanctioned by the theory, but rather are prohibited by it. Thus the debate has centered almost entirely on disputes about the adequacy of utilitarianism as a moral theory in light of our convictions about individual rights, personal integrity, and fairness. The comparative virtues of utilitarianism, as a moral theory in competition with others, have not been at issue, for no competing theories have been available as plausible, well-developed alternatives.

Now the nature of the debate has changed. For Rawls's theory of justice is not merely one more critical attack on utilitarianism. Instead, it gives us an alternative moral perspective— plausible and well developed—and for the first time advocates of utilitarianism must not only defend it against criticisms, they must try to show its comparative superiority in competition with a challenging and altogether different viewpoint. Thus, Rawls has not simply added an excellent piece of work to moral philosophy, he has altered it. And because he has done so by examining the principles of justice, considering them to be the foundation of social order, his work constitutes a landmark in political philosophy as well.

Rawls begins by describing justice as the first virtue of social institutions. He sets out to discover what principles of justice are most defensible, and in so doing he develops a theory that resurrects both the social contract tradition of Hobbes, Locke, and Rousseau, and the rationalism of Kant. For Rawls, justice is the foundation of social structure. Hence all political and legislative decisions must take place within the constraints that follow from the principles of justice.

Unlike the intuitionists who argued against utilitarianism, Rawls is not content to cite instances of injustice by relying on his intuitive sense, case by case, of what is and what is not just. It is not that he denies the existence or legitimacy of intuitions about justice. On the contrary, he is willing to take such intuitions as evidence about our sense of justice. But it is as evidence for a *theory*—a systematic account of why our sense of justice is what it is—that intuitions have a place in Rawls's account.

The primary domain over which justice operates is, for Rawls, the distribution of goods, where "goods" is taken broadly to include much of what one might reasonably aspire to have: wealth, position, opportunity, skill, liberty, and even self-respect. How such goods are distributed in a just society will depend on what principles of justice are reflected in the system of rights, laws, processes, and positions that constitutes the society as a functioning political entity. Thus, a society based on a utilitarian sense of justice will rank as the highest social good the maximization of welfare, whereas a society based on a conception of perfectionism—for example, the enhancement of the lives and abilities of the most able and most fortunate—will permit and perhaps even require the exploitation of the general population for the benefit of the aristocracy, the "supermen," or the exemplars of what humanity can achieve.

Rawls seeks to articulate and defend a theory of justice that accounts for our commonly shared beliefs about what is and what is not just, and then to employ that theory as the conceptual foundation for a system of constraints on human interaction that stands in marked contrast to utilitarianism and has specific consequences for the framing of social, including economic, policy. These consequences are in some ways at variance both with traditional liberal democracy, which tends to reflect a utilitarian sense of mission, and with the tradition of conservative free-enterprise capitalism, which in some instances tends to reflect a perfectionist ethic and in others the ethical perspective of social Darwinism. Indeed, Rawls's theory provides a fresh sense of what social organization should be for, and therein lies much of its interest and importance.

In the development of his theory of justice, Rawls begins with an understanding of human character that he invites us to accept as reasonable. It is easy to do so, for he wishes to be allowed to assume only a few basic points: that each person has some goals, that whatever those goals may be their pursuit is facilitated by having primary goods, and that the satisfaction of human wants depends in part on the possibility of engaging in social interaction with others.

Next, Rawls asks us to contemplate a group of people coming together to negotiate the principles of justice that are to prevail, on the understanding that, although they are free agents in the negotiation, they are to be bound to live by, and publicly to endorse, the principles that result from the negotiation.

Rawls stresses that the negotiation he describes has no historical basis; the description is a heuristic device that he employs
in order to advance his argument. Thus the negotiation is a hypothetical one. Further ingredients in the hypothesis are that
the negotiators are rational agents, each of whom is well informed about psychology, economics, sociology, and the like,
and that each has a rational life plan—that is, a set of goals and
objectives in terms of which he determines what does and what
does not constitute the advancement of his own interest. Further, each is concerned solely to advance his own interests and
is utterly uninterested in the welfare of his fellow negotiators.
That is, he seeks neither to advance nor impede their pursuit of
such goals as they may have; he knows neither sympathy nor
envy, but is steadfast in his pursuit of his own objectives.

Thus far, the scenario is familiar; we envision individuals
who might otherwise be in a state of nature—be it one of war,
confusion, isolation, or just inefficiency—coming together to
fashion a social contract, defining the body politic and specifying its scope and limits. Such notions are featured prominently
in earlier political philosophers, and the social contract theory
of political legitimacy has been viewed as historically important
in spite of its being eclipsed by the utilitarian tradition, at least
within the purview of analytical philosophy. But Rawls adds a
new dimension. For on his account, the negotiators have the additional constraint of what he calls the "veil of ignorance." That
is, they are utterly without knowledge of particular facts, about
themselves or others. Thus, although they have an immense
amount of knowledge of general truths—such as the laws of
physics, the principles of supply and demand in an unconstrained economy, and the effects, say, of social isolation—they
know literally nothing about who they are, what their personal
characteristics are, or what kind of social context they are from.
In short, for all they know, they could be literally anyone—of
any age, sex, race, ability, etc. They know that they have goals
which they wish to advance, but they are perfectly ignorant as
to what those goals are. They are thus completely unable to distinguish themselves from anyone else on the basis of any criterion or characteristic whatever.

The purpose and effect of the veil of ignorance is to eliminate from the negotiation any possibility of the participants

seeking to protect their own special interest at the expense of the interests of others. No biases can occur among rational deliberators beset by the veil of ignorance, since no such negotiator has any idea whether a biased position will help or hinder him once the veil is lifted and he discovers his position in the real world. At this point, a certain dilemma may seem to have arisen, for the negotiators have been characterized both as seeking single-mindedly to advance their own interests and also as completely incapable, as a result of the veil of ignorance, of doing anything to advance their own real, but unknown, interests. Yet this dilemma is not unwelcome to Rawls; indeed, it is essential for the further development of his argument.

The situation in which the negotiators find themselves is called the "original position." They have general wisdom and particular ignorance. They seek to advance their own interests, but are unable to distinguish them from anyone else's. They have no recourse, claims Rawls, but to adopt principles that are optimal with respect to the advancement of the interests of whoever is least favored by the principles. That is, in the original position, the rational agent will realize that, at least as far as he can tell from behind the veil of ignorance, he is as likely to suffer as to benefit from the application of any principles that promote the interests of some more than others. In order to advance his own interests, then, he must favor principles which allow the maximum opportunity for pursuit of one's life plan to everyone—and, hence, no matter who he may turn out to be, to him. A new constraint thus emerges from the deliberation: the principles adopted to regulate the fashioning of a social order must be such that one could rationally agree to live by them realizing that one might be society's least advantaged individual.

The negotiators are free in the original position to consider any and all principles of justice. For example, they may, with Thrasymachus in Plato's *Republic,* consider the view that what is just is what is in the interest of the stronger—that is, of the most advantaged. They may consider the Nietzschean notion that the just course of action is the one that is most ennobling of the species, as measured by the achievement of the most "advanced" of men. Or they might consider the view that justice is harmony with nature, that a natural order is the basis of the principles of justice. However, Rawls says, they will reject all such conceptions of justice. For according to each of them, some member of society will be systematically underprivileged—and no rational negotiator would risk being in such a position. Surely they will consider utilitarianism, but that, too, will be rejected. For, Rawls argues, utilitarianism threatens to oppress some members of society in the interest of social welfare; hence so long as one is unsure that he would escape being thus oppressed, it would be less than rational to adopt a system of principles that allows for anyone to be oppressed. In the end, according to Rawls, the negotiators in the original position must arrive at the conception of justice that he calls "justice as fairness."

The conception of justice as fairness is articulated in two fundamental principles of justice. The first principle concerns liberty. Since enslavement or other deprivation of freedom to act is inimical to the pursuit of one's life plan no matter what that plan may be, a guarantee of liberty will be sought by each negotiator. Since if anyone is deprived of liberty, everyone is threatened by the possibility of being that deprived person, rational negotiators will insist on maximizing liberty for all. The first principle will thus be adopted: each person is to have maximum equal liberty. But further reflection will lead to an acknowledgment that actions engaged in by one person may well restrict the liberty of another. The principle of liberty thus cannot reasonably require the unqualified granting of total liberty to everyone; rather the liberty of each must be constrained by the need to protect the liberty of each. A more refined principle of liberty is thus adopted: each person is to have an equal right to the most extensive total system of equal basic liberties compatible with a similar system of liberty for all.

Having thus established that the distribution of liberty is to be equitable, the negotiators will turn to the question of the distribution of other primary goods. If the world were such that each person could have as much as he pleased of each commodity, questions of distribution would not arise. Instead, each person would simply partake as he pleased of whatever commodity he desired. But the world is not like that, and the negotiators know that scarcity—of material goods and social advantages—prevails. In a context of scarcity, some principles governing distribution are an essential part of a conception of justice as a virtue of social institutions. Again, the negotiators will consider a variety of principles. They will reject systems of distribution that discriminate against selected segments of the populace, no matter what the basis for selection. Each will reject a utilitarian principle, since it does not rule out the possibility that an unequal distribution of goods will leave him relatively disadvantaged or exploited in order to maximize the general welfare. The negotiators may consider a principle that mandates a thoroughly equal distribution of goods, so that no person need worry about receiving less of any good, material or otherwise, than any other person. But they will soon come to realize that they stand to benefit by the introduction of certain inequalities in the distribution of advantages. For example, giving a rural physician an airplane would make him relatively advantaged, but even—and perhaps, especially—the least advantaged among the rural populace stand to benefit as a result, and thus should sanction the inequality. The negotiators will want to allow for such inequalities. But other inequalities, such as tax loopholes favoring the very rich at the expense of others, must be prohibited. If there are to be relatively advantaged positions in society, with the resulting inequalities justified on the ground that even the least advantaged individual is better off in virtue of them, each negotiator will realize that in the real world he may aspire to such positions. But the veil of ignorance will prevent him from selecting principles that will favor his own chances of acquiring them. He must instead provide that such positions be equally open to all, lest he be disadvantaged with respect to them. Thus the second principle of justice emerges: social and economic inequalities are to be arranged so that they are both (a) to the greatest benefit of the least advantaged, and (b) attached to offices and positions open to all under conditions of fair equality of opportunity.

As the negotiators consider the two principles of justice, they will realize that conflict is possible between them. That is, it is possible that a restriction of the liberty of some individuals may constitute an inequality that satisfies the second principle; it may result in an increase of goods that benefits everyone. But Rawls rules out such inequalities, arguing that the negotiators will give the first principle an absolute priority over the second.

Thus, even an improvement in the welfare of everyone is insufficient justification for inequitable abridgment of liberty. Rather, a person's liberty may be abridged only insofar as that abridgment constitutes an essential part of a system of liberties that maximizes liberty for all.

The argument that Rawls offers to support his claim that rational deliberators in the original position would give the first principle absolute priority is an especially good example of the subtlety of reasoning that permeates *A Theory of Justice*. Crucial to the argument is Rawls's conviction that among the primary goods self-respect is central and that a fundamental characteristic of human beings is their desire to express their nature in a free social union with others. He then argues that "the basis for self-esteem in a just society" is "the publicly affirmed distribution of fundamental rights and liberties." [4] If self-esteem is the most valuable of primary goods, and if it is dependent on an equitable distribution of liberties, then no negotiator will risk being in a position that is disadvantaged with respect to liberties, lest he be impeded in pursuit of associations and activities through which to express his nature and thereby to achieve self-esteem.

The first principle is thus an absolute constraint on the formation of social institutions and practices. Within the limits of that constraint, the second principle, called the "difference principle," allows for inequalities, so long as they benefit the least advantaged. There is some reason to believe, Rawls claims, that inequalities that satisfy the difference principle will be of general benefit. He writes: "When the contributions of the more favored positions spread generally throughout society and are not confined to particular sectors, it seems plausible that if the least advantaged benefit so do others in between." [5] But this condition, called "chain-connectedness," is not essential, since what induces negotiators in the original position to adopt the difference principle is not that it assures that everyone will benefit from allowable inequalities, but that the least advantaged will benefit from them.

These two principles of justice, and the priority principle,

[4] *A Theory of Justice*, p. 544. All of the references that follow are to this work.
   [5] P. 82.

constitute the fundamental conception of justice for which Rawls argues. He does not claim that these principles are necessary truths, but that their justification "is a matter of mutual support of many considerations of everything fitting together into one coherent view." The conditions descriptive of the original position, Rawls claims, constitute a plausible basis for the establishment of a theory of justice, not because they are *a priori* true, but simply because they are conditions that we do in fact accept, or can be led to accept, by philosophical reflection. The methodology, then, is "to collect together into one conception a number of conditions or principles that we are ready upon due consideration to recognize as reasonable," [6] and the hypothetical deliberations in the original position are "an expository device which sums up the meaning of these conditions and helps us to extract their consequences." [7] Once we acknowledge the legitimacy of the description of the initial position as reflecting convictions about justice that we share, the argument becomes an exercise in rational choice: given those conditions, what would it be most reasonable for negotiators to choose as governing principles, publicly acknowledged, under which to live? Thus, for Rawls, the theory of justice is an application—indeed, he calls it a part—of the theory of rational choice.

The heavy reliance on the exercise of reason, and on determining the sort of principle one could rationally endorse knowing it would be uniformly applied to all, is strongly reminiscent of the Kantian methodology and the resulting conception of the categorical imperative. For Kant, a categorical imperative is a principle that applies to one in virtue of his nature as a free and rational being—and hence applies equally to all. Critics of Kant have objected that he gives no convincing account of what principle fits that description, and it is this criticism that Rawls takes his theory to circumvent. For the conception of the original position, he claims, provides an argument showing specifically which principles free and equal rational beings would choose. For Kant, it is pure reason that yields moral principles. For Rawls, the principles of justice follow from an argument

[6] P. 21.
[7] *Ibid.*

which incorporates as premises a body of beliefs about human psychology, social interaction, and the facts of moderate scarcity and competing claims. Thus Rawls departs from the pure rationalism of Kant, while at the same time offering an argument that is distinctly Kantian in its basic tone.

Once the principles of justice and priority of liberty are taken as established, the argument next moves to the establishment of a social order within the constraints of these principles. Rawls claims that those constraints will "define a workable political conception," [8] although they will not specify uniquely what the social order should be in detail. They will not, for example, discriminate between social orders within which the means of production or transportation are privately owned and those in which there is public ownership. But they will discriminate between those that are repressive, subservient to vested interest, or discriminatory, and those that function in the interest of providing every citizen with the best possible prospects of pursuing his life plan.

The evaluation of alternative social orders parallels the evaluation of conceptions of justice. Once the negotiators arrive at the selected conception of justice, the veil of ignorance is partially lifted, and they enter the second stage of deliberation. Here, they are to frame a constitution specifying the powers of government and the basic rights of citizens. The original position thus gives way to a constitutional convention, to which the negotiators as delegates bring not only their general wisdom, but "the relevant general facts about their society, that is, its natural circumstances and resources, its level of economic advance and political culture, and so on." [9] It is in this context that a constitution is chosen "that satisfies the principles of justice and is best calculated to lead to just and effective legislation." [10] The constitution, constrained by the conception of justice, will have to protect "liberty of conscience and freedom of thought, liberty of the person, and equal political rights." [11] Thus the principle of justice that has most bearing at the constitutional level is the principle of liberty.

[8] P. 195.
[9] P. 197.
[10] Ibid.
[11] Ibid.

Of course Rawls does not suggest that this description has historical accuracy, nor that it is an empirically possible process for future deliberations. Instead, it is the articulation of a point of view with respect to which actual constitutions can be evaluated as being more or less in harmony with the principles of justice.

Once a just constitution is established, the negotiators move to yet another stage: they become legislators. Now constrained not only by the principles of justice, but by the particulars of the adopted constitution as well, they are to judge proposed bills and policies. Once again, the veil of ignorance lifts further, and "the full range of general economic and social facts" [12] becomes part of the negotiators' knowledge. Personal identity and characteristics remain unknown, however, so that no bias is possible in favor of the protection of vested interests. At this stage, it is the difference principle that holds the center stage. Legislation is largely concerned with the achievement of long-term social and economic goals, and the difference principle requires that "social and economic policies be aimed at maximizing the long-term expectations of the least advantaged under conditions of fair equality of opportunity." [13] Thus, laws favoring the privileged are excluded as unjust, unless they result in benefits which accrue maximally to the least advantaged.

Given the possibility of chain-connectedness, such justified inequalities may well exist, and thus Rawls is no uncompromising egalitarian. He is quite prepared to countenance privilege—not, with the utilitarian, to maximize social good—but only in order to improve the plight of the least advantaged. The justifiability of special considerations, such as oil depletion allowances or farm subsidies, depends therefore on empirical facts about whether or not such benefits filter down ultimately to help the neediest. Such questions are often hard to answer, but their appropriateness has been evident in much of our public life. For example, proponents of an SST, acknowledging that a very small percentage of society would directly benefit from the convenience of supersonic flight, went on to argue that the advantages of undertaking the project would nonetheless per-

[12] P. 199.
[13] *Ibid.*

meate society as a result of the facilitation of high-level commercial and governmental interaction, and through the provision of badly needed jobs. The plausibility of the case is not at issue; what is significant is that its advocates, in making it, reflected an awareness that the claim of chain-connectedness of benefits was essential to their attempt to portray the enterprise as socially desirable. But their appeal was to the general utility of the project—to its tendency to maximize social welfare. If Rawls is right in claiming that our deepest and most widely held convictions about justice can best be systematically accounted for by the two principles he advocates, then no such appeal to the general welfare is sufficient. Rather, proponents of the project should have to argue that the privileges resulting from governmental support of the program would specifically benefit the least advantaged, and thus would make the society more just. And if that condition were satisfied, no appeal to the general welfare is even necessary.

While Rawls is not an egalitarian in the sense that he wants the available economic and social advantages distributed equally no matter what, he is surely an egalitarian in his respect for the value and personal autonomy of each individual. Moreover, he is clearly a redistributionist in that he takes the proper function of government to include not merely the maintenance of a social order, but the achievement of distributive justice by placing the highest social value on the needs of the neediest. Since natural abilities and the circumstances of birth are among the advantages the inequitable distribution of which fosters privilege, and since such inequitable distribution is, as a matter of empirical fact, essentially ineliminable, it is a consequence of Rawls's position that the just society will seek to compensate for the resulting privilege by investing its resources, including the abilities of the most talented, in efforts designed to improve the plight of the least fortunate. Such a view is plainly at odds with the rugged individualism of the unconstrained free enterprise economy, and it is equally at odds with the highly controlled communist or socialist state that submerges the individual's autonomy in the quest for greater social welfare. For Rawls, the first obligation of the social order is the achievement of justice, and the legislative consequences of such a view may differ profoundly from those of a utilitarian view of government as an instrument for the maximization of the general happiness.

Rawls claims two kinds of advantages for his theory of justice as fairness as compared with utilitarianism. First, and most importantly, he holds that our sense of justice is more accurately reflected in his two principles than in utilitarianism. Thus, a moral superiority is claimed for the theory. Second, Rawls argues that the social contract theory of justice as fairness among free and equal rational deliberators is a theory that avoids many of the most troublesome problems that utilitarians face in trying to apply their theory to actual choice situations. For example, even knowing that policy A will benefit more people than policy B does not enable the utilitarian to decide in favor of A, since the benefits under B might be so much more productive of happiness that they would outweigh the broader distribution of benefits under A. The resolution of such problems requires the quantitative comparison of one person's pleasures with another's; yet it is unclear that such comparisons are possible to make in an adequate way. For Rawls, however, no such comparisons are needed; it is enough that we be able to identify the least advantaged and predict what will benefit him.

Still, Rawls's theory raises many questions, and it is not without its critics. A growing body of objections to *A Theory of Justice* is developing, and it is reasonable to expect that the philosophical literature in the near and intermediate future will include increasingly many examples of such criticism. Indeed, it is perhaps in engendering such debate that the book may make its most significant contribution.

Objections may be raised primarily at three different levels. First, one can question the adequacy of Rawls's method. Since his arguments seem to rely heavily on the plausibility of the notions of the original position and the veil of ignorance, some critics are challenging the use of these notions, suggesting that the original position is not really intelligible, or that the veil of ignorance would be immobilizing, with the result that the negotiators would be unable to make any decisions at all. Or one might argue that if the notion of the original position is genuinely a heuristic device, then substantive claims cannot be based on its use. A critic holding such a view would, of course, then focus on the kind of support that Rawls offers, independently of the notion of the original position, for the claims that he illustrates by using that notion.

A second level of objection involves granting, at least for purposes of discussion, the adequacy of Rawls's method in principle. One may then question the correctness of the reasoning that is based on it in Rawls's account. For example, we may accept the view that the description of the original position makes sense and agree further that the negotiators could in fact reach conclusions. But we may then disagree with Rawls about what conclusions they would reach. Rawls claims they would seek always to adopt principles that would protect them against the disadvantages of being society's least advantaged citizens. But some critics of Rawls have already begun to argue that such a view is unrealistic; that the negotiators might well be less cautious, willingly risking some deprivations for a chance to be part of a privileged elite. Or one can accept the essential conservatism of the negotiators as Rawls describes them and still question whether that conservatism would necessarily lead to the specific principles that Rawls espouses. Indeed, even the primacy of the primary goods can be called into question. Might not an ascetic anticipate that an equitable distribution of material goods and power would impose on him more than suits his own life plan? And is it not necessary for the negotiators to contemplate the possibility that when the veil lifts they will discover themselves to be such ascetics, to whom serenity, a sense of oneness with nature, and freedom from entrapment in the affairs of the world constitute the goods of life?

A third level of attack is based on an acceptance both of the intelligibility of Rawls's method and of his claim that the principles in question follow from that method. For such acceptance does not entail an acceptance of the principles themselves. One can grant that the two principles of justice follow, as Rawls claims, from the deliberations in the original position, but challenge his claim that those principles adequately reflect our most deeply held convictions about what is just. For example, we may be unwilling to relinquish completely the view that there is some moral worth in striving toward perfection in pursuit of a moral idea that is independent of any social contract. Or we may be uncomfortable about the absence, in Rawls's account, of sustained consideration of the jurisprudential aspects of justice, such as are reflected in our belief that punishment is appropriate for the guilty, but not the innocent.

Rawls is aware of these objections, among others. Surely, more objections will arise also, as initial reactions to *A Theory of Justice* give way to sustained critical examinations. Whether, in the end, the objections can all be met is unknown. What is certain, however, is that Rawls has given us a powerful new instrument for illuminating social problems. He has redirected moral and political philosophy with a major work that, in the best tradition of Aristotle and Mill, may well admit of as much precision as the subject matter will allow. He has demonstrated conclusively that towering achievements in scholarship are not a thing of the past; and his work—analytic but full of substance, rooted in tradition but novel in approach, abstract in conception yet profound in its practical consequences—constitutes a stunning affirmation of the essential creativity of the human intellect in its ceaseless quest for understanding of the moral and political dimensions of our lives.

Biographical and Bibliographical Notes

HANNAH ARENDT

Hannah Arendt was born in Hanover in October 1906. Her philosophical development was influenced by the work of both Heidegger and Jaspers. She did social work in Paris during the thirties and came to the United States in 1941. She worked first in publishing, and has since held visiting academic appointments at Berkeley, Princeton, Columbia etc., but has been primarily based in Chicago and New York.

Her publications include: *The Burden of Our Time*, 1951 (published in later editions as *The Origins of Totalitarianism*); *The Human Condition*, 1958; *Between Past and Future*, 1961; *On Revolution*, 1963; *Eichmann in Jerusalem*, 1963; *Men in Dark Times*, 1968; *On Violence*, 1970; *Crises of the Republic*, 1973.

RAYMOND CLAUDE FERDINAND ARON

Raymond Aron was born in Paris in March 1905. He wrote his Ph.D. in Germany and afterwards during the late thirties he was Secretary of the Centre of Social Studies at the Ecole Normale Supérieure. During the war he edited *La France Libre* from London and afterwards he was a regular columnist of *Figaro*. In 1955 he became a professor at the University of Paris. Since 1970 he has been a professor at the Collège de France.

His publications include: *Introduction à la philosophie de l'histoire*, 1936 (translated as *Introduction to the Philosophy of History*, 1938); *La Sociologie allemande contemporaine*, 1950 (translated as *German Sociology*, 1957); *Les Guerres en chaîne*, 1951 (translated as *The Century of Total War*, 1954); *L'Opium des intellectuels*, 1955 (translated as *The Opium of the Intellectuals*, 1957); *Espoir et peur du siècle: essais non partisans*, 1957 (one essay, *De la guerre*, translated as

On War, 1958); *Immuable et changeante*, 1959 (translated as *France, Steadfast and Changing*, 1960); *France: The New Republic*, 1960; *Paix et guerre entre les nations* (translated as *Peace and War*, 1962); *Les grandes doctrines de sociologie historique*, 1960 (translated as *Main Currents in Sociological Thought*, 1965–1968); *Dix-huit leçons sur la société industrielle*, 1961 (translated as *18 Lectures on Industrial Society*, 1967); *Democratie et totalitarisme*, 1965 (translated as *Democracy and Totalitarianism*, 1968); *Essais sur les libertés*, 1965 (translated as *An Essay on Freedom*, 1970); *Trois essais sur l'âge industriel*, 1966 (translated as *The Industrial Society*, 1967); *Progress and Disillusion*, 1968; *La Révolution introuvable: réflexions sur les événements de mai*, 1968 (translated as *The Elusive Revolution: Anatomy of a Student Revolt*, 1969); *De Gaulle, Israel et les Juifs*, 1968 (translated as *De Gaulle, Israel and the Jews*, 1969); *Marxism and the Existentialists*, 1969; *De la condition historique du sociologie*, 1971; *Etudes politiques*, 1972; *République impériale*, 1973 (translated as *The Imperial Republic*, 1974).

FRIEDRICH AUGUST HAYEK

Friedrich Hayek was born in Vienna in May 1899. He worked first as a civil servant and was then director of the Austrian Institute of Economic Research. He came to England in 1931 and joined the staff of the London School of Economics. In 1950 he became professor of social and moral science at the University of Chicago. In 1962 he became professor of economics at the University of Freiburg. He was awarded a Nobel Prize for Economics in 1974.

His publications include: *Geldtheorie und Konjunkturtheorie*, 1929 (translated as *Monetary Theory and the Trade Cycle*, 1933); *Monetary Nationalism and International Stability*, 1937; *Profits, Interest and Investment*, 1939; *The Pure Theory of Capital*, 1941; *The Road to Serfdom*, 1944; *Individualism and Economic Order*, 1949; *John Stuart Mill and Harriet Taylor*, 1951; *The Counter-Revolution of Science*, 1952; *The Sensory Order*, 1952; *Capitalism and the Historians* (ed.) 1954; *The Political Ideal of the Rule of Law*, 1955; *The Constitution of Liberty*, 1960; *Studies in Philosophy, Politics and Economics*, 1967; *The Confusion of Language in Political Thought*, 1968; *Freiburger Studies*, 1969.

BERTRAND DE JOUVENEL

Bertrand de Jouvenel was born in Paris in October 1903. He has mostly worked as a journalist and diplomatic correspondent contributing to both French and foreign newspapers. Since 1945, he has been received as a visiting professor at various universities including Oxford, Cambridge, Manchester, Yale, Chicago and Berkeley. In 1966 he became a professor in the faculty of law at Paris, a rare distinction in France for someone who has never presented a thesis. Along with his wife, he directs the Société d'Etudes et de Documentation Economiques, Industrielles et Sociales, which produces some of the major French futurology publications. He has belonged to the French National Accounting Commission, the 1985 Committee of the Plan, and is associated with the SSRC's Committee on the Next Thirty Years.

His publications include: *L'Economie dirigée*, 1928; *Vers les Etats-Unis d'Europe*, 1930; *La Crise du capitalisme américain*, 1933; *Le Réveil d'Europe*, 1938; *D'une guerre à l'autre*, 1940; *Napoléon et l'économie dirigée*, 1942; *Du pouvoir*, 1945 (translated as *Power*, 1948); *La dernière année*, 1947; *Raisons de craindre, raisons d'espérer*, 1947; *Problèmes de l'Angleterre socialiste*, 1948 (translated as *Problems of Socialist England*, 1949); *L'Amérique en Europe*, 1948; *The Ethics of Redistribution*, 1951; *De la souveraineté*, 1955 (translated as *Sovereignty*, 1957); *The Pure Theory of Politics*, 1963; *L'Art de la conjecture*, 1964 (translated as *The Art of Conjecture*, 1967); *Arcadie*, 1968; *Du principat*, 1972.

CRAWFORD BROUGH MACPHERSON

Crawford Macpherson was born in Toronto in November 1911. In 1935 he became lecturer in political economy at the University of Toronto, where (after various positions elsewhere) he is now professor of political science. He has held fellowships at several universities and was President of the Canadian Political Science Association in 1963–64.

His publications include: *Democracy in Alberta*, 1953; *The Political Theory of Possessive Individualism: Hobbes to Locke*, 1962; *The Future of Canadian Federalism*, 1964; *The Real World of Democracy*, 1965; *Leviathan: ed. and intro.* 1968; *Democratic Theory: Essays in Retrieval*, 1973.

HERBERT MARCUSE

Herbert Marcuse was born in Berlin in July 1898. After his academic career in Germany was interrupted in 1934, he accompanied the other members of the Institute of Social Research to Paris and then to Columbia University in New York. He served with the OSS and the State Department from 1941–50. He resumed university work at Columbia (1951), moving then to Brandeis (1954) and later to San Diego (1965).

His publications include: *Hegels Ontologie und die Grundlegung einer Theorie der Geschichtlichkeit,* 1932 (translated as *Reason and Revolution,* 1941); *Eros and Civilization,* 1955; *Soviet Marxism,* 1958; *One-Dimensional Man,* 1964; *Kultur und Gesellschaft,* 1965 (translated in part as *Negations: Essays in Critical Theory,* 1968); *A Critique of Pure Tolerance* (jointly with Barrington Moore Jr., and Paul Wolff Jr.), 1969; *An Essay on Liberation,* 1969; *Five Lectures: Psychoanalysis, Politics and Utopia,* 1970; *Revolution oder Reform?* (with Popper), 1971; *Studies in Critical Philosophy,* 1972; *Counter-Revolution and Revolt,* 1972.

Michael Joseph Oakeshott

Michael Oakeshott was born in Chelsfield, Kent, in December 1901. He became a fellow of Gonville and Caius College, Cambridge in 1924. In 1951 he was appointed to the chair of political science at the London School of Economics.

His publications include: *Experience and its Modes,* 1933; *A Guide to the Classics: How to Pick the Derby Winner* (with G. T. Griffith) 1937; *The Social and Political Doctrines of Contemporary Europe,* 1939; *Leviathan: ed. and intro.* 1946; *Rationalism in Politics,* 1962; *On Human Conduct,* forthcoming.

Sir Karl Popper

Karl Popper was born in Vienna in July 1902. He left Austria in 1937, and became a senior lecturer in philosophy at Canterbury University College, Christchurch, New Zealand. In 1945 he moved to the London School of Economics, retiring in 1969 as a professor of logic and scientific method.

His publications include: *Logik der Forschung,* 1935 (translated as *The Logic of Scientific Discovery,* 1959); *The Open Society and its Enemies,* 1945; *The Poverty of Historicism,* 1957; *Conjectures and Refutations,* 1963; *Revolution oder Reform?* (with Marcuse) 1971; *Objective Knowledge: An Evolutionary Approach,* 1972.

John Rawls

John Rawls was born in Baltimore in February 1921. He was an instructor at Princeton in 1950 and a Fulbright fellow at Oxford in 1952. In 1953 he became a professor at Cornell, moving in 1960 to the Massachusetts Institute of Technology. Since 1962 he has been professor of philosophy at Harvard.

His publications include: *A Theory of Justice,* 1972, as well as many articles in academic journals.

Jean-Paul Sartre

Jean-Paul Sartre was born in Paris in June 1905. His first post was in 1929 as a teacher of philosophy at the Lycée du Havre. Although he never received a university appointment, he published a number of influential works on philosophy and psychology. He served in the army in 1939, was a prisoner of war in 1940. In 1941 he returned to Paris and became a celebrity as the leader of the then fashionable school of existentialism. After the war he founded *Les Temps Modernes* and has lived by writing.

His publications include: *L'Imagination*, 1936 (translated as *Imagination*, 1942); *Imaginaire*, 1940 (translated as *The Psychology of the Imagination*, 1950); *Huis clos*, 1943 (translated as *No Exit*, 1958); *L'Etre et le Néant*, 1943 (translated as *Being and Nothingness*, 1957); *Les Chemins de la liberté*, 1946 (translated as *The Age of Reason, The Reprieve*, 1947, *Iron in the Soul*, 1950); *L'Existentialisme est un humanisme*, 1946 (translated as *Existentialism and Humanism*, 1948); *Situations*, 1947–49, 1964 (translated individually by title); *Les Mains sales*, 1948 (translated as *Crime Passionel*, 1961); *Saint Genet*, 1952 (translated as *Saint Genet*, 1964); *Critique de la raison dialectique*, 1960 (translated in part as *The Problem of Method*, 1963); *Les Mots*, 1963 (translated as *Words*, 1964); *Les Communistes ont peur de la révolution*, 1969 (translated as *The Communists and Peace*, 1969); *Flaubert*, 1971 (originally published as *Les Autres*).

Leo Strauss

Leo Strauss was born in Kirchhain, Hesse, in September 1899. Between 1925 and 1932 he worked as a research assistant in the Academy of Jewish Research in Berlin. From 1932–34 he was a Rockefeller Fellow in the social sciences in France and England. He moved to America in 1938, where for the next ten years he was a member of the graduate faculty of the New School for Social Research in New York. From 1949 to his retirement in 1968, he was professor of political science at the University of Chicago. After leaving Chicago he taught at Claremont Men's College in California and at St. John's College in Maryland, where he held the position of Distinguished Scholar in Residence. He died in 1973.

His publications include: *The Political Philosophy of Hobbes*, 1936; *On Tyranny*, 1948; *Persecution and the Art of Writing*, 1952; *Natural Right and History*, 1953; *Thoughts on Machiavelli*, 1958; *What is Political Philosophy?*, 1959; *History of Political Philosophy* (jointly with Joseph Cropsey), 1963; *The City and Man*, 1964; *Spinoza's Critique of Religion*, 1965; *Socrates and Aristophanes*, 1966;

Liberalism: Ancient and Modern, 1968; *Xenophon's Socratic Discourses*, 1970; *Xenophon's Socrates*, 1972.

Eric Herman Wilhelm Voegelin

Eric Voegelin was born in Cologne in January 1901. He worked in the law faculty at the University of Vienna until he was dismissed by the government in 1936. He went to the United States in 1938, becoming an American citizen. He held various academic positions in the United States, including appointment as Distinguished Professor at Louisiana State University, and in 1958 he became professor of political science at the University of Munich. Since his retirement he has been senior fellow at the Hoover Institution, Stanford, California.

His publications include: *Rasse und Staat*, 1933; *Der autoritäre Staat*, 1936; *Die politischen Religionen*, 1938; *The New Science of Politics*, 1952; *Order and History I: Israel and Revelation*, 1956; *Order and History II: The World of the Polis*, 1957; *Order and History III: Plato and Aristotle; Wissenschaft, Politik und Gnosis*, 1959 (translated as *Science, Politics and Gnosticism*, 1962); *Anamnesis: Zur Theorie der Geschichte und Politik*, 1966; *Order and History IV* (in preparation).